# IN THE
# GRIP OF THE JUNGLES

# IN THE
# GRIP OF THE JUNGLES

BY

**GEORGE HOGAN KNOWLES**
Contributor to the "Cornhill Magazine,"
"The Tatler," etc.

ILLUSTRATED

GYAN

*Published by*

GYAN

Gyan Publishing House
5, Ansari Road
Daryaganj, New Delhi-110002
Phone: 011-47034999, 9811692060
E-mail: books@gyanbooks.com

*Distribution Network*
gyanbooks.com
India, USA, Canada, UK, Australia, France



ISBN : 978-81-212-2103-0 (HB)
First Published, 1932

2nd Impression 2021

*Printed at:* Gyan Press, Delhi.



**In The Grip of The Jungles**
Author: George Hogan Knowles

# IN THE GRIP OF THE JUNGLES

BY

GEORGE HOGAN KNOWLES

*Contributor to the "Cornhill Magazine," "The Tatler," etc.*

ILLUSTRATED

WRIGHT & BROWN

12-14 RED LION COURT, FLEET STREET

LONDON, E.C.4

THE AUTHOR

TO

MY WIFE, JESSIE;

MY SON, AND MY TWO DAUGHTERS,

JESSIE AND BARBARA

THE HIMALAYAS. SNOWY RANGE, DARJEELING.

*Photograph by*
*Messrs. Bourne and Shepherd,*
*Calcutta.*

And down, and down, the darkness falls away,
Like a great cloak torn from the break of day.
Back roll the clouds, which to the valleys cleave
As white gigantic shoulders skyward heave :
Still soaring, till their ghost peaks point away,
Into the clear space of immortal day,
'Th' Eternal ' snows '—where Britain's flag's unfurled—
In dazzling splendour crown the mighty world.

G. H. KNOWLES.

# PREFACE

THE Author owes a debt of gratitude to his brother-in-law and sister, Mr. (the late) and Mrs. B. A. Rokeby—known to their old friends as Mr. and Mrs. B. A. Rebsch of the Indian Forest Service—for their often-time hospitality, and the many thrilling holidays in the Himalayan Jungles he has spent with them and their guests. The Author would also like to pay a tribute to his two brothers, Mr. E. D. Knowles and the late Colonel J. K. Knowles, I.A., and to his sister—a great sportswoman—Miss Nellie Knowles, and to many friends, for their keen enterprise and spirit of sport on many an adventurous tour.

The spring-time in certain of the best Himalayan altitudes, and the winter in the sub-Himalayan country of gorgeous crops and beautiful scenery, compare thrillingly, with their cold, their midday warmth and intoxicating fragrance, with those goddesses of rarest delight, our English spring and summer—when these two seasons of the year conform to ideality, and come dancing in with the blush of their exclusive charms.

India, in the relationship she has to offer, of primrose, cherry, and snow-clad pine, will forever call to Great Britain's sons and daughters ; in whose heart, may that wondrous jewel of their Empire, always have a big place.

# AN APPRECIATION

*By* A. G. HALES

*The famous War Correspondent and Author of the world-renowned "McGlusky Novels"*

I WELCOME this book by my jungle friend, Mr. George Hogan Knowles, partly for friendship's sake, but more especially because it enriches our literature with its wealth of knowledge concerning most things pertaining to the life of India, that land of colour, mystery, romance and adventure, where the bottom seems always to be on the surface and the surface at the bottom of things. If there is a man fully equipped to write a book, or series of books upon India it surely is this author, who has spent over thirty years roaming in that wonderful land. He has left his footprints everywhere betwixt Bombay and the topmost heights of the mighty Himalayas. He has trodden the unknown ways of the jungle and lived the life of the people. Game of all kinds from the destructive tiger downwards have fallen to his unerring rifle, but never for the mere sake of slaying. He has followed the rivers from the sea to their sources carrying withal the photographic eyes of the trained observer, that supreme gift of the writer. All that he has written springs from first hand knowledge, he has given us a book that each can treasure. Gladly do I welcome my jungle friend to the greater jungle of London literature and joyously wish him God speed and good hunting.

## FOREWORD

*By* Mr. Leonard Huxley

EDITOR OF THE "CORNHILL MAGAZINE"

MANY of these stories of the jungle took shape for the *Cornhill Magazine.* Here are tales of real " Shikar "—good hunting and blank days : here actual sight from safe hiding, of battles between the Lords of the Jungle, or the subtly told scene of a half-ghostly chase. The Editor who welcomed these to the pages of *Cornhill,* bids them in their new form win equal welcome from all lovers of wild sport and adventure.

## FOREWORD

*By* Mr. E. Huskinson

EDITOR OF THE "TATLER"

THE jungle stories that I welcomed to the pages of *The Tatler*—which have been republished here—convince me that the author of this book, " In the Grip of the Jungles ", and his Publishers, Messrs. Wright and Brown, are presenting to the world, not only a series of thrilling experiences of big-game hunting in the great Himalayas, and in their vast lowlands of primeval forests, but nature-studies, so blended with stirring incidents, as to give the reading a special interest and value. The author's descriptive powers are of outstanding merit, and, from a literary standpoint, worthy of notice. I shall be glad to see this book a success.

## FOREWORD

*By* THE EDITOR OF "THE AUTOCAR"

IN wishing Mr. George Hogan Knowles' book every success, I write as one who has been privileged to publish some of this author's work. It is specially gratifying to find that a writer with such an attractive style regards his "characters" not as objects for slaughter, but as subjects for close and sympathetic observation. It is his object, not to take life, but to get behind the great curtain that screens an almost invisible world—a world indescribably thrilling in the mighty Himalayas and in the sub-Himalayan country in which his adventurous life has been passed. When stories are told, as Mr. Knowles tells them, as a blend of interesting nature-study and thrilling incident, the reader can enjoy them to the full.

## ACKNOWLEDGMENTS

THIS BOOK contains contributions made previously to the *Cornhill Magazine*, the *Tatler*, the *Autocar*, and to other Magazines; and the author is much indebted to the Editors of the above Magazines for their courtesy in permitting him to make use of his contributions in their present compiled form.

LORDS OF THE JUNGLE SALUTING THEIR GUESTS
(MR. B. A. ROKEBY'S CAMP—CHORGALIA VALLEY—NAINI-TAL DIVISION)

A CATTLE THIEF, SHOT BY MR. B. A. ROKEBY
(B. A. REBSCH). IMPERIAL FOREST SERVICE

*Incident page 87*

# CONTENTS

# LIST OF ILLUSTRATIONS

# IN THE GRIP OF THE JUNGLES

## CHAPTER I

### A MOONLIGHT GHOST

LIKE an English spring when the tulips bloom, and flaunt in gorgeous rows of red and yellow their tempting wine cups, comes the thrilling winter of the sub-Himalayan country with its enchanting crisp air wafted from the mountain heights. Soft, golden rays shed a genial warmth as the day wears to noon ; and then suddenly there breathes the divine heat-wave of an English summer on some North Sea cliffs, that swells—on a billowy green—the white sails of the yacht, and deepens the blush-rose on the cheeks of the fair English maiden.

But lives there a saint who can fathom India—with her breath of Heaven veiling deadly dangers, and her fiery furnace offering a haven ?

It was about the middle of November, and I was spending ten days' leave in the delightful Himalayan Station of Mussoorie, which from a height of 7,000 ft. overlooks the town and the beautiful valley of Dehra-Dun, in the sub-Himalayan country.

A great friend of mine, a big, hardy Irishman—Bill, as everyone called him—was the manager of a large tea estate situated in the western part of the valley, about fifteen miles from the town of Dehra-Dun. Some miles farther west again of his main factory lay a smaller garden called Banwali, the only approach to which was a very lonely road through deep ravines and gorges—embosomed in dense jungle—where, in the past, a man-eating tiger invariably took up his quarters.

When once a tiger becomes a man-eater and ceases to fear man, nothing but solid iron doors can bar him from entering a house.

One such tiger, apparently, had caused both Bill's factories to be closed down, and he wanted me at once. I received Bill's letter by a late post, and made arrangements to leave the following day.

Morning breaks as, shivering on the back of my mountain pony, I start off, accompanied by a Gurkha peon carrying my rifle. The peon is an old soldier called Bacha Sing.

" Look! Sahib," he exclaims suddenly, sweeping an arm over the world as we approach the mighty descent, " that view reminds me of my own beloved country, Nepal! "

Great horizontal bands of grey mist, split by crimson rays as the sun tops the eastern mountains, lie close over the canopy of dense, undulating forest stretching far below, that seems to rise and fall like a heaving sea—the sanctuary of the wild elephant and the big Himalayan tiger! Will-o'-the-wisps, where the streams glitter, play hide and seek below the misty spray; and, like forked streaks of silver, the riotous rivers slice the inclined expanse downwards, until their winding lengths are lost in the distant Siwalik range of hills to the south, that pierce through the misty bars and rise, dark and frowning, against a lemon-washed horizon.

We hired fresh ponies at Dehra-Dun, and continued our journey to Bill's tea-garden.

The rough road soon led into wild country. In front of us lay a winding gorge of sheer rock wall, in the centre of which there lived—inside a spacious cave—a wonderful hermit, a Brahmin priest who had the reputation of being able to predict the future.

At the mouth of the cave stood the tall, well-knit, silent figure in yellow robes.

"Pass on, sahib," the priest said, "your call is urgent!"

I saluted him. "Do not enter the Banwali bungalow without your loaded rifles," he warned. I then saw him bending down to whisper something to Bacha Sing, who seemed to start back in alarm! I knew it was useless to question the peon, as he would be sworn to silence.

Two hours later Bill, his young assistant, Jackson, and I were discussing our plans for that memorable night!

At midnight we were to travel to the out-factory of Banwali—just alone by ourselves—in an old creaking bullock cart, with tinkling bells round the bullocks' necks, in order to attract the man-eating tiger. In the quiet jungles at night sound travels a long distance, and a "sing-song," after the manner of a travelling Indian dancing party—would complete the bait.

The strictest orders were issued to the Gurkha peons of the tea-garden—including my man Bacha Sing, that on no account were they to follow, or to come in search of us. We decided not to risk the lives of any of the staff. Young Jackson had learnt to drive a bullock cart, and would be the bullocks' "tail-twister."

A full round moon is flooding the rough road in front of us with a sheen of silvery light that sparkles on the leaves of the dense jungle and glints on the rocks as we creak and tinkle along in our bullock cart at a snail's pace.

It is about two o'clock in the morning, and we are crawling up a low hill, nearing the gate of the Banwali factory. The valley stretches below us—a vast sea of white, lustrous splendour that blinds the eye! Our big coats and our caps are wet with the heavy dew, and we are chattering with the piercing cold.

Suddenly, from an adjoining hill to our left, the startled bay of a sambur stag comes echoing down, almost choking us with excitement! The bullocks stop of their own accord as the alarm cry ceases suddenly as it came, and deathly stillness prevails, broken only by the drip, drip of falling dew from the forest trees. We listen breathlessly! Yes—there is something! Slowly there comes a breaking sound in the jungle to our left—there is a sudden rush, and we raise our rifles. But only a big black bear dashes across the road to our rear. We take a breath of relief and move on.

"The man-eater has startled that bear—and the sambur too," remarks Bill in a shaky whisper. "We are being followed!"

We pass through the gate and down the drive to the Banwali bungalow, that stands lonely and desolate, like a haunted house—the white walls gleaming in the moonlight.

Young Jackson tells us that he left a bottle of whisky and some sodas on the table in the front room, and we hurry on the bullocks.

But at that moment—great Heavens!

The deafening trumpet of a wild elephant to our right front—where the tea bushes end abruptly—suddenly crashes through the silent jungles. The bullocks come to a dead halt again, as if frozen with terror. The trumpeting is followed by loud trampling—the mammoth is striding into the garden! His trunk is curled up savagely, and great white tusks gleam in the moonlight.

"Quick, Jackson!" I hear Bill exclaim.

But Jackson seems confused; he is standing up on the driver's seat, lost in excitement, to get a fuller view of the wild tusker. Suddenly the bullocks dart forward and bolt in a panic! We see Jackson being hurled in the air, over the thick hedge walling the right side of the road; and the next instant Bill and I are being shaken to bits as we fly up the drive. We speak to the bullocks, we coax them, but they tear madly past the bungalow, and then suddenly swerve right round. It is impossible to hold our rifles! We are swung clean out of the cart and fall heavily to the ground.

We lie stunned for a few moments—half conscious that the cart is rattling down the drive, carrying away our rifles, back in the direction from which we came.

We rise with difficulty and look at each other panic-stricken! Bill is a heavy man and seems hurt. He is limping badly, and I help him along, up the veranda steps, shouting out to Jackson; but through the startling gleam of that awful night only echoes come mocking back—"Jackson, Jackson!"

Bill is unusually silent.

"You must have a drop of whisky, Bill, before we can do anything—speak man!"

My frightened voice sounds far away. I have placed Bill in a chair near the table, and I am about to pour out some whisky with a trembling hand—listening to the wild elephant crashing through the jungle again—when suddenly we see something huge in front of the wide open door.

"What is that?" Bill gasps out queerly. An enormous dark shadow the size of a buffalo looms up as if by sudden magic, obliterating the moonlight. It has a colossal cat's head—am I dreaming? I am about to shout "Jackson," but I am choked, dazed, transfixed with terror. Bill sits silent—staring, staring!

The huge shadow squats down deliberately before us, stretching out two formidable paws and placing them on the threshold of the door. His great tail sways behind, and beats with loud knocks on the shining pavement of the veranda—my God !—in satisfaction of his find. His great head is erect, looking at us, fascinating us—so silent, so still.

Slowly I put my glass down ; it touches the table with the slightest sound, and a threatening low growl like soft thunder gurgles out. There must be no movement—no attempt to run. We are warned.

Silvery rays gleaming on his fierce whiskers, the monster man-eater shows his ghastly fangs in a terrible grin. Hot steam from his heavy breathing penetrates the room. We are helpless—at his mercy. A lifetime seems to be passing. The warning words of the hermit : " Do not enter the Banwali bungalow without your loaded rifles," burn in my brain, and I hear myself thinking : " We couldn't help it."

The monster is playing with us. Has he just killed poor Jackson ? The thought is awful. All we can do is to freeze ; it seems the only hope.

Suddenly—what is it ? Another nightmare ? There are soft creeping footsteps behind me ! I dare not turn to look round, but presently I see something long, like dark steel, coming up slowly, slowly, slowly—now it extends past my right shoulder. But—horrors ! The monster is rising and is emitting again a terrible threatening spit—like a steam-engine. He is taking a stride forward. Heaven have mercy ! Poor Bill ! The next instant there is a blinding flash ! The enormous form swirls up high on to its hind legs, rolls on the shining veranda, and falls heavily over the plinth, as the instantaneous crash of a heavy rifle thunders out, echoing and re-echoing in the distant hills.

Bill jumps up, and we seize the short, dark figure standing behind us.

"What—Bacha Sing!" I exclaim.

"Have you seen Jackson sahib?" fairly roars Bill at the Gurkha peon, in uncontrollable excitement.

"Yes, sahib; he is safe!" Another Gurkha emerges softly from the back door, and the two men explain that young Jackson is locked up in an out-house.

Bill is himself again. In his great joy he lifts the little stalwart Gurkha up in his arms.

Outside the great ghastly man-eater was lying stone-dead, shot through the head. Presently, Jackson came running up the drive, followed by three other Gurkha peons.

The Gurkhas asked Bill's forgiveness for disobeying his orders.

Bacha Sing explained that not only was it against their nature to stop back, but the hermit had ordered them to go. That picking up a spare rifle of Bill's—which they loaded—they took a short cut through the jungle, and reached Banwali bungalow long before we did. When the wild elephant created the trouble they were hiding behind the hedge by the road-side. The hermit had warned Bacha Sing that Jackson would be the victim of the tiger, and that the Gurkha peons had to take "Fate by the horns" and save him.

When Jackson fell over the hedge and into their arms, they gagged and bound him quickly—as, acting against orders, they could not give themselves away—and locked him up in an out-house. They then took up their position again behind the hedge.

The tiger took them, too, by surprise. For fear of hitting us, they dared not fire when the brute was in front of the open door. The Gurkhas stalked round to the back of the bungalow and Bacha Sing acted as he did. Great nerve was required; for had the tiger been suddenly disturbed, he would probably have killed the three of us.

## CHAPTER II

### COMEDY AND TRAGEDY IN THE JUNGLES

IT was about the middle of April, on one occasion, when I took a fortnight's leave to join a shooting party that had been arranged by a Forest Officer and his wife, for some of their friends.

I was delighted at the prospects of shooting in the Ganges Forest Division—the Forest Officer's charge at the time—which was well known for big game. This beautiful stretch of country begins in the western Himalayas, near Hardwar (a great pilgrimage place for zealous Hindus) and comprises a considerable portion of the wild range of the lower hills that are situated on the north side of the great out-gate of the holy Ganges, as it emerges into the plains on its eastern course. On a cold winter's morning, the northern view along the banks of the river leaves an impression of wonderment never to be forgotten. Sometimes—seen through the illusion of a mist-laden morning—when the sun rises and dissolves the snow clouds on the higher mountains, the low, azure hills below, fringed with fleecy drifts of cloudlets, seem to come rolling forward—as if rebounding back from the looming mountain barrier—like high seas of foaming purple, threatening to swallow the distant plains.

Watered by the many mountain rivers that help to swell the mighty Ganges, this fertile, sub-Himalayan country is the home of the wild elephant, and the massively built tiger of northern India, whose fur for dazzling beauty—the male growing an appreciable mane

—is famous throughout this vast peninsula, and even far beyond the confines of the awe-inspiring Himalayas.

The headquarters of the shooting party had been arranged at a camping ground known as " Hathikund," the pool of the elephant, situated in a wild part of the Forest Division.

After a long day's march on the back of an elephant—on my way to Hathikund—I arrived at a lonely, forest rest-house, a camping ground called " Murghatti," with its spacious clearing at the mouth of a wide valley, which opened suddenly to view as one's journey came to an abrupt end round a high spur. The " Chowkidar," or Care-keeper of the Forest Bungalow, was a lovable old veteran, who mothered every white man that happened to arrive at this rather cheerless place, noted for a bad type of malaria fever. He burnt, round my armchair, the refuse (after extraction of oil) of the neem fruit—the neem tree possessing medicinal qualities in its leaves and fruit, which are very bitter—and anointed my hands and bare knees, below my shorts, with the nauseous oil. After the discomfort had passed, I was grateful, for the pugnacious mosquitoes decided to leave me strictly alone. Then the old fellow advised me to drink strong tea, and helped my servant to brew it, indulging in a big mugful himself, with a broad grin and an affable " salaam."

Later on in the evening, I found the fussy old man interfering with my sleeping arrangements. I was looking forward to an undisturbed night's rest. To my surprise I saw my bed, with my precious mosquito curtain trailing on the ground, being carried far outside the bungalow. It was dumped down in several places, and finally, carefully arranged on a clean spot of ground, quite near a large tree, under which the elephant was tethered. The Chowkidar remarked that I would be safest there, out in the open, as the bungalow was, for a time, under the influence of an evil spirit. On being questioned by me, he explained that, within the last ten days, he had killed two huge male cobras inside the house—each time late in the evening—and that, as the female snakes were sure to come in search of their mates, and wander through all the rooms at night, he advised my sleeping a good distance away from the bungalow, taking no risk, not even in the veranda.

In the habits of the " spectacled terror " of India, it is firmly believed—and, with rare exceptions, I have found it true—that, if one of a pair is killed in a certain place, the other one will come there sooner or later—and to the very spot, where it will take up an aggressive attitude. This instinct, which seems to be peculiar to this variety of snake only, is a wonderful thing. It would naturally be supposed that the direction taken by one of a pair, and its whereabouts, after it has wandered at random from its abode in search of prey, could not be known to its mate at home. An uncanny sense of smell might give an explanation; but, after the lapse of days—which is usually the case before the living snake finds the spot where its mate was killed—it would be logical to presume that all traces of the missing snake had disappeared. I have disinfected carefully a whole room in which a cobra has been killed, and yet the mate has come to the precise spot.

The " mahout " hailed my presence in his little encampment with delight; and, after we had all had a " snack "—each in his own fashion—we made a cheerful little party, with the elephant in our midst—to warn us against a prowling tiger—enjoying his dinner of unleavened bread; each large, baked cake being doubled up, with a lump of " goor " (caked molasses) in between, and put into the elephant's great mouth, with tender care, by his devoted keeper and driver. And then, under the refulgent stars of the heavens above, whose purple glow crept into the blackness of the jungle night, we listened to a thrilling tale of the North-West Frontier, told by the old Chowkidar—who had seen service as a stretcher-bearer in an ambulance corps—and one by one we fell asleep. But what a myth seemed slumber! I seemed to have dozed but a few moments, when the maddening cry of that indolent bird, the "koel" (the hot-weather songster), "brain fever, brain fever,"—which has made many an Englishman pack up quickly, and fly back to beloved Blighty before his time—and the sound of breaking branches, as the elephant cracked and chewed his fodder, seemed to be magically responsible for suddenly ushering in the dawn of a new, summer's day. I presented the old Chowkidar with a packet of tea—to his great delight—and we were well on the highway to Hathikund before the sun rose. By ten o'clock in the morning, there came into view a picturesque encampment of large, white tents, pitched in a shady grove of trees, on the high bank of a wide, tributary river, called the "Sona Nadi," or river of gold, whose sands are washed for this precious metal.

That same afternoon, the Forest Officer proposed a visit to some pools up the river—about two miles from camp—for some fly-fishing. He was bent upon giving us a treat of "mahseer" (the Indian salmon) for dinner that night, and felt very confident of a most enjoyable afternoon and a big "bag," as he remarked that the place was hard to beat. There were four of us left in camp; a Major and Mrs. B. making up our party. The other guests were all out in the jungles. We were delighted at the prospects, and, after some tea, we started off on two baggage elephants—the only ones not engaged—hustling them along to save time.

We had quite two to three hours of daylight before us,

when we reached a sharp bend in the river, where the banks were beginning to get steep. Here we opened out our fishing tackle on some large, flat rocks overlooking two big pools, the water falling into the lower one like a miniature cataract, which, half-way down its fall, was obstructed by a protruding grey rock that sent a huge spray all over the wide surface of the pool. Caught by the rays of the afternoon sun, the spray fell like streaks of glittering rain. We were pleasurably entertained a few moments, watching a flight of sand-bank swallows diving low down through the inviting spray and enjoying a bath.

While we were examining all the beautiful flies, trying to make a selection for the afternoon light and the particular season, Major B. scrambled down the high bank, and began to examine the wet sand along the edge of the water.

"As I thought," he said on his return, "there are tracks of many wild animals, including our friend, Hathi!" (the elephant.) The sound of a waterfall is very attractive to all the animals, and must often—to draw a logical conclusion—suggest a thirst when there is none in reality. "What shall we do?" asked the Major—"fish or shoot? If we wait quietly on the top of this bank, we may get a shot at a tiger or a panther, or at least see something interesting. I never shoot over water," he said, "but perhaps for some particular carnivore that has become a danger to human life. There are some tracks of a big tiger down below."

We turned down shooting with one accord; and, while the Forest Officer and Major B. took up their fishing rods, Mrs. B. and I armed ourselves with cameras, in the hope of securing some snapshots. We kept our rifles handy in case they might be needed.

While we were watching, with keen interest, the casts

of the "white moth" that Major B.—fishing just below us—was deftly making, I suddenly looked up and saw a small, black animal ferreting about at the edge of the water—to our left front—on our side of the river. Mrs. B. and I were almost facing a high bank, upstream, which curved round like a semi-circle. The Forest Officer was fishing a short distance farther downstream. The queer-looking animal had, apparently, come out of some high grass to our left, and had sneaked down the bank without our observing it. We thought it was an otter; but, as the animal approached nearer—we being well hidden and sitting perfectly still—we found it was a civet-cat, a nocturnal, carnivorous little animal. It seemed extremely inquisitive and excited about something, jumping up the bank, where it seemed steepest, and slipping down again, with a gentle splash, into the running water. We became intensely interested. Presently it sat down and began to gaze intently at some holes in the bank above its head. Then it suddenly leaped up, clinging to the bank for a moment, with its fox-like snout inside a hole; but there came a landslip of sand, and, at the same instant, a gorgeous kingfisher darted out of the hole. To catch the bird, the civet-cat made a desperate effort; but it fell down below, with the slip of sand, and, lying buried for a moment, it rolled into the water. Then it jumped up and shook itself so comically, that we had great difficulty in suppressing a laugh. Major B. happened to look up at that instant, and by silent head and eye movements, we induced him to glance over a boulder, below which he was screened. He immediately became interested too.

It seemed quite clear that the civet-cat was out hunting, the prey evidently being the eggs and the young of the poor water-birds that made holes in river-banks for their nests. Parent birds seemed to be the object as well, being entrapped in their holes and caught, unless little landslips hurled their enemy down the bank, and they were able to fly out.

The civet-cat was now concentrating its gaze on a larger hole, a little nearer our position. The Major had stopped fishing, and carefully hidden, the three of us were now absorbed in the study of a jungle drama, as fascinating among the lesser creatures as it is among the greater inhabitants of the jungle. The undaunted " civet " stood up once or twice on to its hind legs, and sniffed, and then, bending low, made no mean a spring. It reached the hole, almost covering it; then, to our great surprise— " ugh," exclaiming Mrs. B. with a horrified start—a huge snake, several feet long, shot out of the hole with the suddenness of lightning, just missing the civet-cat, which leapt off the bank to which it was clinging, with so absurd an appearance of shock that a burst of laughter escaped from us. That civet-cat seemed to be ultra-sensitive, for it disappeared with astonishing rapidity. Whether it was the snake, or the sound of human voices that gave it the fright of its life, it is difficult to say. We hoped, however, it would be a lesson to that particular carnivore, and that the poor river-birds would be spared its depredations in future. The snake, we guessed, was a " Dhamin " ; a common, non-poisonous colubrine, which, like the cobra, has a great partiality for birds' eggs and their young. How the snake managed to get into the hole seemed to be a puzzle.

Suddenly, the inspiring crackle of the reel downstream made us look round, feeling very guilty for having broken the soft melody of the splashing waterfall, and disturbed the Forest Officer, who was a keen fisherman; for, we saw his hand—which had apparently been raised in warning—come down quickly on to the rod as the line ran out. A "catch," as it appeared, had taken our host by surprise, while he had been trying to attract our attention; evidently to reprimand our hilarity. Then the fisherman began to reel in, and his rod was bent almost double. "A big 'mahseer,'" whispered Mrs. B., as she slipped down to the edge of the water and tip-toed to the Forest Officer, to help him with the net. The Major and I followed her quietly behind.

The "mahseer" was fighting desperately, while the fisherman, with consummate skill, was defying his catch to break the line. The excitement was fairly at its height, when, suddenly, another thrill, in the sound of breaking branches across the river—where, in front of us, beyond a stretch of sand, the dark forest reared its vast canopy—drew our attention from the fishing, and made us look up, wrapt in the deepest interest. In the glow of the declining sun, the sand over which we gazed—about sixty or seventy paces wide—looked like a sheet of pale crimson. There seemed to be some unusual disturbance inside the jungle, and, while we were trying to guess the cause of it—prepared to see anything emerge, from a wild elephant to a herd of deer—there came the sound of a terrific stampede close to the open sand. It looked as if the animals were on the point of coming out, but we were disappointed. Every now and then, however, we could catch a glimpse of some large creatures running about at the edge of the jungle, just within cover. Then, suddenly, a "sambhur" hind broke, and came galloping full speed across the stretch of sand, heading straight for our direction; but she swerved, and splashing into the river on the far side of the waterfall, she scrambled up the opposite bank and disappeared. The Forest Officer, though trying his best to play the "mahseer" as quietly and as carefully as possible, could not help taking an interest with us, in watching the "sambhur," and lost his fish, which made a sudden dash for some rocks, entangling and snapping the line.

Our sympathies—almost simultaneously—went out for the poor fish, with the hook in its mouth; whereupon, we were immediately hard at work trying to suppress a hearty laugh at our good host's comments—humorously seasoned with sarcasm—on our alleged ingratitude. We were under cover of the all-pervading sound of the waterfall, and could indulge in an exchange of whispers, without disturbing any other animals that might again break cover and show themselves. Everything, however, seeming to have settled down in the jungle—but for an occasional crackle of dry wood—we entered into our host's diversion, and some merry sparring went round. Our giggles became bolder, until a burst of merriment escaped Mrs. B. and myself. A loud noise in the jungle again bringing us to attention, the Major thought it time—with the likelihood before us, of being able to see some more wild animals—to stop the frivolity; and, deserting Mrs. B. and myself, with the intention of being tactful in his arbitration, he decided the issue in favour of the aggrieved angler, by reminding us that it was our turn to suffer the pangs of disappointment, and "fish" for our dinner. This seemed to subdue the angler—but to a point of danger; that is, an eyebrow lifted, as if a slight doubt were entertained as to the good faith of the arbitrator's sympathetic partiality. The pose was suggestive of quite a few other things, and we waited in awful suspense, while the aggrieved angler drew over his personality the cloak of lofty forbearance, and "shuddered," asking us to excuse his catching the Major's waggish spirit. But the drop of comfort intended for the fisherman, in the Major's festive "jeu de mots," had its due effect; for, though our host quieted us with a dignified "hush," he smiled at last, benevolently—

with a touch of relish—and comforted us by explaining (*sotto voce*) that the "mahseer" was a particular adept at working a hook out of its mouth, and that the discomfort of our escaped friend would be of short duration.

The Forest Officer was preparing to try his luck again, for a dainty dish for us for dinner that night, when another stampede, in the sound of crashing undergrowth, made us concentrate on the jungle. A young sambhur rushed out, and fled into cover again. A herd of sambhur, apparently, seemed to be under the influence of some great excitement; and our expectations rose in proportion to the increasing disturbance. We were soon rewarded for our patient watch; for, suddenly, two huge sambhur stags, with massive antlers, came rushing out into the open, one chasing the other. The leading one galloped round in a circle, and then attacked the rear one. The two huge creatures lowered their heads—most ostentatiously, as it seemed—and came immediately into contact, the meeting of the antlers resounding like a bout of single-sticks. The four of us now froze against the high bank of the river, to watch the magnificent spectacle before us. It was a duel between the two stags, who seemed blind and deaf to our presence—a sight worth the sacrifice of the daintiest finned morsel that the sweet waters of that river could produce, advertising their delicacies in jingle and gurgle and spraying trills.

Pushing and straining with their antlers interlocked, nearer and nearer came the two stags—to within a shorter distance of the splashing waterfall, giving us a better view, and raising our excitement to fever heat. It looked as if it were going to be a thrilling duel—a fight to the death; but none of us—by whispered agreement—wishing to see a tragic ending of one, if not both of the noble-looking creatures—however interesting from the standpoint of a nature study—the Major was on the point of clapping his hands and shouting out, to part the duellists—now standing quite steady, head against head—when, to our utter astonishment, the interlocked antlers, suddenly—for a second or two, as it seemed—rose into the air, parting completely from the animals' heads, and dropping back again into their places. It seemed extraordinary. Then it happened a second time, the stags scarcely moving. Then the large, massive horns—still interlocked, as it appeared—wobbled on the heads of the stags in a most uncanny fashion. We could scarcely believe our eyes, and looked at one another for some kind of explanation, until the ridiculousness of the spectacle began to dawn upon us. It looked as if the scene, under our open-mouthed and wide-eyed staring, were undergoing a mysterious change to sudden comedy. It needed but another absurd development to send us—this time—into a fit of incontrollable laughter.

The climax came. Now shaking violently, the interlocked antlers seemed to get unfastened—separating from each other—and, falling on to the necks of their owners, they slipped down the withers of the stags, on to the soft sand. Shying in great agitation, at their own falling antlers, the stags jumped aside in such ridiculous surprise, that our bubbling spirits—suppressed practically the whole afternoon—burst forth at last, and we disturbed the whole jungle with our boisterous roars and shrieks of laughter. With snorts of terror, the scared animals swung round, and, looking grotesquely foolish with their small, bare heads almost lost in the now conspicuous protrusions of their large trumpet ears, they stared in our direction for a few seconds. The sight was an appalling contrast to their antlered magnificence of but a few moments back. Then, turning in a mad panic, they made a dash for the forest, and, with our fresh outbursts of uncouth laughter exploding behind them—

which accelerated their speed—never, in their jungle lives before, could the poor creatures have run so fast.

We heard crashing through the thick jungle in many directions, as if a big herd of sambhur had been thoroughly scared; and, when everything settled down—hushed to evening stillness by the soothing refrain of the waters—we hastened to the spot where the antlers had fallen—wading through the river in the shallowest parts—and picked up the trophies. Though damaged, the antlers were invaluable "souvenirs" to us. Then, as it was getting late, we hallooed out for our elephants.

Jogging back to camp, we commented upon the wonderful afternoon's entertainment to which Dame Nature had been pleased to treat us. In the incident of the falling antlers, we were apparently fortunate enough to catch her ladyship in a jocose mood, for it had apparently pleased her to seize the opportunity at shedding time for the production of a burlesque. Sambhur, in the Himalayan jungles, usually drop their antlers in March, but the Forest Officer said that some stags shed much later. He thought that in the case that had come under our observation—a remarkable scene, to which we had been such fortunate witnesses—the time for shedding had drawn near, and that the fight had brought this about perhaps a few days earlier than it would ordinarily have occurred.

We were seven guns in all, at "Hathikund" camp; including three ladies, who were keen on hunting and could shoot well with both the gun and the rifle. The hunting grounds that had been fixed upon as the most promising, lay on both sides of the main, dividing valley, the river of gold. Each ground was allotted in rotation to each guest. Lent for the occasion, we had several well-trained elephants for our morning and afternoon excursions; the arrangement being to draw lots for the ladies, each man going out in a given direction on a padded elephant, with his lady partner beside him for a second gun. As a rule a trained elephant is a good stalker, and there is no sport so interesting, and so thrilling, as to move about quietly in dense jungle on the back of one of these grand animals, armed with a camera, as well as the usual firearm for defensive purposes. All the denizens of the sub-Himalayan jungles are accustomed to wild elephants, whom they constantly see and meet; and in consequence, though harnessed and stamped with the atmosphere of Man's civilisation, the domesticated elephant, moving about quietly in the jungles, gives rise to no alarm; provided the human voice is not heard. Mounted on the back of a good trained elephant, who knows how to stalk, the naturalist, therefore, touches ideal conditions for the observation and study of animals and birds in their natural habitat. Constant watch, however, has to be kept during such rambles, and great care taken to avoid coming into contact with a wild bull elephant, who, as a rule, makes himself aggressive, unless he happens to be in a particularly good humour.

In the case of a "kill"—of either a tiger or a panther—that necessitates sitting up over a "machan,"* the arrangement was to reserve that particular ground where the kill had occurred, and to toss up for the more or less certain opportunity of seeing—if failing to bag—either stripes or spots.

Trackers were hard at work trying to mark down the greater carnivora and tying up young buffaloes. When some beaten track of a tiger or a panther has been discovered, it is not uncommon to sit up in a "machan" in

*A small platform—with sitting space for one or two people—fixed on a tree at a height of about 8ft. from the ground; the platform usually consisting of a cot or light bedstead woven with rough string.

daylight, in some convenient spot close to the track, guarding a live bait which, as a rule, comes to no harm.

There had been two such opportunities, but the guests had returned disappointed; for, though tigers seemed plentiful, they appeared to be mysteriously evasive. And then there came another opportunity.

News had been brought late one morning by a grazier—quite a young boy—and a "shikarri," that a very big, male tiger had been worrying the boy's cattle; and but for the interference of a huge wild elephant that seemed out of temper, and was doing its utmost to force an issue with the tiger for some extraordinary reason, a bullock would undoubtedly have been carried off by the striped lord. The boy said that all the long grass in a certain glen had been trampled down. That, whenever the cattle fled the tiger chased them; and the elephant going after the tiger, there was a continuous commotion until he (the boy) was able, after great difficulty and personal risk, to rescue his seven or eight head of cattle, and drive them back to the cattle-station, where he had left them in charge of other graziers.

The "shikarri" stated that the tusker had gone off when he came to the place, but he thought the tiger would remain close to the glen on the look out again for cattle, and he suggested that someone should "sit up" in the glen in the afternoon, over a live bait. Some other "shikarries" thought that the opportunity had passed; but the Forest Officer—Mrs. B. and myself being the only guests present in camp that morning—said that it was often at the eleventh hour that the best luck came. He insisted upon Mrs. B. and myself taking the opportunity, and made us sit down to an early lunch while he despatched a "shikarri" with three help-mates, who led the young buffalo and carried the "machan," to have everything in readiness for us. Mrs. B. and I were to give the men a couple of hours to get away before starting ourselves, little knowing what a perilous adventure lay in store for us.

For April, in the interior of the hills, it was an exceptionally hot afternoon when Mrs. B. and I set out on an elephant, with the grazier boy sitting on the pad behind us, to point out the way. A sultry, dust-begrimed haze, partially screening the sun, seemed to clog the atmosphere. Along the far expanse of the valley, in pale shades of lush emerald, tiny shoots of new grass had sprung up around the clumps of blackened, resilient stalks—most of the high grass having been burnt as a check to forest fires—that lashed our elephant's legs, as we turned off the main Forest-Department road to our left front. Dotted about the far expanse of the valley, clusters of tall sissoo trees flaunted their spring foliage in apple green; and on either side of the wide valley, like a vast amphitheatre with its tiers in gaudy colours, rose the brilliantly clad hills in variegated green and russet; in arabesque creations of cream lace—of the famous "sal" tree in flower—abundantly splashed with the scarlet of the "forest flame" that, in magnificent ascendancy, seemed to deepen the brick-red glow of the sky.

About a mile distant from the road we had left, we halted before a small sissoo grove, where the men that had gone on ahead, were waiting with the young buffalo. The "shikarri" instructed the men where to tie up the bait, and pointed out our "machan"; a cot swung high up on a tree standing conspicuously in front of the grove, a little detached from the other trees.

"This monster tiger that I tracked in the morning," said the "shikarri," "will come out either here, or down a ravine half a mile further on, where I shall keep watch"

—he pointed to some high grass in the distance: "but this," he said, "is the more likely place."

Mrs. B. and I climbed up our tree, and, dismissing the elephant and the men, who were to keep watch on the road, while the "shikarri" moved off to the ravine he mentioned, we made a careful survey of our surroundings. We were below a dense forest, which stood on high, rolling ground. This well-wooded plateau, which took a semi-circular bend outwards, like a headland, shelved down to a wide, shallow stream—gleaming yellow—that followed the zigzagging contour of its banks. Our tree stood about three hundred feet or so from the nearest point of the plateau, down which—worn into the steep face of the bank—came an animal pathway. Facing this path coming down, we made ourselves comfortable in the "machan," and awaited events. Mrs. B. had a high velocity, .375 repeating rifle, while I held a heavy .500 double-barrel express.

After a while, we saw some bamboo clumps shaking up on the plateau, and heard an occasional crash. We immediately suspected wild elephants—apparently grazing. Then it happened that the young buffalo below our tree got restless, and managed to get a front leg entangled awkwardly in his rope. It looked as if the leg might easily be broken, and we felt sorry for the poor creature. I climbed down off the tree to release the leg, leaving with Mrs. B. my heavy rifle, which I could not manage to bring down with me. The hefty young buffalo however, refused to let me come near him. He kept up a threatening attitude: apparently as I was a stranger to him. I was making an effort, as quietly as possible, to win him over with friendly whispers and gestures—much to the amusement of Mrs. B. up on the "machan"—when, suddenly, I heard a crow cawing on the other side of the grove, at the back of Mrs. B. I knew that, in looking for food, a crow sometimes followed a tiger; and, to be on the safe side, I quickly crouched low and took cover behind a fairly wide ant-hill, about four feet high. It stood about twenty to thirty paces to the left front of the buffalo. I was sufficiently in front of Mrs. B. to be well under protection of her rifle. Glancing up at her from behind my cover, I saw that she had just looked round, behind her, and, from her warning gesture, I concluded that the tiger was coming, and that my trying to get back to the " machan " was out of the question.

Peeping between two small, pyramidal spires—about a foot high—erected by the thoughtful jungle ants on top of their castle, I suddenly beheld—bent low to the ground—a massive red head, with a shaggy mane drooping over a thick neck. Then, moving most stealthily, with cautious halts in order to listen, there came into gradual view the dazzling drapery in "*rouge et noir*," of that dreaded jungle gambler and cattle thief. An exceptionally pale shade of yellow seemed to run along the low length of his stomach, and a beautiful, checkered tail—like a gliding snake—trailed the ground behind him, a magnificent specimen of a Himalayan monster!

How he sneaks between the trees! Now he is under Mrs. B.'s " machan," and the poor, young buffalo—his only defence his sprouting horns—puts down his little, square head, in plucky defiance. But the mighty King of cats seems to ignore him. Suddenly, putting caution aside, the gorgeous, jungle gambler strides boldly and ostentatiously right out into the open—leaving the tethered buffalo to his rear—and views the open space in front of him with head erect and tail swaying. Now turning slightly with a huge striped shoulder exposed to Mrs. B.'s rifle, he stares with cocked ears in the direction of the jungle path down the plateau. What a target!

Again I glanced up at the "machan," but Mrs. B. shook her head. I knew she was experienced, and I gathered that she would not take the chance offered, owing to my precarious position on the ground; in fact that, for fear of wounding the monster, she would not fire at all, unless some desperate necessity on my account demanded it.

Mrs. B. now motioned her head towards the plateau. At that instant the tiger sat down; and as he did so, I saw to my surprise, a female elephant with a calf, coming down the pathway to the stream below. Then another elephant followed; and then, to my complete discomfort, an enormous bull elephant, with a formidable pair of gleaming tusks, slowly felt his way down to the stream, where the other elephants had begun to splash themselves with water.

Then, suddenly, events came crowding together—crammed into so short a space of time, that scarcely a breathing interval in which one might hope to collect one's thoughts, seemed to have been granted by Hanuman, and by the gods of darkness and thunder.

The air seemed extraordinarily oppressive, laden with fine gritty dust—it was the season for nor'-westers! In the excitement of watching the animals, I had not noticed the gathering storm. All nature seemed disturbed. Towering over the great jungle, colossal trees—like solemn chieftains bowing in silence before the sullen mood of a capricious Empress—dipped their branches in obedience, lest a leaf should flutter and rouse the ominous stillness. Under the mantle of gloom, the elephant herd froze like black boulders, and the tiger crouched lower. The danger of Mrs. B.'s position struck me instantly. The "Dalbergia Sissoo," an inferior rose-wood tree, being peculiarly brittle and shallow-rooted, is very liable to be blown down in a violent storm, or to have its branches torn off. I was therefore, now, as much concerned for Mrs. B., as she was, apparently, for me.

Suddenly, a blinding flash of lightning, followed by a terrific crash, seems to shake the darkening glen. It seems as if a shell-hole must for a certainty have been gouged out somewhere close by. A distant tearing through timber approaches nearer, and a wind sweeps through the grove, then dies down. The tiger rises, turns right-about, and, with long, crouching strides, makes straight for my anthill. My thoughts are surging. "Can the monster possibly have my cover in view? Does Mrs. B. suspect it?" Her rifle is up! The tiger is passing the tethered buffalo, who, with head down—and a front leg awkwardly hitched up—is following the great cat's movements. As I bend forward to do a bolt, a flame suddenly shoots out from the "machan," and I remain crouched, freezing against my precious anthill. The monster tiger is hit! As I see him lurch and fall forward, sudden, continuous thunder from the heavens, drowns his terrific roars. But the great brute is up in an instant, and—horrors!—turns with indescribable savagery on the unfortunate buffalo, whom he is tearing to pieces. I hear the clicking and clashing of metal on top of the "machan," and raise my eyes slowly, shivering in a cold sweat.

Mrs. B. is struggling with her rifle. "Great Scot! has the bolt jammed?" Now she picks up my empty .500 express—she is looking for the cartridges! Instinctively my trembling fingers press against my right-hand pocket, and my heart sinks as I feel the cartridges there. Mrs. B. is again struggling with the bolt of her rifle; the tiger, maddened with pain, charging in the direction of the metallic sound—whenever it can be heard—and returning again, as savagely, on to the mangled body of the dead buffalo. I am shaking in every limb, lest the monster should see me, or hear my feverish breathing.

Then, suddenly, the storm bursts, and I see the " machan " swaying and crashing against the wind-swept boughs. Trying to hold her rifle, Mrs. B. is clinging desperately to the main trunk of the tree; while I am hoping and praying that that creaking mass of timber will stand. Through the ceaseless fury of cyclonic wind and darting streaks of molten lead, the tiger's awful rumbles and roars of pain and anger can be heard, piercing the glen—carried to the elephant herd hugging their calf; for, suddenly, as the flood gates of heaven open, through the lashing torrents of rain, I see the great bull elephant striding uncannily towards us, across the open glen, shaking his huge head and tusks. " Heavens ! " I feel dazed—benumbed. Mrs. B. is clinging to her tree for dear life. Suddenly our two rifles come crashing down, and the tiger—now beginning to stagger—lurches forward in hideous rage, to maul anything he can get: but his arch-enemy, his disputant to the jungle throne, is on him—so rapidly has the tusker come up.

Almost under Mrs. B.'s heaving tree, the fierce elephant—a phantom, a nightmare, in the misty spray of drenching rain that rebounds off him—charges the wounded tiger in a blood-curdling manner. The striped monster swerves—round towards my anthill; but staggers, and turns sharply with a roar, heading for the open glen. As he passes me, I catch a glimpse of blood pouring down his shoulder. With short, lurching rushes, he gets past the dead buffalo, when the great elephant—pulling up almost on to his haunches—heaves round, and, between Mrs. B.'s tree and my anthill, splashes the sodden ground in another terrific charge. His glistening, beam-like tusks are lowered, and, with a shrill blast—like the shriek of a grating axle—he meets his roaring antagonist, who tries to hurl himself on to the elephant's curled-up trunk : but the wounded tiger is exhausted—he falls, and instantly, through the massive heap of tearing claws and fangs, ploughs a great white shaft. The elephant has pinned down his enemy.

The tiger's roars cease, as again and again the striped form is gored—brutally, unmercifully. Then, full height, up stands the mammoth; and, under zig-zagging tongues of flame and passing claps of thunder, he tramples fiercely upon the carcass. And then, as the wind and the torrents of rain abate, the triumphant elephant, pointing his reddened tusks skywards, lifts his trunk over his head—a superb picture of wild grandeur—and, with a loud trumpet, strides back across the glen with a majestic swing. We watch him anxiously, till he disappears, following the other elephants into the depths of the forest.

With two rifle shots in rapid succession, we called up the "mahout" and the men, who had waited loyally on the road, through the thunderstorm. The "shikarri" came up later, shivering and looking very bedraggled. We were all dripping wet—soaked to the skin—and were glad to get back to camp: where, full of excitement, we recounted the terrible experience. The tiger was fetched in that very night. He measured 9 ft. 8¾ in. First blood was Mrs. B.'s; but her obliging "despatcher" carried matters too far, and had deprived her of a magnificent trophy.

We suspected that this tusker and the tiger were the same animals that had come into collision that morning, disturbing the grazier boy; and this seemed apparent the following day, after we had examined the tracks of the two animals, in both the places where they had met. The tracks looked similar. It appeared as if the tusker had been hugging some previous grievance against that particular tiger—possibly for trying to steal a calf from the elephant herd. Elephants in a wild state show as much intelligence as in domestication.

# CHAPTER III

## THE EX-CONVICT

UP in Náini Tál—one of the most picturesque Himalayan (British) towns in India—I was once invited to a bear shoot. It was in the cold month of December, and the high mountains were all covered with snow. The party consisted of a Forest Officer, a young lieutenant nicknamed "Stuffy," a young lady just out from Home, engaged to the Forest Officer, and myself.

A she-bear with two cubs had been located inside a cave on very precipitous ground. Our guide was a hillman named Bhuwan, an ex-convict.

On our way to the shoot, riding up a formidable mountain, 9,000 ft. high—the northern face of which we were going to negotiate—the young lady remarked on the villainous aspect of the guide. "I should be more afraid of him than a dozen bears," she said.

The Forest Officer then told us that, on his evidence, our guide had been sentenced for "dacoity" to two years' rigorous imprisonment, but that, since his discharge—having employed the fellow to help him to make good—he had found him most grateful and loyal.

It being a common experience in India to find a jail-bird among one's employees, the matter was immediately dismissed.

Some with rifles, and all with alpenstocks, the five of us stood bound together on the brink of a vast precipice, down the steep face of which we had to descend.

Yawning at our feet, and stretching far across to the

interminable ranges of lofty white peaks—that touch soft, pearl-tinted clouds drifting on a bottle-green sky—the grey invisible depth of flecked space sweeps across the mighty valley, where, far to the north, lies the dreaded frozen winter of the Himalayan Mountains. The wide base-lines of the nearest ranges are tinged with pale purple—like a shimmering band—that cuts away the white shoulders of the mountains from the depths below, till there looms up a mighty mirage, as it were, of floating icebergs, waiting for a thaw on the frozen tide of Time. And, over the cold, white grandeur, there comes the daring spirit of adventure, defying the mighty gulf and the snowdrift.

Pointing down to a white ledge running across the face of the mountain—about 300 ft. below—the ex-convict leads the way and we crawl down after him. The zig-zagging path is a goat track, with rough steps cut into the rocks down the most precipitous places. We descend leisurely and cautiously, supporting one another by the strong rope until within about 100 ft. of the ledge.

Suddenly, on a pavement of hardened snow, the leading couple slip and fall on their backs. There is a heavy jerk immediately on the rope that brings the rest of us down on the apex of a sharp turn. In a moment the five of us are ploughing downwards through the snow, gathering impetus like lightning. The girl is crying out to us to hold up above, but it is impossible. Should the leading pair slip over the ledge we should all be lost! This terrible possibility, as we go flying down, is a ghastly nightmare. Suddenly there comes a frantic shout, and the next instant I see the ledge just down below me, and space yawning beyond! I close my eyes, and, in the flash of another moment, I bump up against the Forest Officer, who is struggling on the brink of the fearful precipice. But Heaven is merciful! Another shout and a strong pull and we are hurled back in safety under the brow of the mountain. Bhuwan, the leader, by a dexterous movement has just saved himself, and incidentally the whole party, from going over the ledge. Stuffy and the girl are leaning against the mountain side, panting hard, and shivering with excitement.

Unnerved by this hair-breadth escape we creep silently up to each other on that giddy ledge, like the cornice of a castle wall, and decide to give up the bear hunt; but the guide tells us that he could not pick up the old track again in such bad weather, and that we must proceed.

Hugging the straight wall extending along the mountain side of the narrow ledge, we crawl forward, while the wind and beating snow howls down the yawning abyss on our right. As the risk of suddenly meeting the bear on this terrifying cliff has to be taken should she venture out of her cave on such a day, the Forest Officer and I are leading the way with our rifles ready.

Half an hour of crawling, a sharp turn, and we suddenly come up against a fearful chasm breaking the continuity of the ledge-way, across which two pine logs have been laid side by side in apology for a bridge. The gaping pit is a watercourse, about fifteen feet wide, deeply cut into the mountain side like a vertical split in a wall.

We gaze at each other dumbfounded, while the guide explains that over the logs is the only way to safety; that on the other side we should find an easy ascent up the mountain again. We express surprise to Bhuwan that he should have brought us down a dangerous way when an easier descent to the cave existed; but he only grins. We begin to think his behaviour strange. But it is obvious that the bridge must be crossed, and astride too, the body being pushed along very gradually, with the two hands laid on the logs in front, while the legs dangle in space.

Stuffy, the Forest Officer and his *fiancée* cross together in a party, the girl being placed between the two men. With my heart in my mouth, I watch the trio suspended over the awful chasm. The pine logs are rough-barked, which adds great discomfort to the danger. But they are over at last, standing on the opposite side of the divided ledge, and I breathe more freely. To pass over infinite space, as it seems, on such a terrorising inter-medium as two wabbling logs requires a special mentality and nerve power that falls to the lot of few mountaineers. My turn comes next.

I find that the ex-convict has suddenly detached himself from the rope. He explains that he must be free to bring over, in his own way, the rifles and staffs which are left in his charge. The Himalayan tribesmen, being almost as fearless and agile as the chamois, find no difficulty in carrying baggage over dizzy heights. We knew that in two or three crossings, unaided, he could easily bring over all the paraphernalia.

Bhuwan helps, most assiduously, to place me on the logs, and I feel the rope tightening as the three on the other side put themselves into position apparently for a haul. Shuffling forward inch by inch, with my eyes closed tightly, I am told that I am about halfway over, when, suddenly, I hear the girl's alarmed voice.

"What is the guide doing?—stop him!" she cries out.

The next moment from behind me comes the sound of a pickaxe, and rapid blows follow on rock and shingle. The logs vibrate; and there is a sudden bump downwards, as if their base ends had dropped to a lower level. I have almost crossed as I hear the blows being furiously redoubled, when alarmed voices shriek at me to bend forward and hold out my hands. The very instant that my arm is clutched, and I am pulled up on to the other side in safety, down the mighty precipice fall the logs with a thunderous crash! The voices of my companions, shouting blue murder at the guide, are drowned; and instantly, echoes and re-echoes growl across the mountains, and then bark faintly as they die away to the accompaniment of falling stones.

Tricked? Helpless, frozen—speechless with horror at the bare suspicion, we stand facing the ex-convict who sits on the ledge opposite, grinning fiendishly.

Suddenly he speaks, addressing the Forest Officer.

"You, sahib, got me two years' rigorous imprisonment! I but return the compliment for as many days as you and your friends can survive on that desolate and frozen ledge. The mountain on your side is impossible; and so is the high-walled cave at the end of your ledge. The logs were the only retreat."

He laughs diabolically.

"I leave you," he continues, "to the mercy of the bear and her cubs. Go, make friends with them, share their cave and their fate! Your Government—the mighty British Raj—will never hear of any of us again: we just disappear—like spirits." He rises and points to the north. "I depart for Tibet, over that ice-bound border: Salaam!"

Hardly has the criminal turned his back upon us when suddenly, to our breathless surprise, we see a huge black object standing up on its hind legs, attacking him. It is the bear that has come up quietly behind him on the soft snow—unnoticed by any of us—on her way back to her cubs!

There is a yell of terror from the ex-convict as he tries to pick up one of the rifles. But he is too late! With a savage grunt the bear hurls herself at him. Another second and the wretched man is thrown, head foremost, into the yawning chasm. A slight thud—a faint echo—followed again by the rattle of a few loosened stones, and the demon in human flesh and blood has gone to answer for his crimes!

We stare across the chasm at the perplexed bear. She sniffs for a moment, realising that she, too, is cut off from her cubs. Then suddenly she swings round and shuffles back the way she came. We find that the guide's words are true—we are cut off to die—and our only hope of escape is now centred in the bear! We know that she will find a way to her cubs or die in the attempt.

Our anxious eyes are glued upon her.

Up the white face of the mountain she climbs; then turns suddenly, taking a course parallel with our ledge. Now she is approaching the higher course of the deep cataract that gapes at our feet.

Suddenly she begins to scramble up the side of a huge boulder that seems to hang over in the perpendicular bed of the watercourse, as if a touch would send it rolling down! Only now have our startled eyes rested upon it; awful it looks—hanging magically as if by a thread.

The bear is over; but, good heavens, is the great white boulder moving? We gaze up frantically. Something is moving! We hear a slow, grinding sound, and loose stones are falling. Mercy! It is the boulder—moving slowly but surely—cutting into the sides of the cataract! Can the weight of the bear have done it?

The grinding noise grows louder, and we shrink against the wall of the ledge as big stones come hurtling over our heads.

Suddenly, like an avalanche, sustained and awful—as if the very heavens were splitting open—there comes a crashing roar, shaking our ghastly platform as hurricanes of snow fly overhead and glut the ledge. Another terrific crash as the first echo thunders; then other echoes, less loud, subdued, growing fainter and fainter. A gentle creaking, as if something colossal were settling down at our feet; and then—stillness!—solemn, cold, uncanny.

Slowly we rise and wipe our bloodless faces. Can it be true? Yes; the terrible chasm seems covered up! It has disappeared like magic! There lies a great boulder fixed between the protruding ends of the ledge-ways which the pine logs spanned—an easy walk-over! We stare in astonishment, trying to believe what we actually see; and then, as we realise we are saved—by such a wonderful providential occurrence—we almost dance for joy on that giddy ledge.

To our great delight we met a relief party coming down the mountain side to help us up the old goat track again.

We got back to Náini Tál before darkness overtook us, with the greatest pride in our hearts for the daughters of our beautiful country. Through those hours of terrible trial, the strongest man could not have behaved with greater pluck than did the Forest Officer's *fiancée*.

"Never again," said the Forest Officer, as we gathered round a thrilling log fire, "shall I ever attempt to shoot so sacred an animal as a bear."

"And, if ever you change your mind," replied his *fiancée*, "I shall—di—di——"

But we drowned the young lady's unfinished sentence with the triumphant chorus: "For She's a Jolly Good Fellow!"

# CHAPTER IV

## IN A DEAD CITY: A STRANGE PANTHER HUNT

A YOUNG, Indian chief—to whom I was tutor—and I, during one of our pleasant travels in India—tours which, for educative purposes, the Government encouraged—found ourselves one hot afternoon, five miles out of the historic city of Agra, gazing up at the wonderful, monumental tomb of Akbar the Great. Among the successive Mogul Emperors of Delhi, who ruled with autocratic power, the Emperor Akbar is an outstanding figure for nobleness of character. His wonderful reign of fifty years, 1556 to 1605, corresponds, almost, with the dates of Queen Elizabeth's sovereignty.

It was the month of "chait" (the Indian spring), and the pleasance in which we stood—a garden extending to a hundred and fifty acres—held an indescribably subtle fascination in the bloom of scarlet pomegranates, and in the beguiling perfume of white jasmine. From these pleasant surroundings, immediately in front of us rose—pyramidal in form—the high, five-storied, red sandstone and white marble mausoleum, with the afternoon sun playing fiercely upon the red, and the soft white pillars and archways; whose dainty elegance in ancient, Indian carving and fine, arabesque tracery, seemed to be fantastically emerging from radiant beams—as the eye took it in—like a fairy model of exquisite architecture, being set with magic rapidity in a flaming glow.

Beside us stood an old, keen-eyed fakir, whose naked body was smeared with ash from head to foot, and who looked weird, with a broad streak of vermilion across his forehead, and daubs of ochre on his nose and cheek-bones. He watched us intently, marking our interest in the monument and our exclamations of delight, with accompanying utterances of "Ganesh Ki Jai!" (praise be to the elephant God).

"The fakir's praises to the God with the trunk seem very inappropriate," said the Raja to me. "I wonder what he means! This grand, Mahomedan place, or our presence here, has no visible connexion with the Hindu thanksgiving for escape from evil, or for some good fortune; unless the old fellow thinks we are going to load him with gold 'mohurs'."

We introduced ourselves by name, and questioned the scraggy old fakir; whose long grey hair and flowing, white beard swung with the rustling gusts of warm breeze, as he raised his two hands to his forehead in a solemn salute.

"I am a fair judge of character," he said, "and I have summed you two gentlemen up as being keen sportsmen. If I am right," he continued, "I want you to come and shoot an extraordinarily elusive panther, but twenty-three miles from Agra, in the dead city of Fatehpur-Sikri. Those noble courts and palaces, once a wonderful city, built by the great Emperor who sleeps here," he said, pointing up tragically to the beautiful mausoleum, "defy the ravages of time. As all the Emperor's children died in infancy," continued the fakir eloquently, "that great man built that wondrous city in honour of a son who was at last born to him through the prayers of a very holy man;—a son, who afterwards became the Emperor Jahangir, father of the renowned Shah Jehan, the builder of that greatest achievement in marble art, the Taj Mahal.

"No one believes me," he continued with a sigh,

THE SLOW BUT CERTAIN INDIAN BULLOCK-CART

A FRONTIER PILLAR AND ITS USES

" when I say that, about a week ago, a panther came into that rose-pink capital of ghosts. Everybody looks upon me, I am well aware, as a harmless lunatic. It is due to ignorance. The world hurries along a groove of convention, looking aghast at such as have the strength of mind and purpose to stand aside, and to act according to their own lights. Such few are treated as eccentrics, until they are able to gather followers, when the flow of human thought and life is directed into a new channel. But," he said, " I think you are sporting tourists, new to this district, and your views will be unbiassed. You belong to that unique class, the ' shikarri,' who is born with adventure in his soul, and whose outlook on life becomes large and sympathetic. I felt within my spirit that you would listen to me, and would come out to shoot this panther. That is why, in my joy," said the fakir, " I raised my voice in thanksgiving to the elephant God."

" Why are you," I inquired, " an old priest, so interested in this panther, and so anxious it should be shot? And how, if what you say is true, has this panther been living in those desolate courts without water or food? "

" Listen," said the old man. " Some years ago, in the silent Hall of Public Audience, a European child was killed by a man-eating panther. That panther was shot. The child's father, a Government official, was a great friend of mine; and after that sad occurrence, I swore vengeance on all panthers. For this reason, as well as to prove the truth of my statement, I am anxious, before I die, that the beast should be shot."

The fakir then explained to us, that the superstitious village people knew about the arrival of the panther, but were too afraid to speak; and believing it to be the ghost of the returned man-eater, they drove into those silent courts, every second day, a sheep or a goat—which the panther fed upon—hoping thereby to appease the evil spirit. The village folk also embedded a "nand" (large earthenware tub), which they kept filled with water for the brute to drink.

A visit to this wonderful, dead city was on our programme; and convinced that the fakir, though perhaps eccentric, was no lunatic, we promised to be at Fatehpur-Sikri on the afternoon of the fifth day from that date, as we had previous engagements to fulfil. The fakir said he would await us at the "Buland Darwaza:" the highest gateway in India—176 feet above the pavement. He instructed that, on seeing him, we were merely to follow him silently with our rifles. On no account were we to try to speak to him, or to whisper a word within the walls of the dead city. The fakir then followed us out of the enclosure of the Emperor Akbar's mausoleum. I had heard of the sad tragedy of the English child to which the old man had referred. It was quite true.

In those days, there were neither motor-cars nor branch-railways to convey tourists out to historical places of interest; and the Raja and I had come out the five miles in the usual, hired horse "garry"—a sort of hackney coach—a rickety affair, like a gigantic match-box standing lengthways on its narrow side, the four wheels wabbling inwards and outwards, at all kinds of dangerous angles; while the superstructure creaked and swayed in unison.

By the side of a vicious tat with a squint eye—who, the Jehu remarked, was a bolter—towered an uncanny, transport mule, ordinarily immovable. The only way of getting him to go—notwithstanding the persuasion of his fidgety companion—appeared to be a mysterious proceeding of stuffing both his ears with paper; when he would occasionally take it into his head to bolt along with the tat; as the Raja and I had already experienced, with great anxiety for the coach and our safety.

While the driver—an affable son of the Prophet, splendidly optimistic—commenced operations for our return journey, the fakir requested us to give him a lift back to Agra. "Of course," said the Jehu's mate, an acute little boy: but the Raja and I had seriously to consider the matter, for, though the old fakir was but a feather-weight, he might easily, we thought, prove to be the last straw, as it were, on the camel's back.

We proceeded to examine the coach carefully, as we had done on leaving Agra—much to the indignation again of the driver and the boy. Seeing our dilemma, the fakir said solemnly that safety in this world not being in our hands, we had nothing to worry about. "Precisely," interrupted the driver; "and," continued the priest, "if we had more faith in things, however bad they looked, we should get better results."

"Wa-wah!" (splendid) confirmed the small boy.

The fakir finally reassured us by saying that he had sat in that same conveyance a few days ago, with nine other fares, the driver making the eleventh. "We squeezed in," he said, "wherever there was squatting space, on top or inside, and arrived at our destination safely."

"That settles the question—come along," said the small boy. Whereupon we helped the old fakir up on to the shaky coach-box, where he said he preferred to sit. By this time, paper had been duly inserted into the mule's ears, and the pair were tied up with bits of old rope and harness.

"Quick, your honours—get in!" shouted the driver, and we started; that is, we remained where we were after a terrifying jerk or two! We roared out with laughter, the acute boy joining in, and slapping his bare thighs in great merriment.

Many attempts were made to get a move on—during which time—a solid hour—so wonderful was the outburst of wit in the shape of banter and repartee, that the Raja and I had anything but a trying time. We were in tears with laughter. Even the old priest got lively, indulging in philosophic sallies with a grim smile, and stroking his flowing, white beard.

Finally, the old paper was taken out of the mule's ears —which were blown into—and fresh paper rudely jammed in, with little regard for the mule's sensitive organs. The neck was then stroked down with words of great praise: the mule being invested with wonderful qualities of virtue and wisdom. This, for some inexplicable reason, seemed to have the desired effect. Away we went rattling at an alarming speed. When the pace settled down, the Raja and I felt that we were really off at last; but—as the old priest told us—it is always foolish to anticipate either good or bad fortune. We had covered about three-quarters of the distance to Agra—and were congratulating ourselves—when there was a crash, and the Raja suddenly seemed to drop down into a moving chasm, while my feet lost their support and dangled downwards. The bottom of the coach had apparently dropped out, for, to my amazement, the Raja was actually running on the road below: and he had to run several paces, before he could jump on to the seat again by an athletic movement. We shouted to the driver; but we might just as well have tried to shout for help in the midst of a forest fire, with its crashing din. The small boy was curled up on the dicky-box at the back, having forty winks—oblivious to every kind of sound, for, when an Indian sleeps, he sleeps. So we spared our throats from further effort, and propping our legs up against the opposite seat of the conveyance—spanning the orifice inside the coach—we crashed along, till we arrived at our hotel at Agra.

When we jumped out, the acute boy made a careful inspection of the old " garry." He looked all round, then peeped inside, and we could not help laughing again at the expression of wonder and dismay on his face.

" Ho ho ! " he yelled out to the driver and owner. " I thought they were not gentlemen. They've done away with our fine footboards—kicked them out or something, and now they are laughing."

A good deal of talk ensued ; but the old priest taking up the cudgels in our defence, the owner of the " garry " put his hands up in salute, and requested us to engage him for our trip to the dead city on the appointed day. This we agreed to do, provided a safer conveyance was put at our disposal. We then arranged that the fakir was to be driven on to his temple ; and that, on the day appointed, the driver was to pick him up and bring him to our hotel, from where we should all proceed together. The fakir thanked us, remarking dryly that our lucky escape was due to our having taken his advice and put faith in the old coach, as well as in the optimism of its owner.

Punctually at twelve o'clock, on the day we had fixed, the Jehu and the small boy arrived at our hotel, proud of another coach they had brought, driven by a pair that, to all appearances—with a little aid of the imagination—could just about come under the definition of the horse. Anyway, the turn-out seemed to be an improvement on the old one, and the Raja and I got ready quickly for the start off. We calculated—leaving a safe margin—that it would take us four hours to do the twenty-three miles to the dead city.

But the priest had not come. Both the driver and the boy seemed a little mysterious about this. They said that the old fellow had gone on in a bullock cart, early in the morning, as he preferred the old fashion of doing a journey—rolled up comfortably on a pile of straw, and sleeping as he crawled along.

We started off, however, in great spirits, with rifles and lunch baskets; and after a tedious journey, which consisted of a number of halts in shady groves, owing to the dust and the hot sun, we pulled up at last at the foot of the grand stairway of the dead city; in front of us rising the "Buland Darwaza," or High Gateway of Victory, gorgeous, in the afternoon sun, in marble and red sandstone.

And then an extraordinary thing happened, which puzzled both the Raja and myself. The driver and his small mate offered to carry our rifles, and accompanied us up the vast flight of steps: a hot wind that scorched the skin, blowing like a screaming hurricane through the rose-pink capital. It was the off-season for tourists, and the place seemed to be completely deserted. Reaching the top of the pavement, we beheld the aged fakir, standing alone under a spacious, central dome—when, to our sudden astonishment, the driver and the boy dropped our rifles with a yell of terror, as it seemed, and fled, leaping down the stairway as fast as they could go. In a few moments our coach was rattling away in a cloud of dust. We hardly had time to think. There stood the lean, naked figure of the fakir—like a frail statue delicately carved in mahogany—pointing through the colossal entrance into the interior of the dead city. He seemed quite indifferent to the incident that had just occurred. Suddenly he moved forward, and the Raja and I, picking up our rifles instinctively, and loading them, followed the fakir, as we had arranged to do.

We pass within the circumference of great, red, battlemented walls, feeling completely cut off from the outer world. The hot air is laden with fine sand and dust that hangs in front of us like a shining screen, and we lose sight of our uncanny guide. For a few moments we stand confused, rubbing our eyes and almost choking; then, moving on some distance, we see the frail figure just dimly ahead, pointing in the direction of an immense courtyard.

We breathe more comfortably as the air gets clearer; and passing silently down what seems to be a private entrance, we turn to our left under a marble archway, through which the fakir has disappeared, and suddenly find ourselves in a vast quadrangle, from which rises a magnificent mosque. It is the "Jumma Masjid," the most imposing building of the dead city. In the open courtyard stands the fakir, beside a beautiful Cenotaph surrounded by a fretwork screen carved in marble, which looks like fine lace. It is the tomb of the great saint, through whose prayers Jahangir was born to Akbar the Great.

The fakir points solemnly down beside the tomb; then —before we can come up to him—turning and crossing the quadrangle quickly, our uncanny guide passes through a great portico, consisting of white, marble columns, with entablatures. For some reason it seems that the fakir is careful not to let us come too near him. True enough, at the spot—near the saint's tomb—where he pointed down, there are many pug tracks—of a large panther—old and fairly fresh, clearly visible in the thick layers of dust and sand. Convinced now, and thrilled with the promise of an exciting adventure, the Raja and I follow through the portico, and mark our lean guide ahead.

On, on through silent streets we go, now crossing

desolate courtyards and ghostly halls; now through the Dewani-i-khas, or the great Hall of Audience (where the European child was killed by the man-eating panther), with its wonderful marble-laced galleries criss-crossing above our heads. Here and there, as the fakir glides further along and points significantly, lie scattered bones—the remnants of many a meal the panther has enjoyed.

And now we stalk silently across the large chess-court laid out in black and white marble squares, where the mighty Akbar moved his slave girls from square to square, playing human chess. Then, farther on, we glide through the creeper-grown courtyards of the beautiful palaces of favourite wives. The Golden House, a magnificent structure, arrests my own and the Raja's attention; but when we look round again the old fakir is nowhere to be seen. He seems to have vanished mysteriously.

As the strong wind has died down, the silence grows oppressively, and we note with alarm, the dark, lengthening shadows of the walls. But for these sombre shadows, everything seems bathed in a pink glow—weirdly pink—the walls and the pale, marble structures, now running to a deep shade, now to a pale pink. Even the deathly stillness seems pink; as if pink roses had transfused their delicate colours into the hot, congested breath of summer. To be lost, as I once was, in the ancient ruins of Pompeii, seems nothing in comparison to this mocking silence of a palaced world of blush-rose creation. It seems like a fantastic nightmare: in which, surrounded by weird, palatial magnificence, you are dodging about wildly, trying to hide from fabulous monsters that suspect the presence of a human being in their pink city; far removed, in a world of strange things and of terror.

Suddenly, from a wilder-looking courtyard adjoining where we are standing, comes the loud, sharp, yelping bark of the frightened jackal; an alarm cry which, in forest abodes, is a sure sign that some dangerous carnivore has crossed the path of that scavenger and jungle sentinel. From one stately palace to another, through streets, corridors and grand halls, echoes the sharp sound as the animal scampers away barking. Then, deathly stillness again—so pink, so uncanny! We can hear each other breathing excitedly. "Let us call to the fakir," whispers the Raja hoarsely. "No," I whisper back, as we scan the surroundings, hoping to get a glimpse of that gliding skeleton, crested with hoary hair. I feel we need his guidance, lest the panther, hemmed in within such walls, should attack us suddenly, before we can take him by surprise.

Suddenly, a soft sound breaks the solemn stillness. "What is it?" asks the Raja in a whisper. We listen intently. "Lap, lap, lap!" It comes from the direction of the adjoining courtyard—where the jackal barked—that appears to be a network of jungle. Some animal slaking its thirst! All the feline carnivora lap like the dog, and the Raja glances at me with a pleased expression, for, in the jungle game of "I spy," the advantage lies with the combatant that is the first to place his opponent's position. As there is no sign anywhere of the old fakir, with rifles cocked, we stalk up on tiptoe to a small archway in front of us, and peep into the adjoining courtyard, which is overgrown with grass and shrub, with a creeper-covered pavilion in the centre. To our immediate front, this courtyard seems to open out to a large space, with the ruins of outhouses and servants' quarters dotted about; but to our right it is divided by a long, low wall, covered with riotous creepers. On the other side of this wall, there appears to be a smaller courtyard.

"Lap, lap," again comes that tell-tale sound—undoubtedly from the smaller courtyard! Then, all of a sudden, against the pink background of a high wall, on the farther side of the smaller courtyard, the hoary head and dark shoulders of the fakir seem to rise up mysteriously. It looks like a bronze setting—a life-size cameo, that has suddenly been hoisted up, for our inspection, over the low wall running along our right front. The appearance being deceptive, it seems impossible to guess how far, within the smaller courtyard, the figure is standing; but we are fascinated with the cameo, for there, slowly and deliberately, the head seems to be nodding, as if signing to us to come on. On the left side of the long, low wall we mark a broken archway; and, stooping low, under cover of this wall, we stalk up to the archway carefully, listen for a moment, then dart quickly through. In the front of us a thick bush hides the view. The loud beats of the lapping stop immediately, and the rattle of a single leaf is the only sound that breaks into the solemn stillness.

The nauseous smell of a carnivorous animal seems to hang heavily in the air, and for a moment or two we wait in breathless expectation. Then, quickly, we side-step to the right of the wide-spreading bush. Instantly a loud, hissing growl greets us! Barely twenty paces in front of us, a huge panther, sitting beside some water—it is the buried earthenware tub!—springs quickly to attention. His long tail is swaying and flapping the ground in anger. A small, grassy space, leading up to the high wall, with an archway again on the left side, lies beyond the beast.

Not a moment is to be lost; but as my rifle goes up I notice with anxiety that the fakir—who seemed to have completely vanished when we entered the courtyard—suddenly, at the critical moment, comes gliding in through the archway to the left of the high wall, which rears up on the other side of the panther and appears to completely imprison him. Horrors! the foolish man seems to be advancing, and we dare not fire for fear of a ricochet—from that high, stone wall in front of us—hitting him. "Run!" I shout to the fakir in desperation; but a rush from the infuriated panther at bay instantly drowns my voice. The Raja is down, with the spotted brute on the top of him! The muzzle of my rifle, swinging round instinctively to the onslaught, is almost touching the open jaws of the fiend, and I pull the trigger. Through the silent city echoes the roar of the report, then it dies away like the far sound of a distant landslide in the Himalayas.

"A good thing the shot was through the brute's head," said the Raja, as I helped him up. Though he had had a narrow escape, he was fortunately not hurt. "That stupid fakir," he added, "must be a lunatic after all, if he hadn't the sense to retreat when he saw us in front of the panther."

We were, however, delighted with the bag, and looked expectantly round for the mysterious old fakir, hoping he too would be very pleased at our success; but again the old fellow was nowhere to be seen. This time, for some extraordinary reason, he had apparently deserted us altogether. Standing over the dead panther in the sunset glow of those desolate surroundings, we shouted to the wizened old man for some time; but only the echoes, which seemed more startling as evening approached, came back to us. There seemed to be such a mystery about the whole business. We could not understand how it was that the panther did not attack the old fakir, who, when he appeared as a cameo, must have been inside that small courtyard, and close to the savage animal. We could conclude only that the weird fellow, being an expert stalker—some ascetics spending a lifetime in the jungles—sneaked in through the archway to the left of the high wall, and managed to take up a position—very risky—behind the panther, while the animal was preoccupied drinking water. There were certainly some clumps of fairly high grass behind the panther, but even granting this cover, the old fakir apparently accomplished a wonderful feat in stalking. When—after nodding to us—he saw us coming, he must have stalked out of the courtyard again, returning as he did—for some extraordinary reason—when I was on the point of firing. His stupidity might have led to a dreadful tragedy. Covering up the dead panther with leaves and branches from the bush that had screened us, we prepared to depart, having decided either to return ourselves from Agra to pick up the "bag," or to send a "shikarri" for it in a hackney "garry."

A huge yellow moon had risen over the dark, battlemented walls, along whose embrasured parapet ran a phosphorescent ribbon of silver; as if the ghostly city, so sacred to history, had suddenly been invested with the glory of a magnificent halo that seemed endless in circumference. Guided by the great, luminous dome of the Gateway of Victory, we found our way out, hurrying as fast as we could go, with the echo of our footsteps behind—as if the sleepers of Akbar's long-dead civilisation had suddenly awakened, to chase us out of their holy sanctuary.

No vision of our hackney "garry" greeted us, and puzzling our heads over the strange behaviour of the Jehu and his mate, we shouldered our rifles and walked, hoping to pick up at least a bullock cart on its way to Agra. But after a three-mile walk we were glad to see our hackney coach encamped on the roadside. To our surprise the driver, trembling with fear, immediately fell at our feet and implored our forgiveness. We thought he was repentant for having run away and deserted us, but again he surprised us by saying that, for fear of losing the day's fare—which meant a good thing for him—he had told us an untruth in the forenoon : that the fakir had not gone to Fatehpur-Sikri early that morning in a bullock cart, as he had stated, but had been called away by God ; and that God, who was so great—" Allah ho Akbar ! " he exclaimed—had shamed him into making the humble confession by bringing him face to face with the spirit of the fakir, to warn him (Khuda Bux, the driver) against telling future untruths.

We asked the man to be more explicit.

" The fakir died at Agra," he said, " two days ago, and was cremated on the banks of the river. It was his 'bhoot' (ghost) we saw under the Great Gateway this afternoon, and the boy and I," he said, " were so dumbfounded that we fled in terror."

We were fairly taken aback to hear this, and made all the inquiries we could the next day in Agra ; but the result was not satisfactory. We could find no priests of the brotherhood, and were told that all the members of that particular fraternity had suddenly disappeared from the precincts of Agra. It was believed that they had gone on a visit to one of the many holy places in India that they periodically attended. All that we could glean was that an aged fakir had suddenly been taken ill, and had died. Some named our priest-guide, while others named somebody else. The Raja and I thought—and some wise old heads agreed with us—that it was quite possible that the brotherhood, in order to keep alive their reputation for supernatural powers—which that class of mendicant professed as a divine bestowal—had taken advantage of the death of some other fakir, and had given out the name of our guide, being aware of the appointment he had made with us.

It is well known that there are certain classes of mendicants, who, for the purpose of advertising their powers, will get away with a trick if they can, whenever an opportunity occurs ; but for all that, they do good work among their believers. It seemed impossible, however, to clear up the matter ; and the Raja and I carried away with us the great mystery—as to whether the fakir, whom we followed, was of this earth—of human flesh and blood or an apparition from that unknown world, come to claim fellowship with Akbar's sleeping citizens, who sleep for ever in that city of ghostly magnificence—that dreamland city that stands in the shadow of a mighty age, to mark the handiwork of a great Emperor, and the rise and fall of a great nation. An Empire that, in the circuit of unfathomable time, has passed on to the sacred trust and keeping of Britannia, who, obeying the chime of Heaven's ordination, arose on the great waters of the world, and answered the call of the East.

# CHAPTER V

## THE GREAT "GANGA!"

LOOSED from his high, eternal, snow-clad home—creeping from the droning, astral silence of frozen solitudes and sliding the avalanche; and, roaring down precipices in many an echoing cataract; and—lower, mocking the stately pines in silver-tongued cascades with child-like glee—limpid, resilient falls that bathe with sparkling spray, the graceful bracken and the tender maiden-hair; and, where the laughing tributaries join, gliding silently through the secret haunts of purling brooks—where the lily of the valley enchants the love-sick bee—down, down at last, into the lower world, comes the great life-giver of Hindustan, plunging and swirling in the radiant joy of Ind's generous spirit. Through mighty forests he sports, splashing the elephant herd; and, by Palace, mosque and temple, he reflects on his calm bosom, the glory of lordly cities. And, far and wide, he enriches the sub-Himalayan lowlands with their sun-baked plains of pasture and agriculture; that thirst, where the monsoons weaken, for the spread of his refreshing waters.

Many beautiful legends and beliefs seem to be borne, like the bright marigolds that float in profusion, on the flower-decked foam of these waters. Where the river passes through the wilder parts of the country, the remote village people sing songs, which, their legends say, are the songs of the river. One song of promise swells on the flowing tide, in picturesque romance: "Whosoever

—irrespective of nationality, caste or creed—should be engaged near my banks—within such distance as to hear the sound of my waters—in the quest of some knowledge, or in the destruction of some dangerous beast, for the benefit of mankind, the same shall be protected by my spirit."

Thrilling stories are told of Kings, and other great personages who have hunted on these inspiring banks, and have had miraculous escapes. On hunting expeditions in the Ganges Forest Division, and in other places near the river—apart from my own personal experiences—I have been witness to some wonderful incidents of hair-breadth escapes; not only in hunting, but in other pursuits as well. On each occasion, after the particular danger had passed, the "shikarries" have run to the river, and have raised a handful of its waters to their foreheads, in a most impressive thanksgiving. A memorable incident comes back to me, with all its horrors:

July, and the heavens have opened in grim reality. In the opening demonstration of the monsoons, June's extravagance in the first welcome deluge that brought promise of a normal year of prosperity, has been nothing in comparison. All nature is in harmony with the requirements of man, and the mighty Ganges is overflowing with bountiful contributions. Plunging and creaking through these turbulent waters in Eastern Bengal, a river steamer is trying to make headway against the vast current. Indian passengers crowd the lower decks, the top or boat deck being reserved for first-class passengers; among whom an occasional Englishman may be met with.

An hour ago, before we steamed away from the river calling-station where the Darjeeling mail train deposits passengers from Calcutta—who are making a river trip—

I met a friend, G. P., who was a junior tea-planter from Assam. We found that we had both been invited to the silk factory of a mutual friend for a few days' change ; a custom prevailing among planters who, periodically, visit each other in turn. The silk factory lay about fifteen miles up the river, on the starboard side or northern bank. We hoped to reach our landing-place by lunch-time, if no dangerous river bores obstructed the skipper's movements.

G. P., "pour passer le temps," had brought up from the lower deck an emaciated old snake-charmer who was an inveterate opium-eater. An indigo-dyed turban, and a saffron garment that hung on his lean body, decorated him weirdly. With his mesmeric flageolet and two baskets of snakes, he was a source of general interest in the planting community. The skipper, a Britisher, passed and said : "Wonderful old blighter ! " Jogi was the snake-charmer's nickname ; he too, was on a visit to M. C. Sahib, the manager of the silk factory, with whom he had large snake dealings. Was he not, even now, taking to the Sahib a deadly cobra, freshly caught (?), for which he would receive Rs. 10.

So we were all three visiting M. C., with whose hobby —snake catching and venom collecting—we were all acquainted. M. C. was a keen, scientific naturalist—fearing no creature of the lower creation—who had learned to play the magic flute, and to handle poisonous snakes induced out of their holes. His research room was stocked with bottles of methylated spirits, containing interesting specimens of both known and unknown snakes. Phials of amber-coloured venom, which he had himself extracted, were kept locked up in a glass-fronted cabinet. He spent his spare time in experimenting on fowls and rabbits, with a view to discovering a cure for snake-bite. His companionship was most educative.

The large, ferry steamer arrived at last, and there stood M. C. on the high bank of the river, with his factory looming up above a clump of mango trees. He sent out a factory boat to meet us, and was delighted to see that we had brought "Jogi." M. C. at once proceeded to uncover the basket in which a young, light, cloudy-grey cobra—the spectacled terror of India—was hissing. The brute struck out, and M. C. had a very narrow escape. "Fierce youngster that," he said, laughing, while the snake-charmer reprimanded him for carelessness.

But the snake had tilted the basket, and, before the snake-charmer realised what had happened, the cobra was out, and escaped into a large, deep hole quite near the spot. M. C. was disappointed: he said it was the lightest marked cobra he had seen—the lighter the more venomous—and that he must have it. Notwithstanding the loss, he handed Jogi a ten-rupee note. Before we moved up to the bungalow for lunch, the programme arranged was that we were to come down to that spot in the afternoon—after tea—to enjoy a swim in the fresh, flood water, and to see how a snake was caught. M. C. said he would fetch the cobra out of the hole with his own flageolet, catching it with his bare hands, after the snake-charmer's fashion. It was excellent practice he told us. G. P. and I were keen on the bathing, but, after what we had just seen—almost a dreadful tragedy—we suggested instead, a game of golf on M. C.'s sporting jungle course; but he was not to be dissuaded.

Late in the afternoon, decked out in our airy, bathing costumes, the three of us walked down to the river, G. P. and I having an animated discussion with M. C. about the unnecessary risks he ran in person. But there was no shaking his determination to catch, in its own free habitat, this particular, fierce young cobra. The snake-charmer had been dismissed, and was told that on no account was he to be present at the ordeal. M. C. said that the critical eye of such an expert would embarrass him.

From the snake's hole—about fifty paces from the edge of the river—the high bank recedes down to an inlet of water; a fair sized river-bay, where a thick, red current of liquid mud swirls in, and dies away into shallow back-water. Standing over the snake's hole on the high bank, M. C.—having examined the exit—has commenced to play his flageolet. Under his instructions, G. P. and I are seated on the ground about fifteen paces in front, facing him and the weird background stretching beyond. Against a leaden sky emitting in the distance, intermittently and noiselessly, flashing fangs of lightning that dip into the yellow bosom of the river, M. C.'s figure—athletic in his bathing costume—sways uncannily, now slow and now fast, to a discordant fandango. The shrill notes of his brass instrument pierce the low groaning of the rolling tide to our right, and intermingle hideously with the symphony of swirling water, and the tinkling splash of crumbling sand-banks. Not a breath of air stirs, but our own heavy respiration. Moist and clammy we feel glued to the spot, and M. C.'s instruction to freeze like statues—whatever might happen—seems easy to obey. His life, he had said, might depend upon our strict obedience.

Suddenly, we see a long, sinuous creature gliding out of the hole, and M. C. steps back a pace or two. As a climax is reached in a hoarse fanfare of blasts and trills, the long, light-grey body begins to curl, the head of the snake lifts and the hood expands. Higher it rises in a graceful curve, proud, arrogant, with the mighty power of death in its hidden fangs! And now, as the cobra's forked tongue darts in and out, a change comes over the spirit of the music—for M. C. can play the flute well—

and the fearsome hood sways in sublime motion to the beautiful, rhythmic strains of Barcarolle.

Suddenly, the measured beats of the symphony die away, and M. C. drops his flute quietly behind him, on to the soft grass. The next instant, the open palm of his right hand moves in front of the hood for a few beats, in harmony with the cobra's swaying—whose musical talent seems to mark no difference between the harmonious measures of Barcarolle and the symphony of the breaking waters. Suddenly, the swaying hand shoots up vertically, and, close over the spectacled hood, the fingers make a smart, snapping noise. In a second the hood contracts and down slides the head. As instantly, down shoots M. C.'s hand, and a wreathing lashing mass of pale grey, and then white marble streaks—as the snake's abdomen swings round—is lifted up, well above the ground. It seems as if the nape of the snake's neck were grasped by M. C.'s fingers.

But, as we gaze terrorised, suddenly, the awful, wreathing body coils round M. C.'s forearm with the grip of steel bands, and, to our horror, we see the oily head of the snake slipping from his grasp ; the purchase of the shining grey body, with its powerful contracting muscles, acting as a leverage to draw out the head. M. C.'s face grows ashen as he tries, with cool deliberation, to unwind the cobra's body with his left hand ; but the coils fly back like steel springs, and M. C., probably realising the importance of not irritating the brute further, makes a rush for the shallow bay. We follow in the greatest anxiety. Land snakes dislike water... If, before the brute draws its head out, M. C. can sit down in the water, his life is saved. But—he is too late—the cobra's head is out ! and G. P. and I stand benumbed with mental agony at the edge of the shallows.

Suddenly, from behind us, like a ship on fire on the far

expanse of reddened water, a gorgeous monsoon sunset bursts through the clouded west. Bathed in the red flare, motionless stands the pale figure of M. C. in his sea-beach tights, knee deep in the madder muddy-bay. The diabolical snake is curled fiercely round the now-extended, frozen right-arm—wound round from the wrist to the armpit!—the angry head, with its full-dilated hood—free to strike at any moment—being flung back at an acute curve. The black, forked tongue protrudes within a few inches of M. C.'s frozen hand, and the eyes, struck by the flaming rays from the west, shine like ruby beads—lidless, diaphanous, unearthly eyes that glow with the merciless doctrine of fiends and devils. Dare a finger of the hand move or tremble!

But what's that?—a dark figure, with a drawn knife, emerging from the high bank across the bay?

Warm blood suddenly courses through my veins, as my heart leaps with unbounded joy. G. P. gulps audibly and stirs, but steadies again. As swift as a darting panther with silent pads, the emaciated figure—bare to the waist—has reached the glowing, red water. Now he is moving stealthily in the liquid mass. Can M. G. hold out another few seconds without stirring? He seems unconscious of anyone behind him.

Nearer, and nearer creeps the figure. Now the shrivelled, bronze form bends low with his long knife raised, and poises for a second behind the motionless hood or the cobra; who, with fiendish glee, is defying M. C.'s nerveless steadiness of hand! The sharp edge of the blade scintillates in the evening glow. Suddenly it flashes, and a clod of something grey is hurled through the air and splashes into the water.

I heard G. P. shouting: "Good Jogi—wonderful Jogi!" as we rushed into the water and watched the snake-charmer unwinding, off M. C.'s arm, the headless body of that ghastly snake. The brute, though a young snake, had attained the age, M. C. said, when the poison glands are fully developed. It measured three and a half feet in length.

"You didn't want me present," said the snake-charmer, "but," he said, anointing his forehead with the holy water in which he stood, "in every drop of this there is the benevolent spirit of the 'Ganga,' whose mandate I have but obeyed. That spirit has saved you, as it is writ; for you are trying to benefit all mankind. When you discover a cure," he said, "the cobra will be our best friend, for then we shall not fear him."

"My faith," said M. C., "is in the wonderful faith of these Ganges people.—Whatever the object of worship," he added, "I believe in the mass faith of a people, if the idea be praiseworthy."

# CHAPTER VI

## A FIERCE JUNGLE BATTLE

ON one occasion I was shooting in the lower hills of the Himalayas with a young Raja—to whom I was tutor at the time—and a great sportsman, Major B. We made a very early morning march to an encampment in a very wild part of the jungles known as "Hathikund," in the Ganges Forest Division. The Raja and I were leading the way, mounted on a female elephant, while Major B. was close behind riding on a tusker. Under the intense brilliancy of a magnificently jewelled sky dawn was breaking, and under that serene spell in the early hours—so spiritually absorbing—we were moving leisurely along a broad fire-line that crossed a flat plain covered with high grass.

We had scarcely gone two miles when suddenly we heard two or three sharp barks on the road ahead of us that sounded like wild dogs. We were interested at once and hurried forward. We left the road and stalked round to the spot through the high grass. It was getting sufficiently light to see, and we were suddenly surprised to find two wild boars standing in the middle of the road and defending themselves against a pack of jungle dogs. To suddenly come upon a jungle battle is something not to be missed—an opportunity of a lifetime—and we took up a very careful position on our elephants to watch the proceedings. All the inhabitants of the jungle being accustomed to wild elephants our presence passed unnoticed.

The two boars were on their mettle and kicking up clouds of dust. Suddenly there was a yelp like a war cry from the dozen or more dogs present, and they rushed upon the pig. For a moment the sturdy defendants seemed to be entirely overwhelmed, but with the burly obstinacy of their race they ripped to the right and left, trying to push forward at the same time. Two dogs were actually carried along a short distance on the back of one of the boars, while some two or three dogs were lying on the road *hors de combat*.

It seemed evident that the boars would soon be borne down by the little blood-thirsty creatures, when suddenly one boar broke away into the high grass on the far side of the road. Some dogs followed, but after a short interval they came racing back. This struck us as being very strange, for the wild dog has no mercy and will run his victim down to death. Suddenly bright crimson rays shot across the grassy plain from the great fiery globe that reddened the eastern hills and hung over their summits. Surrounded and torn by the merciless dogs, the poor boar on the road had his head poised up in the agony, as it looked, of a last effort.

We decided to shoot at the dogs in order to save the poor pig. The elephant on which the Raja and I were riding suddenly became restless, and up went Major B.'s rifle; but, before he could fire, we saw the mahout quickly grip his arm and point to the right, into the grass, over the struggling mass below. Major B.'s rifle went up again and we followed the direction anxiously, but could see nothing in the dense high grass. A few seconds and a tongue of flame darted out of the cold steel barrels with a crash, followed, to our great surprise, by the deafening roar of a tiger!

The red dry grass in front of us is immediately a rustling and shaking expanse of stampeding animals, and with the exception of a few of the bolder dogs standing at the edge of the road and panting with their tongues lolling out, looking fiendishly at the poor boar, all have disappeared.

We hear the loud savage growls of the tiger continuing, and we move in that direction. We push our two elephants over the forest-line, where some dying dogs are struggling beside the collapsing boar, and have moved forward about a hundred paces through the thick grass, when in a small open clearing we suddenly come face to face with the tiger, hit apparently by Major B.'s shot, in a death-struggle with the boar that had escaped. We could now understand the reason why the dogs that had followed him had so promptly returned.

Both the tiger and the boar seemed to be badly wounded, and in pain and rage are tearing fiercely at each other. In the surprise of the moment our elephants swerve badly; but the mahouts are plucky and know what to do, handling them firmly and silently. It strikes us instantly that it is a tigress, from her size and general conformation. She is on top of the boar, who throws her off suddenly, with a wonderful exhibition of strength, rushing forward immediately and ripping her terribly in the bowels. With fierce gasping roars in rapid succession the tigress springs again—but she is facing us, and we are immediately seen! There is no possibility of a shot from off our turning and twisting elephants; and now as quick as the sweep of a sharp-edged blade she leaves the pig, and we see the gorgeous flash of black and red flaring in front of us, while a few chance shots pass wide of the mark! Instantly—before we can realise what has occurred—she alights on the trunk of Major B.'s swerving tusker. As her huge open claws and teeth are embedded in the frantic elephant's soft flesh, a loud shriek of pain escapes him. The tigress seems to be clinging savagely just below his forehead, and the mahout, looking down upon her furious steam-spitting jaws, is close enough to be spluttered with reddened froth.

The next instant, a deafening roar from Major B.'s maddened elephant shakes the very ground, as he swings round on to his hind legs. He stands bolt upright for a few seconds, and then comes down with a great thud on the ground with his fore-feet in his mighty effort to shake off the huge cat. The mahout and Major B. are clinging desperately to the pad as they are hurled up and then twirled round with the fury of the elephant. Major B.'s rifle is flung out of his hand, and it crashes into the high grass.

Suddenly the infuriated tusker turns his blood-besmeared trunk towards us, dripping with the hideous mess from the awful wounds in the bowels of the tigress, and falls on to his knees to crush her. The spectacle is a terrible one, and the mahout is now in imminent danger of his life. He can hardly keep his seat at the steep angle of the tusker's suddenly conceived and frantic stratagem; and Major B., with his left arm around the mahout's neck, is trying his utmost to keep him from tumbling off and being crushed to death along with the tigress, who now must sooner or later let go her grip.

My heart beats like a sledge-hammer as we see the huge tusker about to stand on his head, as it seems, and it looks as if he must take a somersault! We shout to Major B. to try to jump off to one side, while we are doing our best to persuade our elephant up to rush the tigress when she springs away, as we expect her to do any moment in order to save herself.

But no! The tigress is fighting with the ferocity of a mother that has cubs. Suddenly, as we expect the worst to happen, the tigress loosens her grip and falls under the trunk of the elephant! Streams of blood pour down the tusker's forehead and trunk, and splash the white fur which the tigress shows underneath as she lies struggling on her back with her protruding claws striking the air in fury. Her hind-quarters seem to be under the kneeling weight of the tusker's head and trunk, and she is apparently pinned. The Raja is sitting in front of me, and now raises his rifle quickly, trying to take a careful aim at the head of the tigress roaring and spluttering close in front of the tusker's curled-up trunk. The shot is a risky one, but something must be done, and I let the young Raja take it.

The roars of the tigress cease as the sharp report of the rifle echoes through the hills. At this instant we see Major B. scrambling down off the pad so dangerously inclined forward. We immediately bring our elephant up cautiously behind the tusker, and make her sit down quietly some thirty paces away to pick the Major up without delay. Major B. has scarcely reached our elephant when the tusker suddenly rises to his feet, and fortunately for us and his mahout—who has held on with the greatest pluck—begins to pommel the dead body of the tigress who has received her quietus from the Raja.

Immediately Major B. had scrambled up on to the pad of our elephant, we moved away rapidly about two hundred yards, in case our immediate presence should give the excited tusker cause for further irritation and attack. In the absence of other tuskers to help quiet an enraged elephant the best thing to do is to move away quietly if there is time, and to leave the mahout to deal with the temper of his animal.

The mahout fought desperately with his elephant, using his formidable "gajbag," or iron hook, freely, and hurling upon him such a vast vocabulary of abuse that we were struck with wonder at the unlimited possibilities of the Hindustani language. The mahout waxed, and waxed so eloquent that the tusker, appearing to be constrained to listen, ceased his trumpeting. Within an hour's time he was so far calmed that he stood quietly, and looked as if he were, in reality, ashamed of his conduct towards his mahout.

We called to his plucky driver to take him on to a river a short distance ahead, where we could wash his wounds while we waited to pick up the fallen rifle and to pad the tigress, which we found in a terribly mangled state. Her skull was a pulp, and nearly all the bones in her body appeared to be broken. It was a bad light in the early morning. The tigress had moved the moment Major B. had pulled his trigger. When the shot hit her the wounded boar was in all probability crossing her path at the time, or in close proximity, and she must have turned upon him in rage. We looked for the dead dogs, but found to our surprise that they had disappeared. They were apparently devoured by the pack.

On arriving at the river we were glad to see that the tusker's wounds were not as dangerous as we expected to find. It seemed evident that the tigress was in a considerably enfeebled state, which was fortunate for the elephant. Tearing up an old tablecloth—obtained from one of the morning carts that had come up from camp—we proceeded to bandage the tusker's trunk. He behaved very quietly, sitting down in the water and allowing us to do the needful—though it was the mahout alone who dared give him any further pain.

CHURKA, NEAR NEPAL TERRITORY
WHERE THE TIGER HUNTS THE SWAMP DEER
(The Author's wife, the Author, and his two brothers)

SOME FINE SAMBUR HORNS : DEER AND PANTHER THAT
RAID VILLAGE CROPS AND GOATS

# CHAPTER VII

## AN ILL-FATED GLEN

FAR to the north of Lucknow—the capital of that old, historic Province of Oudh, over which a King once ruled in prodigal splendour—lies a remote tract of glorious country; the sub-Himalayan district of Lakhimpur. Touching the wild borders of the Himalayas, where the dreaded brigand and the huge tiger of northern India find a harbour of refuge, and, adorned with the glamour of thrilling, historical legends, this district calls alluringly to the big-game hunter. It was here, in these wilds—long before the advent of the Honourable East India Company—along the high borderland of deep, jungle recesses, that a powerful Nawab—whose jewel-hilted sword rested in its scabbard in the presence only of the Moghul Emperor of Delhi—built, regardless of expense, formidable forts in support of a deep intrigue to kidnap into his territory, a beautiful Princess of the Himalayas; news of whose wonderful beauty and independence of spirit had spread far and wide. Owing to the iron conservatism of caste, the Mahomedan chieftain could never hope to win, by legitimate means, the hand of the fair Princess; and he treated with reckless scorn the consequences of incurring the fierce anger of the King of those mountain territories.

In a central stronghold—from which a line of forts, manned by the flower of his army, extended through the jungles to the east and west—the great Nawab, in company with his commander-in-chief, spent weeks on end in all seasons of the year, hunting the tiger and the panther, while awaiting from the mountain heights news of the progress of his dangerous intrigue. Tradition narrates that the Princess, tired of the close watch kept upon her—through the influence of her jealous *fiancé* —on account of her great beauty, was enamoured with the romantic adventure; and, as proof of the favourable reception of the Nawab's amorous avowels, she sent him, through his spies, a painted portrait of herself, promising,—if there were no hitch in the working of his secret plans, to put his courage to the test. One night, cleverly disguised, she left the royal palace of her aged father, the King, and fled with the Nawab's ambassador and his secret agents.

It was not long before the plot was discovered. Notwithstanding his infirmity, the King of the mountains led, in person, his sturdy hill soldiers down to the plains, in pursuit of his fugitive daughter: but, the main body of his army being led astray through treachery, he was captured near the Nawab's jungle forts. Though a prisoner, the mountain King was treated as a royal guest, being paid all the honours due to a great sovereign. In his wrath, however, he publicly insulted his host, and, as old as he was, the King challenged the great Nawab to a private duel. The Princess, penitent for her conduct and tortured with grief, followed the duellists and their seconds to a glen—an open clearing, in dense jungle. But, when the combatants drew their swords, the handsome Nawab, a warrior in the prime of life, suddenly flung his weapon down, and, throwing himself at the feet of his royal prisoner, exposed his bare breast to him, saying that he would rather die and lose his happiness in this world, with the Princess as his wife, than harm a single hair on the grey head of such a brave King. Upon this the Princess rushed up, and, prostrating herself across her lover, implored her royal father's mercy and forgiveness.

Touched with his daughter's appeal, and the noble sentiments of her chivalrous lover, the King ordered the lovers to rise, and, as a token of his forgiveness—and sufferance of the Princess's conversion to Islamism—he silently placed the hilt of his sword in his daughter's hand, and turned his back to walk away. But, at that very moment—Fate striking a blow to cloud the happiness of the lovers—a savage tiger, that had been wounded by some soldiers amusing themselves hunting, suddenly rushed across the glen, and killed the aged King before he could be rescued.

In due course, holy men from the two kingdoms came, and, cursing that jungle clearing—with the invocation that whosoever should pass through it would meet with sudden death—they laid with brickwork, horizontally on the ground, a large figure representative of the evil one. And to this day may be seen the old ruins of the grand Nawab's jungle stronghold; on the site of which now stands a double-storied, inspection bungalow for Forest Officers, called the "Fort." About a mile north of this bungalow, in the depths of the Government reserved forests, crumbled pieces of brick are still supposed to be found in an open depression, where the grass is stunted. From the "Fort," or inspection bungalow, a fire-line runs north, through the high tree forest, crossing a portion of this, apparently fated, jungle clearing; for, strange to say, not a few tragedies and narrow escapes from various causes, have, from time to time, occurred on this road—either close to the clearing, or on the site itself. The saddest tragedy of all was the case of a young Forest Officer, who, within six months of his arrival in India, was killed outright on the very spot, by a falling tree.

I had shot in the vicinity of the "Fort" on one or two occasions; always avoiding this glen, through force of habit more than any sentimental reason. But on a subsequent occasion I happened to defy the legendary curse. I joined a Christmas party at the "Fort" for a ten days' shoot. Several guns made up the party. In view of the superstition of our shikarries and elephant drivers, we treated the glen as forbidden ground, and allowed a detour to be made, whenever we had occasion to make use of that particular road, or forest-line.

One afternoon—it was a Sunday too, I remember—I took out shooting a young Lieutenant—alluded to as P. —who had arrived in camp only that morning. A pad elephant, a staunch female, had been put at our disposal; and we started off. The other guns elected to rest in camp that memorable afternoon. P. was full of curiosity about the ill-fated jungle clearing, and, his keenness to go through this glen and test it, inspired me to make the venture. Our mahout, however, a son of the Prophet—a fine, old, bearded veteran—refused to even entertain the idea; so, in the face of the old fellow's solicitations, we determined to make the adventure on foot. "Why tempt the great Allah," he said, "who has permitted, for some reason we mortals do not understand, certain things to come about in certain places. It is all for the good of mankind; and our holy men do say, that there is more in superstition than meets the eye," he said, warning us seriously. But we had no personal objections, and insisted upon going.

We follow the forest-line down—the elephant moving solemnly—until we come to a well-known bend in the road, within about two hundred yards of the glen. Here we insist upon the elephant's sitting down, in order to dismount; and we are about to alight, when, suddenly, some cheetal (spotted deer) call furiously in the jungle to our left. They are terribly alarmed at something. The elephant gets fidgety and stands up again. "Don't go," pleads the mahout; but we insist dogmatically. For some extraordinary reason, the elephant, as staunch as she is, begins to give trouble: she is not inclined to obey her driver. The mahout punches her on the head with his iron "gajbag," and, the moment her knees touch the ground, P. and I slip off the pad with our empty rifles (in movements up and down "machans" and elephants' backs, weapons being unloaded for the sake of safety). But what can have happened to the elephant? For no more apparent reason than the alarm cry of some cheetal, she gets up in a panic, and bolts before the mahout has had time to unfasten our cartridge bags and hand them down to us! Madly rushes the elephant through the forest, in the opposite direction to the calling cheetal. We stand and gaze after the trumpeting creature, astonished and alarmed. With empty rifles and no ammunition, we are helpless. I suggest walking back to camp. "No," begs P. "Let us stalk up quietly and see what has disturbed the cheetal—it will be some fun!"

In the excitement of big-game, one sometimes loses one's better judgment. Hugging the left side of the forest-line, I lead the way, while, in single file, P. follows excitedly, close behind me. Suddenly, in a red-hot panic, the herd of cheetal disperse in all directions, some rushing desperately across the road in front of us. Almost simultaneously, a short distance on ahead—still to our left—we hear a thud of something falling heavily. I whisper that I think it is a cheetal that has just been seized by a panther; and we move on in breathless excitement, treading as noiselessly as possible through the sun-lit patches of the lengthening shadows. Now we are within a few paces of the "clearing." How still, all of a sudden, the jungle becomes! Cautiously we move forward, until I set foot on the forbidden ground.

Instantly, like a sudden blast, there comes the fierce intake of a dreadful breath, followed by a deafening roar that pulls us up to a dead halt, with the blood freezing in my veins. It is a monster, savage tiger—horrors!—that has just killed a cheetal stag at the corner, to our left, where, between the road and the open glen, the high tree forest terminates abruptly. The monster—for a mighty creature he seems with his massive head and shoulders—gorgeous in bright red and black stripes, is standing over his kill, to lift or drag it into the heavy jungle. We are standing right in the open before him, disturbing him at his most savage moment. Instinctively I feel that nothing but successful jungle deception—to stand still! —can save us. It is the practice of wild animals when confronted with sudden danger—the law of the jungles! I don't move a hairbreadth; and I am hoping and praying that P., behind me, won't make a mistake—that he will see the urgency of following my example. To turn my head round, however slowly, and whisper a word of caution, would mean instant death! I am praying that no breeze, however gentle, may spring up; for the slightest rustle of grass near us, would be sufficient to provoke the tiger further, and cause him to hurl us into eternity. We are dressed in khaki that blends with the jungle coloration; and my fervent prayer, that this mighty creature may be deceived—if but for once in his lifetime—makes the veins throb in my temples: life seems so precious! Suddenly, with a stretch that seems to double his size, the huge tiger squats down deliberately, and, with a great paw on his kill, snarls at us in great gasps, like steam from an engine—shooting out spasmodically. I can almost count the long, white whiskers that fly back with each terrific grin; as a low, continuous, gurgling sound—like the deep, bass pipe of a great organ, exhausting its last vibrations round the high columns of an echoing cathedral—makes the ground tremble beneath us. His yellow fangs project like hideous tushes. His claws are extended full length, and his tail is lashing the short grass furiously. And now, as he takes stock of our statue-like presence with ears thrown fiercely back, his great maned head (the Himalayan mane of the big male) moves round alternately; one moment, slowly away from us, and the next moment swiftly and fiercely back, as if he suddenly suspected an aggressive move on our part. These head movements, with terrible snarling and spitting, are repeated, until I feel my knees quaking, and my nerves gradually collapsing. I seem to be alone; and I feel I cannot hold out much longer. The time that is passing seems to be interminable; and a dreadful feeling seizes me, that something must happen, or I must give vent to a scream—whatever the result may be!

I am suddenly conscious of the measured sound of something moving slowly and heavily on the ground—somewhere, beyond the tiger, inside the forest to my left: slight sounds of branches being swished aside—along the edge of the glen—seem to follow. The huge tiger hears! With a sudden, sedate calmness of expression he turns his great head away—from me. And, now, noiselessly he rises, showing his superb size and might; and, with his ears pricked forward, he faces the direction of some fresh interference. How magnificent he looks!—like a vast picture in oils, on a background of sunset gilt. Fresh blood seems to be tingling in my veins, as I feel myself now lost in admiration. But suddenly the tiger charges out of the picture, with a roar like a clap of thunder! An elephant trumpets, and there is the sound of a scrimmage. Someone tugs at me from behind; and the next thing that I am aware of is, that I am racing down the forest-line in the direction of camp.

"I thought you were never coming," said P. as we

halted for a moment, and looked at each other, pale-faced and out of breath. How we enjoyed that little rest with the camp fires in view! Suddenly, from inside the forest, our gallant mahout's voice rang out in an order to his elephant, and, reassured, we hurried on to camp.

Later on the mahout told us that, when he came in search of us—after stopping and quieting his elephant—he saw us standing, heard the tiger, and, guessing the trouble, he stalked his elephant up from the opposite direction, in order to draw the tiger away from us. Being an experienced mahout and shikarri, he manœuvred his elephant out of the way when the charge came. We had a lucky escape; as it was entirely a matter of accident, that the tiger in his charge selected the elephant first, and not us.

## CHAPTER VIII

### A CLEVER JUNGLE DACOIT

I WAS once shooting at the foot of the Náini Tál hills, in the Terai Forest of the Himalayas, with a brother-in-law of mine—Mr. B. A. Rokeby—who was, at that time, the Forest Officer of the Náini Tál Division. Mr. Rokeby—or Mr. Rebsch, as he was known in the old days—was a great sportsman, and was well known all over northern India as a keen naturalist. During his career in the Imperial Forest Service over a hundred tigers had fallen to his gun ; and he was a reputed authority on the habits of wild animals. He held a very open view, and firmly believed that the feline species could boast the best brains in the jungles, and that their cleverness was often uncanny.

In camouflaging, in order to secure its game, a tiger or a panther will sometimes depart from commonly established habits, and will exhibit an originality in ways and means of attainment that would almost match the inventive powers of a human being. Few are the sportsmen who have troubled to lift the veil behind the beaten track of the orthodox manner of hunting, and who have penetrated into the unseen life of the jungles with its secret movements and alarm cries, for the sake of study rather than the boast of trophies. It is a pity from the standpoint of scientific progress ; for the result is that the ordinary sportsman—even with an experience of twenty-five years or more in India, and with perhaps a great show of trophies—is the first to disbelieve in an uncommon incident which has not come within the pale of his experience. The only appeal to him seems to be the " bang " and the " drop," and everything else is ruled out as fiction.

The naturalist, purely and simply, is handicapped; he relies a great deal on book information, and his tour in a new country is too brief to put him in the way of information, penetration, and opportunity. He lacks, too, the necessary impulse of the true sportsman, whose inherent love of seeing an animal in its wild state leads him, or should lead him, into avenues of adventure in which information is won by mighty patience and hard experience.

It was in the middle of May, when the hot winds blow through the parched jungles and scatter the winged seed of the famous sal tree (*Shorea robusta*) far and wide. The dry leaves in the forest lay densely thick on the ground.

Mr. Rokeby and I were encamped on the high banks of a dried-up river, and had to get water for camp from holes dug in the sand.

The magnificent moonlit night drove sleep from our eyes. The sultry heat of day had penetrated into the night, and seemed to ooze from the molten sheen of silver that poured down on the low hills in front, and over the phosphorescent sea of vast rolling forest, whose glittering canopy covered the plains below.

It must have been about two o'clock in the morning, and my brother-in-law and I were reclining in long armchairs in front of our tents—glistening white, like large cones of dazzling snow—when, suddenly, an old Mohammedan carter with a long beard and a longer face—who seemed to be cut and bruised about the hands and feet—presented himself with one of our forest guards. Some of our servants, whom the cartman had awakened, were standing behind. They were all in a state of considerable excitement.

"What brings you here, Abdulla?" inquired Mr. Rokeby as the old carter saluted. "At this hour of the morning you should have nearly reached your lumber camp, my friend. What will your master say?"

"Huzoor!" said the old stager, who, in the lonely hours of night, had gone through many thrilling experiences in the jungles with his two white bullocks as his only companions, and who feared neither wild elephant nor tiger, "I have spent all my life in these forests, working for contractors and conveying the baggage of many 'Sahibs' from camp to camp at all hours of the day and night, but never before have I found a tiger so daring as to demand a seat in my cart, and to climb up behind, uninvited, without any regard for my bullocks, who were already burdened with my timber merchant's baggage."

We burst out laughing, at which the old carter seemed to be mortally offended; he drew himself up at once and stood, grave and dignified.

"You may believe it or not," said the carter, "but it is a fact. I have walked back eight miles, driving my surviving bullock before me through the deceptive moonlight, and but for his wonderful sagacity I might have tumbled over the high river-bank and been killed. I mistook the road, and was forcing the 'life of my life' down the edges of a deceptive cliff when he suddenly refused to proceed, and tried to instil wisdom into me with violent kicks, so that I had to obey his wishes, and I turned back. Allah be praised!"

"Then the tiger has killed one of your bullocks?" questioned my brother-in-law.

"It is so—alas!" he exclaimed.

"But tell us exactly what happened. Were there any other carts with you?" asked the Forest Officer.

"Yes; but the other carts are all right; and may the

drivers be visited with plague for leaving me all alone," he added. "Owing to the heavy load my noble bullocks dragged behind, and, the bright moonlight twinkling and dazzling in my face, I closed my eyelids. My two dear children toiled over the rough way and rocked me into a sound sleep. I dreamt presently that I was being attacked by 'dacoits,' and was fighting desperately with this small stick of mine to safeguard my master's things, when I fancied that some of the 'dacoits' jumped up behind, and my cart tilted upwards; and then, in the bamboo cage next to me, my master's ducks and fowls made such a noise that I awoke with a start—but too late! An enormously big animal had a paw on my neck, and I was pinned down. I immediately knew it was the big demon 'shere' (tiger) of this valley that had baffled your honour on many occasions; for none other could have been so daring as to jump into my cart! He deliberately walked over my body and gave me a low warning growl, commanding me to lie still. I was obliged to obey the monster, under whose stride I felt like a pygmy, and lay quite helpless."

"But are you quite certain it was the tiger?" questioned my brother-in-law.

"The tiger!" exclaimed Abdulla. "Is there the single mark of a claw on my neck?" he queried. "Your honour knows that the cat tribe tread with their soft pads only—unless enraged—being acute enough never to give away their guilt! Besides, there was his warm breath on my face and body, like hot steam from the cooking pot; the overpowering smell peculiar to his kind and, last but not least, his warning growl!"

"Well, what happened then? Go on," said my brother-in-law.

"When the cart tilted up with his weight behind, my oxen of course were released from the yoke; and taking a few paces forward they stood still, very much confused. It was then that the demon walked over me and brought the front part of the cart down again with a great thud, which I thought would have overbalanced him; but no, he squatted calmly on the driving space allotted to your poor humble servant and watched my frightened bullocks stampeding down the road."

"I wonder if it is true," I asked. "I am almost prepared to believe anything from our many extraordinary experiences in these jungles."

"Go on," said Mr. Rokeby to the man. "Let us hear his story."

"With the bullocks gone—which the tiger made no attempt to follow up—I made certain he would fall back upon me and that my doom was sealed. But to my great surprise he just stretched down to the ground like a great cat, and walked a few paces up the road very casually. His huge dark form, clearly visible in the moonlight, turned broadside on, and then passed silently to my right into the heavy jungle at the edge of the road. The silence was most oppressive, and I was startled at the sound of my own agitated breathing. I was determined, however, to follow in the direction of my bullocks; and I was just about to alight from my cart when, to my surprise, I heard my bullocks stampeding back towards me at full speed. Calling to me in terror, they came trembling right up to my cart. I was just about to speak soothingly to them when, suddenly, I caught sight of the tiger's form again, standing on the road close behind them. But somehow this form appeared to be a little smaller. I thought it was the deceptive light, when to my horror the larger form, like a great shadow, glided suddenly out of the jungle and seized one of my poor children. It seemed as if he had been waiting deliberately for this, and was hidden within a few yards of the spot where my bullocks had come to a standstill. A feeble low escaped my poor child that was caught, and then I heard him fall heavily to the ground. My remaining child rushed past me and the cart in a panic, and I followed after him, down the road in the direction of camp."

"The tigress driving the game up to the male!" said my brother-in-law. "It is quite a common practice among tigers and panthers during this time of the year, the mating season."

"But the tiger tilting the cart up to release the bullocks!" I exclaimed—"that's a bit thick!"

"My experience teaches me," said Mr. Rokeby, "to keep a very open mind with regard to accounts of the doings of wild animals. Though Indians are very much given to exaggerate an incident, this carter's story is quite within the bounds of possibility. Experience once gained—in the first instance, either by some accident or as the result of some action for an immediate end or purpose—is quite sufficient to give that opening that intelligence needs, in any lower creature, to develop instinct into the higher order of reasoning powers, as great and wonderful as the mentality of the most advanced human being. This tiger, I suspect, is a lazy old fellow," continued Mr. Rokeby. "Stripes, remember, acquires great cunning the older he grows, and with it he gets alarmingly bold. It is fortunate the jungles here are so well stocked with game or there would be many a man-eater attacking these camps of ours."

My brother-in-law said that he had previously received information from his forest guards about a big tiger—reputed to be very bold—who indulged in depredations along the main roads of this part of the Forest Division, and thought this tiger must be the same animal.

The old carter and the forest guard then informed us that this was not the first occasion on which this huge tiger had tilted up a cart in order to release a pair of bullocks; that he had acquired this habit owing to the inconvenience of getting the grip under the neck when a bullock is yoked, and the trouble involved in extricating the body afterwards from under the weight of the cart.

"I can quite understand that," said Mr. Rokeby. "I would put nothing past him if age or some other infirmity has driven him to become resourceful."

"Hazoor," said Abdulla excitedly, "come at once in a cart while yet the stars are scintillating in the heavens, and see for yourself whether I speak the truth or not. I will be your driver and the tiger will jump up behind to tilt the cart!"

"The chance of a lifetime!" exclaimed my brother-in-law.

The suggestion was seconded by me in great excitement. We knew the old carter to be a most experienced and reliable man, and his proposal certainly gave promise of considerable sport. We immediately went inside the bungalow to change our pyjamas to khaki shorts, while a smart servant, after expressing himself with doleful misgivings at the prudence of our decision, hurried off to prepare some tea. My brother-in-law ordered the biggest cart in camp to be brought out at once, with a pair of good bullocks; and ordered that a pad elephant should follow our cart behind—after we got in—at a safe distance of about half a mile, in order to be ready to pick us up in case of any serious trouble with this old demon tiger, as the natives of the place believed him to be.

We sat down to a very early "chota hazarie" that was laid outside in the moonlight, and fortified ourselves for the adventure that lay before us.

"I propose carrying the 'machans' with us on a

second elephant, if it should be necessary for us to 'sit up' on the road some distance from each other. My idea," continued Mr. Rokeby, "is that this demon will be lying up after his feed and won't trouble about another cart till seven or eight o'clock in the morning—supposing that he is viciously inclined! He won't kill again for the sake of hunger before tomorrow afternoon."

"Then you don't consider the chance a very good one!" I exclaimed.

"Yes—I do," replied my brother-in-law. "I am much impressed with the carter's story, as I know that many an old tiger takes to killing from sheer vice—even when he has fed to the full; and I think for this reason that the chance is well worth a trial."

"It is strange," I said, "that a tiger in these forests, so well stocked with game, should trouble himself about cart bullocks along a public road, however vicious he might be—unless, of course, he is very old and incapable."

"The graziers from the plains have taken their cattle to other grazing grounds," said my brother-in-law, "and that only leaves the wary and active deer, which perhaps this demon is unable to catch."

The bullock cart in which we were to make the adventurous journey had been brought up, and Abdulla, the cartman, was waiting in readiness to drive the cart, while his own surviving bullock was held by a peon. But we had hardly gone a few hundred yards from camp when Abdulla's bereaved bullock broke loose from the peon and came scampering down the road after us. We had to call up several men to have him surrounded. We seated ourselves comfortably again in the cart, with our rifles by our sides—assured that the troublesome bullock could no longer follow us—when, from the jungle at the back of our camp, there suddenly came a deep lowing sound.

Abdulla jumped off the cart quickly, and declared frantically that his lost bullock (killed by the tiger) had called to him; that it was his ghost undoubtedly.

The companionless bullock the men had surrounded now seemed to become mad with excitement. He rushed furiously at the men, trying to break the circle.

Abdulla rushed up. "Let my child go," he shouted, "to find his brother."

Mr. Rokeby and I walked quietly up to the crowd. The cartman seemed strangely affected. Again at the instant, through the stillness of the glittering night, came a deep gurgling sound, followed by a soft lowing. We listened in breathless astonishment, as we knew at that hour of the night all the camp animals were locked up, and none could have strayed out.

Abdulla seized his bullock, that was restless even in his hands. It apparently wanted to rush off into the forest in the direction from which the lowing sound proceeded —now faintly again, and now in louder, trembling grunts of fear.

My brother-in-law dismissed all the attendants present but a shikarri and Abdulla, the cartman; and then a strange, uncanny presentiment seemed to grip us in the deathly stillness that prevailed. We calmed Abdulla's excited impatience with the promise that we ourselves would walk up in the direction of the lowing, following him and his bullock, to find the ghost.

"I feel certain," whispered Mr. Rokeby to me, "that the tiger has followed Abdulla and his remaining bullock here to camp; and that this deep, peculiar lowing is the tiger's camouflage. He is actually mimicking the bullock's call to draw him into the jungle. On previous occasions

I have had similar suspicions, but have not had an opportunity of putting them to the test. A tiger is often very persistent in following up his game, and I would not in the least be surprised to discover that my suspicions are true. The tiger is capable of emitting a variety of low guttural sounds, some of which lend themselves eminently to the imitating of a bullock's challenge or to his call of distress. The tigress has apparently secured the bullock that was killed, and the tiger is determined to get this one which poor Abdulla has saved."

We abandoned our first plan; and now, in accordance with another one, we immediately set to work.

My brother-in-law, followed by Abdulla and his bullock, went straight down the high banks of the river; after having arranged that the cartman should take his bullock into the middle of the river-bed, and there, in open moonlight view, pretend to be in difficulties with it. Mr. Rokeby was to keep in the background, in the shadow of the bank, ready with his rifle in case the tiger—if it really was stripes—followed the cartman and his bullock over the open river-bed. The shikarri and I were deputed to stalk into the deep jungle in the direction of the lowing, which now seemed to come from nearer the river-bed.

Crackling the dry leaves as much as possible, the shikarri and I stalked carelessly through the black shadows and the brilliant patches of moonlight, making a semi-circular route to keep the animal, whatever it was, between us and the river-bed. We had covered a distance of about 200 yards from camp when I suddenly recognised the nauseous smell of a tiger. In the dense undergrowth the air was heavy and oppressive, and the smell was unmistakable. I now felt certain that my brother-in-law's suspicions were correct, and that the bullock's call we had heard had come from no other beast than the tiger. We moved forward noisily, to drive him into the river-bed. The lowing sound had ceased now entirely, and presently we emerged on to the cliffs of the river. From the high bank we had a glorious view of the expansive white stretch of sand; and to the right of us, just dimly visible, we beheld the cartman and his bullock awaiting the expected attack on the top of a hillock of glittering sand.

Suddenly, from the high bank, under our very feet, as it were—a great dark object shot silently and swiftly across the white expanse. It swerved to the right and distinctly crouched. Then forward again it moved, getting less and less perceptible. A few moments of tense excitement gripped us, and then a thunderous report seemed to shake the high river-bank, as I recognised the crash of my brother-in-law's heavy 12-bore rifle; crash upon crash followed as the echoes resounded through the hills, till they died away like the rumble of a distant landslide. A fierce grunt responded to the shot—then agonised roars awoke the silent jungles. We scrambled down the bank, and, keeping close in the shadows, came up to my brother-in-law. Abdulla with his bullock had beaten a hasty retreat under the high bank.

"A spine shot, I'm afraid," whispered my brother-in-law. "We must walk up and put him out of his pain at close quarters."

This we did. He was a magnificent tiger, measuring 9 feet 8½ inches in the flesh, with a beautiful sub-Himalayan mane on his neck.

The strong circumstantial evidence—in fact actual evidence—confirmed us in our belief that a tiger can, and actually does when occasion demands, imitate the call of some animals, such as "Sambhur," cows, and bullocks, in order to attract his prey. A panther, too, will mimic the call of smaller animals. It is common knowledge that a hyæna is master of this system of camouflage ; and there seems no reason why a doubt should exist in the case of tigers and pánthers, that are much cleverer than hyænas, with a wider aptitude for camouflaging.

# CHAPTER IX

## A ROGUE ELEPHANT

A FOREST Officer's life is a lonely one, and usually he and his wife, if he happens to be a married man, are always glad of company—to have friends who are keen on shooting come and stay with them. For eight or nine months out of the year the Forest Officer is in camp, moving about in his division, inspecting his forests and controlling scientific operations, and when the hot weather comes he has an anxious time protecting his forests against fires. The larger and more valuable forest areas are reserved, which means they are closed to cattle-grazing and the public generally.

The administrative charge is a large one, with a responsible staff of subordinates under the Forest Officer's control, such as rangers, forest guards, peons, and watchers. The whole Forest Division, consisting of some hundreds of square miles, is mapped out and divided into large blocks, which are sub-divided again into compartments by straight, neatly-cut fire-lines. It is often a Chinese puzzle to know where you are when you suddenly emerge from a dense compartment on to a fire-line, particularly on a cloudy day. At intervals, along important boundaries and frontiers such as Nepal, broad, hundred-foot fire-lines are cut.

On special occasions, when big shoots are organised, a number of elephants are borrowed from landed proprietors. The Indian landlord is a keen and generous sportsman who is always ready to oblige a shooting party, while the opportunity affords valuable experience and training for his elephant.

On one occasion I was on a visit to my sister, who was in camp with her husband in the lower Himalayas. My brother-in-law was the Forest Officer of that particular division, and the place at which we were encamped was one of his wildest outposts, famous for wild elephants. It was early in December, and my sister had several guests stopping with her for a few days.

A dangerous wild tusker in the division had become notorious. He was an exceptionally big bull elephant that had apparently gone " must," and had left the herd, becoming a solitary wanderer. He had killed two wood-cutters, and not a few forest officials had had some narrow escapes. My brother-in-law had reported the matter to the Government, and requested that the rogue elephant, being a danger to the public, should be notified for destruction. Under the forest regulations wild elephants are especially protected, with a heavy penalty in force for shooting one without a licence ; and it was while we were awaiting the sanction of Government to this elephant's destruction that the following incident occurred, nearly resulting in four of us being killed—my two sisters, a young Lieutenant B., and myself.

It was about four o'clock in the afternoon, and the four of us mentioned above, sitting down to tea, were the only ones in camp, the other guests having gone out shooting. My brother-in-law had been out on work the whole day and had not returned. A married couple had left early in the afternoon to sit up over a tiger's kill, and we proposed going out for a walk to meet them on their return. News had been received that the rogue elephant had been located that morning some fifteen miles away to the west, and though the walk we proposed along a hundred-foot fire-line lay in the same direction—down which road the tiger-shooters would be returning—we looked upon the walk as quite safe to take. It was not likely the rogue elephant would be anywhere near camp till the following day, assuming that he would be moving leisurely, even if he travelled in our direction.

My two sisters and Lieutenant B. started off for the walk, leaving me behind to follow them up as soon as possible, as I had to give some orders in camp about the elephants, which I had been deputed to do.

In a commanding position—overlooking a small valley —the forest bungalow stands on the brow of a low hill, with well-cleared space all round. In front of the house, beyond the valley, stretches a vast undulating canopy; and above this rolling sea of green, in progressive altitude, the higher ranges of hills struggle to peep over each other's shoulders like curious giants. A golden cloud glows in the west, and the soft purple tints of the afternoon shimmer with slanting beams of crimson that break from the half-screened sun and criss-cross—now fading in the deep valleys to a pale suggestion of salmon, and now glinting on bold rocks that have wedged their way into daylight from their environment of dense undergrowth. Down from the bungalow I follow a bridle road that winds through high, close-growing timber—prize "Sal" trees—towering up on either side of the narrow way, like solemn sentinels, without a flaw in their magnificent straight boles. Passing through the wood, the road emerges into the open valley. A roughly constructed bridge crosses a clear crystal stream murmuring pleasantly between moss-grown rocks. On the other side of the bridge I follow the road that rises again to join at right angles a broad 100-ft. fire-line that, parallel with the stream, runs along, interminably as it seems, to the east and west through dense jungle; those vast primeval forests that have manned India's mountain defences from the remotest periods of history, defying, with their deadly fevers and wild beasts, the invading foe from the north.

Following the footprints of my two sisters and Lieutenant B., I turn towards the west and walk down the broad fire-line. The party have got away a good distance in the short time it has taken me to follow them up, and I coo-ee two or three times, but there is no reply. My voice sounds unearthly in the stillness of the forest; and I am about to move on quickly, when suddenly, some distance in front—round a bend of the fire-line—I hear terrified screams and a man shouting. I recognise the voices, and a horrible presentiment seizing me that my two sisters and Lieutenant B. have suddenly come face to face with the rogue elephant, I run down the fire-line as fast as I can. All I have in my hand is a walking-stick, and I know that Lieutenant B. is no better equipped.

As I get round the bend of the road I can see straight down the broad vista. Something dark and huge seems to be blocking the view, and I see three figures standing, and seeming to sway in front of the enormous black object. I can now hear my sisters' screams distinctly. Never have I covered the distance of about 200 yards quicker in my life. And then, as I come up within short range and take in the scene, I stop almost unconsciously, breathless and aghast; feeling as if I have suddenly been transported by some evil spirit from a pleasant walk in romantic surroundings into the middle of a terrible nightmare.

There, Lieutenant B., with wonderful pluck, is waving a thin cane in front of the trunk of an enormous wild tusker. Behind him, my two poor sisters are clutching each other in terror and screaming wildly. Each time they attempt to move back in order to run, the horrible monster with his huge terrifying tusks—projecting in front like two white enamelled beams—makes a savage thrust forward, and they stand still in terror. The brute seems almost on the top of them, but for some inexplicable reason hesitates to carry home a charge. He must have stepped out of the jungle suddenly and taken them by surprise.

In a dazed way, unable to utter a sound, I stare at my shrinking companions, and though my stupor could only have lasted a few seconds, an age seems to have passed, eking out its awful agony, before I regain my breath and self-control, and realise that something must be done—quickly, or we may all be killed. The next instant, supporting Lieutenant B. with a loud shout, I reach my sisters and draw them back, flourishing my stick under the huge elephant's trunk as I come up by the side of my sisters' brave rescuer.

On my sudden onslaught the brute throws his great ears forward, and hesitatingly takes a step in retreat. We instantly instruct my two sisters—keeping up continual shouting—to take cover behind us: to move gradually backwards, and then turn and run. They obey us in frantic terror, while we try to stand firm and shout imperiously at the elephant till our lungs are almost fit to burst.

Looking up at his great head we concentrate desperately on his murderous eyes, like small red marbles, and wave our sticks high in the air. The brute has only to put out his trunk to grab us. But we begin to see red too, and it is a fight of human will-power against the ungovernable instinct of wanton savagery. We know that our lives are at stake and we must drive the brute off. The slightest wavering or hesitation and we are lost!

With a sudden thrilling consciousness of strength that seems to grip and nerve the mind and body—as if a just and merciful God had flashed down into our souls the power to frustrate the wickedness of capricious Fate—we move forward boldly, and with redoubled shouting, fight fiercely for every inch of ground, every precious second.

Back swerves the monster, shaking his head and tusks furiously, and back, farther back! as on we press, making good every bit of ground, determined to strike the brute with our flimsy sticks. Suddenly the rogue—for it is the notorious elephant undoubtedly—swings round with a roar, and raising his trunk and tusks high, is apparently about to rush into the jungle, when some half-naked coolies emerging at that instant on to the fire-line from a forest cart track, arrest his attention. In a second he turns on them, and the men being taken by surprise, one poor wretch is seized, while the others scatter in a panic, yelling in terror.

Evidently the elephant recognises the variety of human being he has killed before—our escape in all probability being due to our foreign appearance—and a ghastly tragedy is now enacted before our eyes.

We have scarcely had time to think, and can do nothing but shout as desperately as before, now at the rear of the beast, to try to save the poor coolie, as, screaming wildly, he is lifted up in the trunk of the elephant. Mad with rage, as if by his forced retreat before our bold front, the brute throws the poor victim under his great feet and tears off his limbs.

The ghastly spectacle makes us feel sick and faint. A moment more, and the elephant flings the body from him, and turns, facing north, as we take cover at the edge of the fire-line behind him, trying to raise a shout again; but the sickening reaction leaves us spluttering and trembling.

Suddenly the revolting monster raises his tusks and trunk, dripping with blood, and emitting an angry roar, crashes into the forest. We hear him smashing through the dense undergrowth, trumpeting as he goes.

Looking as white as ghosts we emerged from our cover and decided quickly what to do. The brute might return at any moment and intercept the party returning from the tiger's kill. Lieutenant B. ran back towards camp to see to the safety of my two sisters while I climbed up a tree to keep a look-out for the rogue and to warn the people coming home. It was not long before I saw their elephant coming down the fire-line, much to my relief. It was fortunate they returned when they did, or a much worse tragedy would in all probability have been the result, as the rogue tusker would have charged their elephant at sight notwithstanding any shots they might have been able to fire.

I led the guests back to camp along a short cut through the forest to avoid running any risks, while they questioned me about the trumpeting they had heard.

We found my two sisters and Lieutenant B. in a collapsed state in camp with my brother-in-law attending to them. Some days later the sanction of Government was received to the destruction of the rogue elephant; but it was some time afterwards that the brute was finally tracked down and brought to account by a special party armed with heavy rifles.

In my brother-in-law's opinion our escape was due to our foreign appearance of dress and colour, to which the wild elephant was unaccustomed and treated us suspiciously in consequence.

A beautiful encampment in the Sub-Himalayan Forests

*By kind permission of*
*The Thomason Engineering College,*
*Roorkie, U.P., India.*

A TRIBAL DANCE IN SKIRTS—IN REVERENCE OF MOTHER EARTH

A PICTURESQUE CROSSING IN THE JUNGLES. MRS. J. ERSKINE AND LITTLE DAUGHTER

*Photo by Mr. J. Erskine.*

PICKING UP THE LOST SPOOR OF A TIGER

# CHAPTER X

## IN THE HIMALAYAN JUNGLES: NATURE'S DRAMATIC STAGE

*The starry-plumed bird, and the elephant herd,*
*And the bee as he murmurs along;*
*The rush of the hind with a panther behind,*
*And the monkeys in language strong!*
*The bounding stream and the pool all agleam*
*Where the gorgeous flies buzz and dip;*
*The mahseer's splash, and the spoon and the dash,*
*And the rattling reel and the slip;*
*The tiger's roars when you're lying out-doors*
*At night—and the wild flowers' scent!*
*The sambhur's bay, as he hurries away,*
*And the moon-light glint on your tent;*
*Are things,*
*Eclipsed by no sphere of health, study or cheer*
*On which man's soul may be bent.*

IN the glorious month of January, with its sensational nip in the air of Indian frost and magic, I was once invited to a "special shoot" by my brother-in-law, Mr. B. A. Rokeby, the Forest Officer. I was tutor at the time to a young Raja who was included in the invitation, and whom I took along with me. He was a minor of about nineteen years of age, under the Government Court of Wards Department. Mr. Rokeby's Forest Division was situated in the lower hills of the Himalayas, and the shoot was organised by him in conjunction with a great friend of his, a Colonel in the Indian Army, alluded to as Colonel H. The Colonel was a wonderful all-round sportsman, with expert knowledge of "shikarcraft" and keenly interested in natural history. He and my brother-in-law had much in common to bring them together in the hunting field, and I looked forward to a most interesting holiday; for I knew that with those great sportsmen and kindred spirits, the shooting of animals—but for sheer necessity—would be put very much into the background, and in the foreground would rise another great opportunity to see wild animal life and to study the great drama of the jungles.

In the matter of big game hunting, where there is so much to interest one in "nature study," there is nothing so disappointing as to find one's jungle companions blood-thirsty shooters who vie with each other in that unsporting and unintellectual ambition to secure a "boastful bag," with all its petty jealousies and noisy pretensions. In this great department of "Sport," shooting and hunting, there are two distinct classes of sportsmen of opposite extremes. The avaricious type who takes the jungle in his tour to shoot all he can, and who sees nothing; and the extreme true type who takes a tour in the jungle to see all he can, and who shoots nothing. This last-defined class, highest in degree, leads on to the various degrees of true sportsmen who shoot, more or less, but always with the greatest discrimination, showing consideration for life of every description; a sentiment which should be borne in mind by every Britisher beginning a career in India, or in any other part of our wide Empire where opportunities for big game shooting are presented.

At our first encampment, where we spent about ten days, wild elephants seemed to be numerous, and had become a nuisance to timber merchants and their carters for some weeks before our arrival. An exceptionally big rogue elephant that had apparently been turned out of the herd, and seemed to be everywhere, had caused a general panic in camp; and, as the shooting of wild elephants is strictly prohibited—unless a particular rogue be declared a public danger by special notification in the Government *Gazette*—we decided to shift camp to another hunting ground. On one occasion, shortly after our arrival, Mr. Rokeby had a narrow escape from the tusker. He was taken by surprise, without a gun or rifle in his hand to fire off in the air. As a rule, wild elephants are easily scared by gunshots or any unusual noise, and with simple precautions one is ordinarily quite safe with a firearm. But, as the Indian shikarri says: "The jungle is the jungle, and one never knows what danger might be lurking."

For hunting and marching we had four trained elephants lent by my young Raja's estates and other Indian landlords; but as we intended to keep to the main forest roads for our "headquarter" encampments, Mr. Rokeby brought out his trap and horse for an occasional luxury ride.

Colonel H. was accompanied by his chief servant, Bahadur Khan (valiant leader), a wonderful major-domo. This fellow, who had recently joined the Colonel's service, was a great braggart, though an attractive character, with the air of the smart Mussulman trooper. His moral sense seemed to be a little warped, but he was true to his salt. He professed great admiration for the Raja, and praised him unstintingly for his refined taste and good things. This affable factotum seemed to be particularly struck with—and in fact quite envious of—a handsome silk turban beautifully embroidered with gold, which the Raja prized and wore on certain occasions.

Having heard that our "dak" runners, who were

bringing our post and supplies from a distant railway station down in the plains, had arrived at a range outpost six miles away, and had fallen ill, Mr. Rokeby had, early that morning—our last day at this particular camping ground—sent off Bahadur Khan in the trap to fetch the things. This great factotum had begged to go, and the Colonel, desiring to test his servant's capabilities, suggested that he might be sent. The relieving party, who were all Mahomedans, consisted of Bahadur Khan (the major-domo), the syce (groom), and the groom's mate. Bahadur Khan had been entrusted with a gun, but with the strictest orders that it was to be used only for defensive purposes—to fire in the air should the rogue tusker or any other wild elephants be met with and become obstructive. Servants are never allowed to shoot and disturb the ground; the shooting of game, moreover, being strictly regulated in the Government reserved forests. The trapper was a steady old horse, accustomed to the jungles; and as a watch was being kept by the forest staff on the rogue elephant—who, only the previous day, was reported to be suddenly conspicuous for his absence—there was no cause for any anxiety. But Bahadur Khan had been instructed that, on his return journey—if there should be any fresh news of the tusker being anywhere in the neighbourhood of the main road—he was to commandeer two forest guards from the range outpost to accompany him back, driving at a walking pace in order to keep together in a party.

As already mentioned, it was our last day at this forest encampment; and a day in the jungles crammed with more thrills I have never known. It was a beautiful morning when we sat down to *chota-hazarie*—about two hours after Bahadur Khan had driven off in the trap—and, as news had been received that shoals of "mahseer" (the Indian salmon) had come down into the crystal pools of a delightful hill river that encircled our picturesque encampment—lying in a green valley surrounded by dense forest-clad hills—we decided to spend the forenoon playing the wily "mahseer." The Colonel chuckled with delight. He was a great fisherman and, among other accomplishments, a connoisseur in everything pertaining to the table. He promised us a sumptuous fish banquet that memorable night, served up with mayonnaise sauce of his own recipe; and it was not long before the four of us—the Raja in great spirits with rifle in hand to keep guard while we angled—were opening out our flies and spoons on the melodious banks of rock-tossed spray and swirling pools, the site selected being about a mile away from the small forest bungalow and our tents.

We had been fishing for about an hour with great success, when suddenly we heard stampeding behind us, and turned round to see a sambhur stag, with magnificent antlers, making a dash for the river, pursued by six or seven of those blood-thirsty little dacoits of the jungle, the wild dog. The chase had apparently passed quite close to our encampment. The stag, whom we let pass, plunged into the rushing waters and disappeared on the opposite bank. We drove off the dogs that returned in the direction of camp, and instructed the Raja—to his great delight—to follow the dogs and shoot them. We picked up our rods again, and shortly afterwards heard two shots fairly close to camp. We hoped that the Raja had done to death at least one of those mischievous little fiends who are so destructive to deer life.

Another two hours or so were spent in the delightful thrills of throwing the fly and trailing the spoon, when, suddenly, we were again disturbed by an uproar of voices, and to our surprise beheld all our camp servants racing towards us with dishevelled turbans flying in the air. A forest peon in khaki uniform and a green turban was leading the excited, gesticulating crowd. We had forgotten all about the Raja, who had not returned.

"The mad tusker! Killed, *all* killed—five people and 'tum-tum' and horse hurled over precipice!"

We gleaned all this to our great alarm from the spasmodic cries of terror as the servants approached. Reeling up hurriedly and leaving our tackle and game-bag to our attendant present, we heard what the peon—who seemed to be the cause of all the trouble—had to say. Though this peon had only recently joined the Forest Department he was intelligent and sensible. He reported excitedly that he had come through the forest on to the main road leading to camp; and about two miles from our encampment had just seen the trunks of five bodies, all hideously mangled, lying by the roadside; that the "tum-tum" and horse had been hurled down the precipice. He said that the monster rogue elephant, besmeared with blood, was standing in the middle of the road gloating over his terrible work. "I stalked cautiously down to the valley to escape detection," he said, "and hurried here to camp to give the dreadful news."

"Be careful," said my brother-in-law, unable to disguise his agitation. "Are you sure you're not depending upon your imagination for the facts?"

"It is the solemn truth," swore the peon, "or may I, too be annihilated this instant."

He stood up convincingly to a hurried cross-examination, and though we could hardly give credence to the report—knowing how, more often than not, even the best of Indian menials were given to excessive exaggeration—yet we received a shock brimful of dread, lest a tragedy, however less in scope, had really occurred. It looked as if Bahadur Khan and his party were on their return journey, and that the five people included the two forest guards who had apparently been commandeered.

"My poor major-domo," sighed the Colonel. "Let us hope there is some mistake and that this is not the poor fellow's first and last experience of the jungles."

While we hurried along to camp, I made inquiries about my young ward, the Raja. It seems he had shot a jungle dog, and on hearing the peon's dreadful news had insisted upon going on ahead (to the place) in company with two of his private servants. On hearing this, I was greatly perturbed, as I was directly responsible to Government for my young ward's safety. He came from a fighting family who could boast time-honoured traditions, and I knew he had it in his blood to throw his glove to death itself, and stand up, single-handed if need be, to tusker or tiger.

On reaching camp we found the whole place deserted. Our "shikar" elephants with their mahouts and charkattas (mates) were all out. Elephants fetch their own fodder, and when not under orders for a hunt are out during the forenoon. Many bullock carts for baggage are kept on hire during an itinerancy, and all the drivers—most useful men in the jungles—were also out, grazing their bullocks. Even the inevitable camp rag-tag and bob-tail were absent.

In the circumstances, if the rogue elephant had tasted human blood and had become a fiend incarnate, a crowd to make a noise, in addition to firing off guns, was strongly indicated, and we turned with an appeal to our household servants. Our corpulent cook, who was enthusiastically active up to that moment, collapsed with sudden spasms of colic. The other servants dispersed quickly, complaining of low fever, headaches, and bilious attacks. They were sure some dreadful epidemic had suddenly seized camp. The forest peon went after them heroically, with great assurances of being able to rally them. He disappeared in the direction of the servants' encampment, calling out: "Friends, the Hazoors (your masters) are going to risk their lives, would you desert them?" But that was the last we ever saw or heard of that peon again, and in due course his name was expunged from the Forest Department pay-roll.

Our anxiety at the peon's behaviour—of apparent panic—had greatly increased. We felt that, had there been no truth in his statement, he would have come along and attempted to argue out the matter, and would cheerfully have faced a reprimand rather than lay himself open to instant dismissal for desertion. Scarcely had we armed ourselves with guns and rifles and started off, when we heard two shots in the distance which seemed to come from the direction of the tragedy. The main road wound along steep hillsides, with the river rushing below us through a vast gorge. Along some bends of the road bare precipices yawned to a depth of about a thousand feet or more, and the three of us—alone—hurrying at our fastest walk, discussed the danger of suddenly meeting the rogue tusker round any such ugly corner—wild elephants and carnivorous animals finding the forest roads most convenient. We heard a third shot and, after covering a few hundred yards at the double, we suddenly came face to face with one of the Raja's servants—beating his breast and calling out "hai hai!" (a wailing exclamation). He fell at our feet in breathless terror, and moaned out that the sight was *awful!*

"What sight?" inquired Mr. Rokeby in hoarse, anxious tones.

"The arms and legs of four people scattered all over the road, and one poor forest guard rolling in agony and crying out for help; and," he added, trembling, "the Raja is standing bravely facing the blood-stained murderer. I bolted off to call you. Quick, Hazoor, or there will be another death!"

Terribly agitated, we left the man kneeling where he was and quickened our pace to a run. We had proceeded about half a mile further on, halting now and again for breath, when just round another bend of the road we met the Raja's second servant. He, too, fell at our feet. "I was hastening to you," he shrieked. "Quick, Hazoor! the Raja has been seized by the elephant, and I heard my young master exclaim: 'You brute!' The two forest guards and Bahadur Khan are lying there torn to little bits, the syce is rolling in agony, terribly wounded, and the brave mate is limping back to camp with an injured leg. You will meet him round the next bend."

Truth or lie, we knew not; but being in a state of doubt, we had to do our utmost, and with what energy we had left we tried to sprint. The Colonel and Mr. Rokeby kept up wonderfully for their advanced years, close to my heels; but we were soon out of breath. While resting for a few moments, we suddenly heard some rustling on the hillside above our heads, and glanced up surprised to see the injured (groom's) mate skipping down a slope, as active as a wild goat. The moment he alighted on to the road and saw us he tried to break back, but we seized him.

"Now, you'll just speak the truth," said Mr. Rokeby severely. "Has any one been killed, and is the Raja in danger?"

"One poor forest guard is a mangled corpse," said the mate in tragic tones, putting up his hands in the attitude of prayer. "The other guard is wounded. The brave Raja drove the mad elephant off the road, but fainted after the effort. I left in haste to call you. The wounded forest guard is trying to persuade Bahadur Khan and the syce to come down from off a high tree, where they climbed up and tied themselves to boughs with their turbans, lest they should fall if fear benumbed their limbs."

We had heard before of such amusing safeguards being practised in India by city inhabitants when scared in the jungles. The mate assured us that the horse was lying dead at the bottom of the precipice, but that the trap, with the wheels in the air, was safely balanced on a giddy ledge just below the road. All this news was certainly less dreadful, and we began to breathe more hopefully, though still obsessed with considerable anxiety, as it was quite possible that someone had bitten the dust if a close encounter with the rogue elephant had taken place. We made the mate return, taking care that he walked in front of us; but he, too, proved to be a shabby deserter. Keeping about thirty paces ahead of us, he suddenly dived into the jungle where the valley sloped gently, and we saw him no more. But, some weeks later, he wrote to Mr. Rokeby from his native village suggesting that the groom should be sacked for cowardice, and that he, the badly treated, misunderstood mate, should be favoured with the post.

Continuing at what remained of our best speed, we had covered a further mile or more of the winding road—of good width for the hills—when we suddenly heard excited exclamations and, to my great relief, we came face to face with the Raja smoking a cigarette, with his gun ready to fire off if necessary. Behind him stood the Colonel's great major-domo, Bahadur Khan, who came forward—bare-headed—and saluted, *a la militaire!*

"What's the trouble?" jerked out Mr. Rokeby, panting and addressing the Raja. "Has anyone been harmed by the rogue elephant?"

"No rogue elephant," announced the Raja, highly amused. "All quite safe."

"What!" exclaimed the Colonel with a strong

suspicion of disappointment in his voice. "No rogue elephant! no one killed? No one even disabled, wounded, harmed—nothing?"

"Well," said the Raja laughing and pointing to the hill-side, "the groom up that tree is slightly scratched."

"Good!" exclaimed the Colonel as he collapsed against the hill-side. Mr. Rokeby and I followed the Colonel's example, the Raja flopping down in sympathy with us and laughing merrily. A few moments' rest, however, revived our spirits and opened to view the humour of the whole occurrence—one of many farces in which I have taken part on the jungle stage of comedy. We lit cigarettes to soothe our parched throats, and looked around. A short distance down the road the trap and horse loomed up, dangerously near the edge of a cliff, but quite intact—the old four-legged philosopher resting in his harness, with his ears in the normal position of contentment! True it was that one man, the groom, was tied up to the bough of a tree. While he was being unfastened by the forest guards, our attention was drawn to an incident that developed into a grand finale. The valiant Bahadur Khan—who had apparently taken up his position under the tree after saluting us—began to taunt the unhappy groom for cowardice.

"I suppose," said the major-domo with a sarcastic bite, "you are an upholder of the old Indian proverb that 'it is better to live than to die in heroism'; as in the one case—you'll argue—one might be of some help to one's companions in trouble, while in the other, one could be of none! A fine face you'll have to show to our noble masters when you come down."

We could not refrain from laughter, while the major-domo, apparently taking our hilarity for approval and applause, coughed loudly with satisfaction, and was about to chide the poor groom again when Colonel H.

summoned Bahadur Khan to our presence. The Raja then explained to us what had happened.

The party were on their return journey, Bahadur Khan having brought along the two forest guards from the outpost, though the road had been reported safe. It appeared that a wild cow-elephant with a tiny calf had been seen on the wayside, and though the animals had hurried away down the road in the direction of camp, they had left the party behind them in a great panic. The mate had disappeared up the hillside, while Bahadur Khan and the groom had entreated the two forest guards to help them up a tree, and bind them fast with their turbans. The Raja said that within the first two miles—the place having turned out to be about three miles from camp—his two servants had deserted him, first one and then the other; and that, proceeding by himself, he saw the wild elephant and calf coming down the road and he frightened them away with a few gun shots. He said that he continued alone down the road, shouting out to the party till he reached the spot. It seemed that the two forest guards, on being questioned aside by the Raja, had confessed to him that, on hearing his shouts, Bahadur Khan, thinking that rescue was close at hand and ashamed of being caught tied up a tree, had got them (the guards) to untie him quickly, and made a great show of bravery when the Raja appeared. Bahadur Khan, it seemed, had been deaf to the entreaties of the poor groom and had actually given orders—being in charge of the party—that the unfortunate fellow should be left tied up for exhibition.

The Colonel then ordered Bahadur Khan to produce his turban for our examination.

By this time the groom had been brought down off the tree and, on hearing the Colonel's order, he took it upon himself to act for the major-domo, who began to look crestfallen. Dashing off suddenly, the groom came back with a gorgeous silk turban!—delighted, apparently, at the opportunity offered to retaliate on Bahadur Khan.

"By my ancestors!" exclaimed the Raja in Hindustani, "may I be buried alive if that's not my best ceremonial turban."

We roared out, and shook with laughter at this turn of affairs, the groom and the forest guards joining in. Wiping away tears of laughter, my young ward turned with an appeal to the Colonel.

"Don't sack Bahadur Khan," he implored; and, expressing himself in Hindustani, added: "He is a character that'll keep us delightfully alive throughout our tour. I suppose he merely borrowed my turban for a little peacockery out of camp."

After a severe reprimand, the Colonel ordered his major-domo to restore the turban—carefully washed and ironed—as soon as possible to the Raja. We then drove back to camp and sat down at once to a thoroughly enjoyable, though late, lunch.

In the afternoon Mr. Rokeby and the Raja went down again to fish, while Colonel H. and I, anxious to explore some unbeaten tracts of forest, set out riding on a single-pad elephant to revel in the delights of a quiet stalk. The Colonel sat in front, near the mahout, while I had the more comfortable seat behind him, commanding the rear outlook as we jogged along.

We take a course due north. In front of us, high and massive rise the northern range of dark green mountains —great giants that peer over each other's shoulders with bare, shaven summits set with flashing brilliants of amber and purple hue, where the soft, golden rays of blue-tinted winter pick out exposed rocks. Our way to the dense forest that stretches down from the vast mountain slopes and covers the interminable valleys to our immediate front, lies across a low formation of hillocks, clad with high sambhur grass and straggling trees. This dry, rolling ground seems to be well stocked with pea-fowl that fly up suddenly—sometimes from under the trunk of our elephant—with a loud rustling and flapping of uncouth wings. So disturbing becomes this frequent nuisance that our elephant, though a steady female, gets her nerves upset. Suddenly, near her hind legs where the bird had been lying close, a beautiful peacock rises with a crashing noise, flaunting a long tail in full, starry plumage. This is too much for the elephant, who swerves to one side, trumpets, and bolts. Helter-skelter we fly downhill—for an elephant can travel, occasioning great discomfort and danger to the riders—straight for a low, open glen where the grass is shorter. Using the flat part of his hooked spike on the elephant's head, the mahout brings her to a standstill near a clump of bamboos, but not without considerable difficulty. While at the halt, trying to calm down the elephant, we suddenly hear close by—just on the opposite side of a hillock to our right—the alarm cries from some "cheetal," the graceful Indian spotted deer. Some carnivore, we know it is certain to be, trying to stalk the quick-scented deer—a tiger, perhaps, or a panther! The elephant standing still instinctively, quietly we wait, with rifles ready and bated breath, commanding the open glen in case the animal, whatever it may be, should break across. Suddenly we hear a stampede of deer, breaking away opposite to our position. A short interval of silence follows, breathlessly expectant, while the Colonel and I strain our eyes and ears in every direction; but we can neither see nor hear anything! We are about to move round again, to look for the disturbing carnivore, when suddenly the disappointed roar of a panther awakes the seemingly slumbering jungles. Jungle fowl cackle, flutter up and speed away over the glen. Rising heavily and thundering on to tree-tops, numerous pea-fowl raise their cat-like "me-ows" and shriek in a discordant, ear-splitting chorus. With ringing clicks of wing startled green pigeon shoot over our heads; and flights of noisy parrots cross and recross over the trees. Expecting the panther at any moment to emerge silently somewhere close by, we wait patiently till the roaring ceases and the jungle bedlam dies away. When all is still we move the elephant forward to take up a fresh position, when, to our surprise, we see a poor, limping hind cheetal get up from under the bamboo clump standing like a great fern in front of us. Our elephant's slight rustle through the grass has apparently disturbed the hind. She seems to be badly hurt or wounded—possibly by some small carnivore unable to kill her—and, looking pitifully in our direction as if expecting to be sprung upon by the panther—of whose proximity she seems to be undoubtedly aware—she staggers forward, limping along slowly as if in great pain. We follow behind quietly in hopes—before putting the poor creature out of her misery—of catching the panther *in flagrante delicto*, should he happen to be hidden somewhere close by and see her.

Deer seldom look higher than their own level on the ground; and, seeing the grass move and hearing the occasional rustle of our creeping elephant behind her—for a panther is often careless in his stride if he considers his prey an easy catch—it seems evident that the hind cheetal thinks the spotted carnivore is on her track, and she struggles hard to keep out of range of a sudden rush. We have followed the poor hind over a hundred yards when, heading straight for some dense jungle, she suddenly becomes alert, and, to our utter astonishment, bounds off with a kick in the air as lively as a two-year-old Derby winner in the pink of condition.

"Wah!" exclaims the mahout. "What miracle is this? Allah, ho Akbar!" (God be praised!)

"Some camouflage," whispers the Colonel to me, reprimanding the elephant driver for raising his voice. "I have an idea; back we must go to that bamboo clump."

In the greatest excitement we turn the elephant round and, after considerable searching—so cleverly did the hind cheetal zig-zag us about and confuse our direction—we at last locate the spot. Making the elephant sit down the Colonel and I jump off her back, and there, to our surprise and wonder, in a tuft of grass under the bamboo clump lies a glossy, tiny baby cheetal scarcely a day old!

Apparently thinking the panther was coming on to them, the poor mother cheetal had jumped up, pretending to limp and be an easy prey, in order to draw the panther away from her young one; risking her own life in the daring camouflage. Science has made but small strides into the deeper mysteries of the great jungles. It is a life full of wonder, with its hidden, multifarious activities—a life almost as mysterious as the invisible world that, in the interests of our present day, is being explored with indefatigable perseverance by our great modern spiritual scientists. No one may even hope to enter the theatre world of the jungles and behold even a few of the countless screens raised in turn, without first paying the high fee for the indispensable passports; the purest quality of good "intention," self-sacrifice, and unremitting patience. We were well rewarded for withstanding the temptation to round up the panther at once when he roared and to try to shoot him.

Suddenly, a fair distance away to our left, we heard a sambhur stag's alarm call, and it was apparent that the panther had taken that direction. Covering up the baby cheetal carefully with grass and leaves, we hurried off in the direction of the baying sambhur, little dreaming that we were to be so fortunate again as to be eye-witnesses to another thrilling camouflage. We lost the direction of the sambhur, who had stopped calling, and had proceeded about half a mile when we heard the noise of shaking branches on ahead, and knew we were approaching monkeys—the black-faced Hanuman of ancient Indian legend. We stalked up very carefully, as deer are invariably to be seen grazing under monkeys, who throw down tender leaves and fruit. We kept away from the particular trees in order not to disturb the happy family of monkeys, but within range of a good view. Some clusters of grass and a few large grey rocks were scattered about the foot of the trees. Some monkeys were on the ground, some squatted on the rocks—all engrossed in eating. Those on the trees who could see our elephant seemed to approve of our unobtrusive presence. After a prospective survey, Colonel H. drew my attention to a large dog monkey sitting on the ground huddled up, with his back to us. The spot chosen seemed to be a cunning one, under shelter of a rock near the foot of a tree, with some tall light grass which could be used as a screen, partly surrounding the animal. Owing to his frozen attitude we were particularly interested in him. Watching this fellow closely, we suddenly noticed a slight lifting of his hitherto imperceptible tail, that seemed to be too straight and dark-coloured for a monkey's curled appendage, and we immediately became suspicious. But, as evening was approaching, the light was most deceptive; besides which, knowing how quick monkeys are at spotting their enemies, we felt sure that they would know if any danger lurked near them—giving their wonderful alarm cry that never lies—and we should have put aside our suspicion had there been even a gentle zephyr blowing. But it happened to be unusually still, and we discussed, *sotto voce*, the possibility of monkeys becoming so absorbed in their feeding as to lose sight of danger for the time being when there was no movement of air to carry a warning, monkeys being as much dependent on the sense of smell as on the faculty of sight. In a family together, particularly when feeding and off their guard, there are always at least two or three monkeys detailed for sentry duty, ready to give the alarm cry should they sense danger; but on this occasion the sentries, if supposed to be on duty, were evidently overcome by the temptation of the luscious fruit and were grave offenders against the trust of their fellows. I have no doubt but that the delinquents were severely punished afterwards, for suddenly a breeze sprang up from the direction of the huddled-up creature under our suspicion.

Immediately there is a great commotion in the Hanuman encampment. In the fading light deafening alarm cries—loud, hoarse coughing—ring out, while our elephant simultaneously gives the indication of the close proximity of some dangerous carnivore by beating her trunk on the ground. The place is now alive with rushing and scrambling grey creatures, coughing in spasms and darting up tree trunks. From the shaking and rattling branches overhead the steadier and deeper nasal chorus of alarm echoes through the far jungle, warning other monkey families and arousing the sympathy of those ubiquitous alarmists and scandalmongers of the jungle, the pea-fowl, who join in with their raucous flourish of trumpets from every point of the compass.

In the noise and confusion the mahout is trying to keep our elephant steady, when suddenly we see a big, belated monkey dashing blindly for the tree, at the foot of which lies the rock and our marked animal. In the flash of a second, with elastic ease the deceptive, huddled-up creature unrolls and sweeps round. There is a terrorised cry from the monkey, followed by sudden, complete silence; then comes the faint, muffled sound of a tussle, and a few seconds later the realisation of the tragedy amidst a worse bedlam! Up goes the Colonel's rifle, and breathlessly I wait till a spot of blue flame in the dusky light brings a crashing bark, silencing everything but the shrieking pea-fowl.

It turned out to be a female panther. We did not think that she was the same animal that had roared during the earlier incident that evening. Leaving the poor monkeys to bury their dead, we padded the "bag" and found our way back to camp by the dim light of a half-moon. But that we saw the panther's clever camouflage —simulating the appearance of a monkey—we could not have believed it possible.

Before dinner that memorable night Colonel H. had found the time to prepare his promised mayonnaise sauce, and we were half through some wonderful fish courses—the result of the day's angling, which gave the camp a treat as well—when we heard excited conversation going on outside among the peons and the cartmen who were loading the advance carts for the night march. The Colonel's major-domo came rushing in to say that Mr. Rokeby's two milch cows and a calf, that was about two days old, had been carried off by somebody or something. Mr. Rokeby had received confidential official information that some dacoits had been traced by the police as having escaped into the jungle—a harbour for them—in our direction. Thinking it quite possible that these dangerous outlaws had slunk into camp and committed a theft, we armed hurriedly and went outside.

The young Raja—who had had his dinner in his own

caste fashion—was surrounded by a crowd, listening to what the cow-boy had to say. The boy was most emphatic about having seen a ghost, an awful-looking creature, dancing under a sal tree at the back of the cow-house. All our Hindu servants and followers were seized with superstitious dread. It looked like a trick on the part of the dacoits to give the thieves time to get away, and we were moving off to see if there were any truth in the report of the theft when a mahout came up from the elephant lines to say that he had just seen the two cows grazing near their encampment. How long the cows had been out of their house he could not say, but he had looked into the shed and the calf was not there. This put quite a different complexion on the matter.

The crowd supported the cow-boy, whom they knew to be innocent and truthful, declaring the calf's kidnapper to be a ghost. The great Bahadur Khan was again in considerable evidence. He expressed his opinion that a ghost was merely an optical illusion, whereupon the Colonel, much to the Raja's amusement, ordered him to lead the way with a lantern. Leaving the cow-boy—who was too frightened to come along—and the crowd behind, we proceeded to the cow-house, situated in a lonely spot a little apart from the main encampment. The Raja was carrying a second lantern behind us.

The front door of the cow-shed was open, and the small calf was not in its little mud square on the right-hand side of the room where it was kept at night. On the left-hand side of the room broken ends of grass-made ropes were attached to the pegs where the cows were kept fastened. It was apparent that some animal had entered and carried off the calf, frightening the cows who had broken loose.

With due precaution we proceeded to the sal tree, some thirty or forty paces behind the cow-shed, and Bahadur

Khan was ordered to lift his lantern up higher. As he did so he suddenly gasped, turned on his heels and bolted, dropping his lantern in his panic; for there, robed in white, behind the tree trunk—the deceptive beams of a dull moon giving the vision a ghostly appearance—a strange, narrow figure, half risen from the ground, as if trying to struggle up to an upright position, swayed from side to side like a young, slender-limbed Hindu widow bemoaning the loss of her departed lord.

"It *is* a ghost—an ill-omen!" whispered the Raja to me excitedly.

Rubbing our eyes as if they had suddenly played us false, we stared in utter bewilderment at the desolate figure, so dread yet pitiful in its aspect and, for a moment or so, we too caught the spirit of the panic, glancing pale-faced at one another. Then silently the Colonel took the lantern from the Raja's shaking hand, and directing the light downwards on to some obscure shadows, there came gradually into view a huge, dark length of body—as thick as a giant creeper—working on the ground in slow muscular movements.

"A python!" exclaimed Mr. Rokeby.

We immediately stepped nearer, and to our great astonishment saw the big snake's head that had apparently somehow got through a tear in a large, gleaming white cloth which was partly wound round his fore-length, draping the horrid reptile in an extraordinary manner! We shot the brute at once and tried to solve the mystery. He was gorged and was undoubtedly the culprit who had swallowed the calf. He had evidently been trying to rid himself of man's encumbering garment by struggling and swaying as he raised himself.

More lanterns were brought as the camp crowd now gathered round us. Bahadur Khan, who had recovered from his panic, helped to retrieve the white cloth, and suddenly held up a wonderful length of something which, though mud-stained and torn, was all silk, embroidered with gold.

"Bury me again—alive," said the Raja, "if that's not my best silk turban!"

We held our sides and roared with laughter; the crowd dispersing discreetly, trying to suppress their outbursts of merriment.

"But how the—the—could it have happened?" exclaimed the Raja in amazement, joining in our laughter. "My allowance from the Court of Wards," he said, turning to me, "will have to be doubled in the jungles to meet such subsidiary expenses."

Bahadur Khan said that, as instructed, he washed the turban carefully and put it out to dry on the top of some high grass standing in front of the cow-shed; but he admitted having forgotten all about it. The cow-boy said that when night came on he picked up the turban, noticing that there was a tear in the centre of it, and thinking it to be somebody's loin cloth—as the light was dusky—he took it inside the cow-shed. As he had been called to help load the night carts, he hung the turban hurriedly across the two short upright posts that stood on either side of the entrance leading into the calf's mud-square. The boy said that the turban slipped down the posts and got caught about half-way down by nails or something; but he let it remain where it had fallen and hurried off, leaving the front door of the cow-shed open till his return for the night. It appeared that some three hours later the boy came back with a light, and while searching for the cows he saw the ghost under the sal tree.

We examined the narrow entrance leading into the calf's "sanctum," a rough square made of mud walls about three feet high. Two short bamboo posts stood on either side of the entrance, and, true enough, more than half-way down the posts some nails protruded about a foot off the ground. More than half the width of the turban must have lain on the floor, blocking the entrance into the mud square.

We could only surmise that the turban got torn in the forenoon by the ill use to which it was put during the wild elephant adventure, and that the python, having slipped into the cow-shed when no one was about, frightened the cows who bolted out of the house. In going after the calf the python must have got entangled in the hanging turban, having managed to get his head through the tear either on entering the square or on his departure, after swallowing the calf. Folds of silk would readily cling to the slimy, viscous surface of a snake's skin, so that the more the python struggled the greater must have been his dilemma! It was one of those extraordinary, accidental incidents that come about sometimes even in the most prosaic course of human life.

# CHAPTER XI

## UNDER CANVAS WITH A RAJA: NETTING DEER AND A CAMP DISASTER

IN the olden days, in the great stretch of primeval forest at the foot of the Himalayan mountains—particularly in the "Sewalik" range of hills and east of beautiful Dehra Dun, all along the Náini Tál Terai, as far as the Lakhimpur or Kheri district—the great Emperors of Delhi used to set forth in the glorious winter months on hunting and shooting expeditions. In addition to tiger shooting and elephant "kheddas"—the "pit" system of catching wild elephants being frequently in favour in those great historic days in Upper India—a great sport indulged in was the netting of the beautiful spotted deer or "cheetal," which overran the higher glens and the Terai Forests below the hills, in countless numbers. In that "ancien régime," tradition has it that the display of splendour, when pleasure was the direct object of an expedition, was unsurpassed by any other kind of pageant; such as spectacular processions, Royal tours for administrative purposes, and the necessity of display consequent upon warfaring campaigns; all of which, in ancient Eastern monarchies, had the sole object of impressing the people—friends and foes alike.

All the chief nobles from every province of the vast "Moghul" Kingdom would receive a Royal summons, on pain of incurring the great Emperor's displeasure—which might mean anything—should submissive and punctual obedience, whatever the sacrifice, not be considered a compulsory obligation. From many hundreds of miles great and small chieftains, and Rajas and Zamindars of every status and degree would travel by day and by night, each with his retinue of soldiers and shikarries, to reach the great capital by the appointed time. The Ministers of State would assemble all these "blue blood" of the land in a vast encampment, until the arrival of the great day when, with the vast splendour of the Emperor and his personnel, all would move out from Delhi in an overwhelming and glittering procession of many miles in length.

Unfortunate would be the poor cultivators through whose villages and lands the Royal hunting and shooting expedition would mark out its course of travel, for the selected locality in the jungles. Not only had the Emperor and his Ministers, and all the great and small nobles of the kingdom with their innumerable servants and followers to be fed and kept as the mighty host moved along by easy marches every day, but the almost countless animals, elephants, horses, and cattle, had to be maintained. The crops for miles and miles around, within the circumference of each length of march, would be devastated and laid waste to a blade of grass. Durbars would be held and "nazaars" (gifts—in money, in kind, in goods) taken, and the small farmers and the cultivators would be reduced to beggary and starvation by the conclusion of a day's march.

What a different aspect is presented in the India of to-day, with its great protection and prosperity under the benign and mighty rule of the gallant British people! In British India there is no poor cultivator residing in the most distant and the wildest corner of the Empire, who has not felt the blessings of the great protecting arm of the Britisher—be it official or non-official—and who does not live in complete confidence as to the safety of his life and property;—a confidence that has gripped the "real" India, and that, like the sound of temple bells, ever awakens in the hearts of the people a feeling of thankfulness for the benevolent reign of our Sovereign :

*Emperor, whose pow'r this region vast commands,*
*No race more proud of King than ours of Thee!*
*Beneath whose flag unconquered swells each sea,*
*And roll the roaring oceans round thy lands.*

*By town or desert, 'neath the sunset's rays,*
*Where e'er the humble ploughman rests from toil,*
*He knows no foe can raid, no plunderer spoil*
*His full ripe fields, the gladness of his days.*

*In grass thatched hut he fears no lawless crime,*
*Save where the tiger roars ere night's begun——*
*Where far and wide thy grandest regions run ;*
*Ind's mighty Forests saved for countless time!*

*Of rich or poor, upon each racial brow,*
*No mists can veil the sunshine of the free ;*
*From dreaded 'Thug' secure beneath the tree*
*The traveller finds a welcome solace now!* *

Even to this day vast herds of the graceful "cheetal," abound in most of our sub-Himalayan forests protected by Government. Dangerous as it is, the netting of deer is a most fascinating sport; provided the butchery indulged in—when the object is not to take the animals alive—were only left out of the programme.

A great friend of mine, known as Shikarri Diggs, and I were once fortunate enough to be eye-witnesses to the

*These four stanzas are an extract from a poem written by the author, and addressed to His Majesty, the King Emperor of India, on the occasion of His Majesty's Durbar in Delhi, in 1911.

sport. Some years ago, in a district in Oudh, now the United Provinces, Diggs and I were invited to a shoot by a big Indian Zamindar friend (a large landowner), who had extensive estates and possessed a wide extent of sal forest stretching far north, to the foot of the Himalayas. We were joined by an officer in the Opium Department, who, along with his wife, had also been asked to the shoot. The lady was as keen as we men were on small and big-game shooting, and was a capital shot with both the gun and the rifle. This Zamindar, or Raja as he was called locally by his people, was very anxious to show us this ancient sport of netting deer, and we gladly accepted his kind invitation.

We encamped the first night of our arrival in a large grove of wide-spreading mango trees, quite near the Raja's residence. It was a picturesque spot—rolling, undulating country, covered with the young tender Indian wheat and gram crops all in dark green, stretched on all sides of the grove of trees; and, with the field hedges lining some parts of the scenery, one could easily imagine oneself in delightful Kent again—between Canterbury and Margate—looking out on to the young English wheat, barley and oats at the end of spring. It was the month of December, some ten days before Christmas, and the weather was cold and bracing with a nice crisp feeling in the air. Here and there small hamlets nestled over the distant view, among clumps of bamboo and graceful plantain trees, which, as soon as the eye rested on them, gave one a wrench, and brought one rudely to realise that this was the East, and that beautiful England lay thousands of miles away, across many seas. It is strange that, even in the best climates of Eastern countries, however green the grass may be, it is never the same beautiful emerald shade as the Englishman is accustomed to see in his own country. How one misses that delightful green, even with the variety of coloration over a distant view when harvest time is approaching, and the ancient, sombre-looking windmill stands out on some interesting brow of rolling English scenery. Now and again a feeble reminder brings a lump to the throat, and makes one feel sad and disconsolate!

We helped the Raja, on the first night of arrival, in his arrangements for the big hunt the following day. The programme was that all the Raja's elephants—some three or four—should be sent on to a camping ground about two miles away, where we were to spend the next two or three days. We were to leave early the next morning on horseback, riding the short distance into the next camp, where the elephants would be waiting to carry us another three miles, to a spot in the heart of the jungles.

It was a delightfully cold morning the following day, when we set out after "chota-hazarie" (morning tea and warm toast) on our fidgety horses. We mustered a cavalcade of six altogether, including the Opium Officer's wife, and enjoyed a bracing, thrilling gallop for the first few furlongs before pulling up rein for a walk. A soft sun, like a crisp sheen of gold, lay over the green fields to the right and left of the white dusty road ahead, and began to awake the sleepy bullock cart drivers curled up on top of bags of merchandise, or lying inside their carts on top of thick paddings of straw, covered from head to foot in rough black blankets and dirty thick white cloth. Strings and strings of creaking bullock carts are passed along the district roads of an early morning, each pair of bullocks moving at a snail's pace (ox-nose to tail-board of cart ahead), and all depending upon the acuteness of the pair of bullocks of the leading cart. They follow one another behind in a long line—sometimes half a mile long—with their drivers and sometimes the merchant himself, or other occupants, in the unconsciousness of deep slumber. Very often, through tiger infested jungles, they travel all night in this manner, quite unconcerned as to what may happen, with complete confidence in the intelligence of their bullocks or buffaloes.

We arrived in camp about nine o'clock, after dallying on the way, and mounted our elephants for the remainder of the journey. The Raja was in high spirits as he took us along, explaining the method of netting deer, until we reached a clearing in the jungle where a number of tame "cheetal" stags—which were fine animals—were awaiting us, in charge of their keepers. We now took to our horses that had been brought up behind.

"I am now going to introduce you to a grand old India hunt," said the Raja, "the sport of our ancient Kings! These are my trained champions," he said, as he pointed to the gram-fed stags, some of which had beautiful branching antlers, measuring 35 and 36 inches.

We suddenly heard village drums and the shouting of men, and were informed by the Raja that the noise came from a band of beaters who were driving a herd of spotted deer into an open glen close by us. A strip of forest intervened, so that we could see nothing; but the Raja and his men presently led us out to an open spot, and concealed us, horses and all, in a thick clump of shrubbery, from which we could see down the open glen without being seen by the wild animals. We dismounted here, holding our horses firmly in order to keep them quiet.

Very soon, a big herd of "cheetal" emerged into the open, the members of which stood about scattered, some grazing, and some looking steadfastly in our direction. The stags, most of whom looked warlike and powerful, came loitering up behind, as if they ignored danger of any kind. The tame champions, who were brought into a position facing the wild herd, were now let loose, and they immediately advanced at a proud trot, shaking their beautiful antlers.

The challenge was taken up at once by the watchful guardians of the wild herd, who came forward with a similar threat to meet the Raja's stags. The wild ones hesitated a moment, however, as if puzzled whether the strangers came as friends or foes. But it was not long before the matter was decided, and the parties quickly attacked each other—the wild stags bounding up fiercely, with their heads lowered when within a short distance of their adversaries.

Their antlers soon met in a resounding crash, and all interest was at once centred on the fierce contest that waged between the tame and the wild creatures. The former, as formidably built as the free-rovers, appeared to be specially trained to stand on the defensive; which they did with admirable skill. The object of this, as the Raja whispered to us, was to reduce the wild stags to a state of fatigue by inciting them to constant attacks—in order that, when the time came to approach the combatants, the danger to the shikarries might be lessened. It was not a case of sham warfare, but a fierce struggle of the most desperate nature.

The moment soon arrived for the shikarries to advance; and, as a number of them on foot made their appearance, hugging the edge of the forest, with long gleaming knives in their hands, and strongly made nets of thin rope, the hinds and young prickets of the herd—and a few larger stags that were not participating in the battle—instantly took flight. The big wild stags were too fiercely engaged to trouble about the danger threatening them from behind. To steal round to the rear of the combatants, getting between them and the forest—in order to cut off the retreat of the wild animals—was the desired objective of the plan. The huntsmen succeeded in their efforts; and the spectacle that now lay before us was thrilling and blood curdling, as the sinister looking shikarries stole up cautiously from behind, with heads and backs bent low, moving softly, step by step, over the bright green sward.

The clever manœuvring of the trained stags, to keep the wild ones so engaged that their hindquarters would be in a direct line with the advance of the shikarries—to prevent the slightest chance of a glimpse behind—was an exhibition of such wonderful intelligence on the part of those animals that it seemed quite incredible; we could hardly believe the indisputable evidence of our own eyes.

Altogether, there were six wild stags engaged with six tame ones; and twelve shikarries advanced in couples, in open order on the same alignment, the deploying interval—to use military terms—between each unit of two men being twenty to thirty paces.

We saw the tame stags pushing and butting to the right and left; and we were astonished when the Raja told us that his trained champions were not only arranging to cover the men, but were adjusting approximately the same uniform distance, laterally, between themselves with their contesting opponents as the lateral space between each advancing unit of shikarries. He told us that the tame stags, the moment they came into contact with the wild ones, noted the lateral distances of the advancing men, and immediately put the battle line into the same order. He said that their sense of exact distances was baffling to human understanding; and he remarked here that the antelope and the goat had been observed to possess the same mathematical sense. We saw, to our utter surprise, how skilfully the tame stags were treating us to an example of this wonderful sense, and were, in fact, manœuvring in unison with the men, at every stage in the attack, to suit the whole plan of battle. The right flank of advancing men had nets, and the left, knives. In each unit of two men, one man—who in every case was a powerfully built athlete—was empty handed; his duty being to catch the net on the other side of the stag, when thrown, and to pin it down; and, in case of mishap, to seize the horns of the wild stag in order to save his companion, with the net or knife, as the case may be. The trained athletes constantly practise with the tame stags, fighting with them, and seizing their antlers of a sudden, at which they become wonderfully dexterous.

The shikarries were now close behind the desperately engaged wild stags; and those with knives on the left flank, with a sudden swift stroke with their weapons, hamstrung their brave victims, and hurried away. Three of these poor animals, so dealt with simultaneously, unable now to withstand the pressure brought to bear by the unhurt champion deer, fell helplessly to the ground.

Meanwhile, among the right flank of men who were net-bearers, two succeeded in throwing their nets with great skill, and a couple of fine stags were held and pinned down, the animals being thrown to the ground by the crafty movements of the men: but in this flank, one unit of men narrowly escaped being gored to death. They were suddenly attacked by the only stag that was able to get away. As the net-bearer was on the point of throwing his net, one of the brow horns of the wild stag broke off, and the tame one, who at that moment was pressing hard against his opponent's horns—the two antlers being interlocked—was impelled forward with great force, and fell on his knees behind the wild one. The infuriated wild stag switched round instantly, and coming face to face with the two shikarries, who were completely taken by surprise, charged home with a loud snort! Being thoroughly experienced at the game, the two men flung themselves down, and lay face downwards, flat on the ground. The stag's sharp horns, however, ripped the back of the thighs of the net-bearer, causing great gashes down both his legs. But for our timely aid, as we mounted at the Raja's request and came galloping up, the wild stag would undoubtedly have killed one of these men.

The tame stags were then called off. The evidence of the severe fighting was plainly marked on their gored chests, from which blood was flowing freely; but, capering about joyously, and tossing their heads, little was the concern they appeared to show for their wounds. Instead of allowing the shikarries to kill the poor hamstrung stags in their usual fashion, we had them shot; and the Raja himself admitted that he did not like, and discouraged, this most unsportsmanlike part of the hunt. It was a wonderful sight to see the captured stags being carried away, their limbs and heads being closely folded up in the nets. They were placed in bullock carts and driven off to the Raja's residence, where they were to begin their training with the tame stags. The Raja told us that, once they became accustomed to their new surroundings, it took but a few weeks to train them, as they were most intelligent creatures.

The following morning our good sporting host, the Raja, announced that he had made arrangements for a duck shoot, and that we were to proceed after breakfast, about 10 o'clock, to a large swamp some two or three miles from camp, in the opposite direction to the belt of sal forest where the spotted deer were netted.

At the appointed time of starting, we heard the tom-tom of village drums accompanied by a great shouting of men, which came from the direction of the Raja's residence two miles away: our servants duly informed us that the Raja was about to appear in our camp, in a motor car which he had lately purchased in the city of Lucknow, and of which he was very proud—the "Howah Garry," or the mysterious four-wheeled vehicle which was drawn by the demons of the wind (in place of horses) who roared in anger when the wheels refused to move forward, being worshipped in awe and respect by all the people, who had never in all their weirdest folk-lore heard of such a thing!

A vast cloud of dust approached, heaved along with the din of tom-toms, shouting and the fanfare of trumpets, sufficient to rend any cloud but an Indian dust storm. The elephants that had arrived earlier in camp began to get distinctly restless; and a remarkable apology for a trapper—which in a more civilised stable would have served the purpose of an excellent harness rack—that was tied on with odd ropes to the suspicious-looking shafts of a rickety two-wheel trap cocked one ear forward, and with the other one lying back savagely denounced the whole cause of the dust and din with a fierce scream and a plunge in the air, which released him instantaneously from his creaking and shaky burden behind. He careered round camp, with his groom lying stretched on the ground, which upset our own saddle horses. Two of the latter broke loose, and the three horses dashed about madly, while the dust of the approaching tumult began to encircle our encampment. This was all too much for the three panicky elephants. They shook their head and trumpeted, while their mahouts swore hard at them—hurling abuse at their prehistoric ancestors. But it was no use! The demons of the air apparently were having a day out! The elephants lifted their tails and bolted from the uncanny camp, making a bee line through our wide-spreading tents. In terror of being trampled, our servants and camp followers rushed madly about; and we had to dispense with the politeness of waiting to receive our expected host, in whatever way he chose to usher himself into camp. We had been in roars of laughter until the elephants stampeded!

"Bolt!" suggested Diggs, "by the Marrowbone Stage!" And we did; Shank's mare was not in it! The mango-trees were thick enough, thank goodness, to hide behind. The Opium Officer's sporting wife flew, and we followed after her. From our various positions behind trees—while the wild duck were waiting to be shot two and a half miles away, we beheld the devastation. The dust and the tumultuous crowd with the Raja, arrived just in time to add to the confusion. The elephants literally tore up the camp. The tent ropes and pegs over which they trampled were burst and flung into the air, and down came the tent poles with resounding crashes. The dust got worse and filled the whole mango grove like a fog. Screams and yells were heard all over the place, and we thought at least a dozen people had been killed. Everybody seemed to be running madly away from the sudden demon invested encampment. Never had Diggs and I experienced such a pandemonium! With the final disappearance of the elephants and horses, the tom-toms and the crowd, the heavy dust began to lift, and when we stalked out of our hiding places we beheld the poor Raja sitting alone in a dilapidated old "Tin Lizzie"—which was probably the first car of the first model ever turned out—with three burst tyres out of the four. He was looking about him terrified, staring all round the encampment, with two of the tents levelled to the ground, broken furniture and crockery, and pots and pans lying scattered all over the place.

"Good morning, Raja Sahib," said Diggs.

"What has happened?" gasped the Raja.

"The elephants and horses took fright," explained Diggs. "Perhaps they've never seen your motor car before."

The Raja breathed more easily and joined in the laughter, after which the cause of the whole trouble was disclosed.

The car had never moved an inch by itself since the day he had paid 1,000 rupees for it. He lived in hopes of its going some day—so did his people! The noisy crowd, with the drums and the flourish of trumpets, etc., etc., was only the attempt of the people to awaken the demon sleeping in the bonnet of the car. A great crowd would always collect willingly to push the car (and so help the demon) whenever the Raja wished to use it; and the disaster in camp was only due to the car being pushed from the Raja's residence to our tents.

"You see," said the Raja, "I was most anxious to do you the honour of taking you along to the 'Duck jheel' (swamp) in my car. The crowd would have been delighted to push us along the two or three miles and to see the duck falling to your guns all over the place. Come along," he said; "if the engine won't go, we have no lack of two-legged ones and will soon arrive at the shooting ground."

He would not hear of us using the elephants or riding. It would take time, he told us, to calm the panic-stricken elephants and catch the horses; and he straightway despatched two men to reason with the crowd and to bring them back.

In small groups of twos and threes the men returned, and soon collected again in a vast crowd, when the Raja assured them that "the demon" was calmed down and they need have no fear.

There was no petrol in the tank, but the Raja said that there never had been any, and assured us that that little matter, along with the burst tyres, was of no consequence in the least.

So we started—and it was a start!—after leaving instructions to our servants to rig up the camp again as best they could, and to send out another lunch basket as soon as they could get ready some more roast fowls and hard-boiled eggs. The nice lunch basket prepared by the Opium Officer's wife had been left on the ground outside, and had been trampled upon by one of the mad elephants.

In order not to disturb the duck on our approach, every effort was made to prevent the crowd from shouting and yelling, as they pushed us along. We were drowned in white dust and had to stop every few hundred yards and scamper out of the car in order to breathe. The Raja appeared to be quite accustomed to it, and seemed to be swallowing enough dust to go a few weeks without any meals.

But all this inconvenience and the dreadful shaking was instantly forgotten when a flight of pin-tail, like a sudden gust of wind, swept over our heads and was gone. As we came into view of a lower reach of land we beheld a great mass of high swamp grass and rushes, and flight upon flight of dark triangular lines rising and falling over the tops of the green and yellow stretches. And suddenly, from far as it seemed, came a thrilling chorus of quack, quack, borne on the morning breeze—clashing in every variety of harsh and penetrating guttural of the wild duck's cry. A flight of the greylag geese arose and circled round the centre of the "jheel," settling again.

We stopped at a small hamlet almost hidden by lofty bamboo clumps, drooping gracefully over the thatched mud huts, and began hastily to gather up our guns and cartridge bags from the motley crowd; quickly we marched off on foot to a bend in the huge swamp, well screened, where about a dozen or more small "dug-outs" (log boats) were awaiting us. The small log boat is punted by one man only, with a long pole, while the shooter sits in the centre of the boat with his bag of cartridges in front of him, and balances himself carefully. There is room for two only in the small dug-out.

The Raja instructed the boatmen as to the position of each gun, and warned us all, at the last moment, that the swamp was full of snub-nosed crocodile, waiting for any one who should be so unfortunate as to fall into the water, and that we must guard very carefully against being capsized. This rather took the gilt off the gingerbread, as it takes very little to capsize the tiny "dug-out," and one might easily make a disastrous mistake in the excitement of shooting, with the sudden swinging round that is necessary for fast moving duck. One's life seemed to be entirely at the mercy of the puny little, dark, half-naked figure standing at the bow of the boat, balancing himself lithely with the long pole in his hands. But these boatmen are expert and seldom make a mistake.

The guns were fairly well scattered over the swamp, as far apart as possible, hidden in the long grass and reeds. Diggs and I were the only shooters using the 20-bore gun, and we challenged the 12-bore. We had all along obtained wonderful results with the 20-bore, and had beaten many of the 12-bore records at every kind of small game, both in killing power—for on the average the losses with a 20-bore gun are much less—and in range. I have known many fine shots in India, and experienced sportsmen, who have given up the bigger bore for the smaller one, and have even used the 28-bore most effectively for game birds other than snipe and quail. One can get very accurate with a 20-bore gun, and the concentration is apparently more effective for long shots.

Skirting the swamp on nearly all sides, the Raja had

placed shikarries with "muzzle-loading guns" to keep the duck on the move, and after an hour's wait in our hiding places some far-away shots suddenly rang out.

From all round the far-reaching swamp a mighty quacking and rumbling is simultaneously heard, followed almost immediately by successive crashes of moving and settling birds. Another few shots ring out and then thunder rolls by as the rising of millions of wild duck at one and the same time merges into a long drawn roar which can be easily heard a mile away.

And what a sight now greets the eye! The sun is almost as effectually obliterated as if a vast cloud had suddenly spread over the sky. Flights of mallard, pin-tail, gadwell, and the red-headed pochards whirr and dash over our heads, flying first low over the reed tops until toll is taken. And then, seeming to come from every point of the compass, flight upon flight at various heights swish by. Bewildered birds in small flights, and in threes and fours dive past and dodge the guns at a terrific pace. The white-eyed duck and the spotted bill appear to be the boldest, and constantly pass low over the guns. Fusillade upon fusillade split the air, and duck and teal come hurling down with a loud splash in the water. The spare boats are working hard, some in the high reeds and others chasing wounded birds out in the open water, and all seem to be getting piled up with a bag. My gun gets too hot to hold, and I have recourse to a khaki-coloured handkerchief. After a while, we call to each other to cease fire as the birds are flighting away. This is done at intervals to allow the duck to return. We shoot on till late in the afternoon, when the Raja calls out that it is time to give over and return to camp. We direct the boatmen; and now comes the excitement of greeting each other on high and dry land to compare notes and our various bags. As the loaded boats arrive, they are emptied by dozens of men who come up from the crowd, and each gun lines out his duck and counts his bag.

There were over two hundred true duck between seven guns, Diggs having got the biggest bag of seventy duck. I was fortunate to be second with over fifty, and the Opium Officer's wife third with thirty-eight. The Raja was greatly surprised at the lady's shooting, and was rapt in admiration of her sterling qualities as a sportsman. By the time we left him he was prepared to reconstruct his ancient inherited beliefs in regard to womankind in general and their capabilities. Of the miscellaneous bag there were several grebe, both the lesser and the greater, and many shovellers, which are quite good eating early in the season, when there is plenty of water and weed feeding along the edges of the "jheel." There were two swamp partridges—one shot by Diggs, and the other by the Raja—five snipe and one quail. It was rare to find the swamp partridges right out in such deep water; and rarer still to find a quail in among the duck, so far from the banks of the big "jheel." But for a few mallard, gadwell, pin-tail, white-eye duck, the partridges, snipe and quail, the bag was divided among the village people who had helped to push the car. We returned to camp on elephants, and as we had had no lunch we were glad to sit down to a high tea late in the evening which necessitated missing dinner.

# CHAPTER XII

## ON THE WAY TO BUXAR: AND A TERRIBLE TIGER STORY

*In the jungle world, th' official has hurled*
*His files straight out of the door,*
*And protected the poor, by following the spoor*
*Of the tiger and bear as before;*
*As in the days when, good milit'ry men*
*Ruled Ind with great Akbar's lore.*
*But one mustn't burn at any strange turn*
*The "red-taped" official takes,*
*When he flies to the chase with a harassed face*
*And the jungle his soul awakes:*
*For you, good reader, in the ranks, or leader*
*Of men in whatever sphere,*
*Would do just the same, and play the old game,*
*If you breathed the wild atmosphere.*

ON the occasion of this six weeks' big game shoot, which I had arranged with my great friend—already introduced—known as "Shikarri Diggs"—a nickname that suited his uncanny insight into the jungles and knowledge of wild animals—and my brother, Colonel J. K. Knowles, I was stationed in Bengal. Shikarri Diggs and my brother will be alluded to in the narratives that follow, as Col. J. K. and Diggs.

Early one morning, in the middle of March, my friend Diggs and I, started off in our cars from Bengal to reach the Cantonment Station of Bareilly—about 800 miles distant—where we had arranged to meet my brother,

Col. J. K. in order to discuss our camp outfit and our future movements. Our wives and families, whom, at the same time, we were going to conduct to the hills from Bareilly, had gone on ahead of us by train. The hot weather had come in rapidly, as it usually does after the month of February, but we were certain of good staging bungalows at every seventy or eighty miles along the wonderfully kept grand trunk road, where we could obtain shelter from the fierce, hot winds that commenced to blow, and periodical rests along the route of our long journey. We had two cars between us—the Standard and the Ford—each of which we took in turn to drive for reasons of the pleasant change on such tours, and the experience gained in driving a car of some other style and make than your own. We started off with the intention of doing 225 miles a day and reaching our destination on the afternoon of the fourth day; and we succeeded in keeping very exactly to the programme, under conditions of heat and "bad going" in many parts of the road that are trying to the best of engines and tyres. Both these makes of cars behaved excellently—particularly the English Standard, which was a third-hand car, having run over 30,000 miles.

After a halt at Bareilly for three days and nights, which was a regrettable but unavoidable slice off our leave, my friend Diggs, and Col. J. K., my brother, left for the Western-Himalayan Government Forest Division in the Bijnor District, to get the first camp ready at Buxar; a fascinating spot on the banks of the Ramganga, one of the many tributary rivers that rise in the Himalayan mountains. They took with them the Standard and the Ford which had brought Diggs and myself from Bengal, while Col. J. K. had his own car, the Angus Sanderson, which, of course, he declared to be the best car in the market! He had already despatched many bullock carts with servants, tents and baggage to Buxar, to await his arrival, where four trained shikarri elephants, kindly lent by some Rajas of the neighbouring districts for the occasion, were to meet him. We had drawn lots as to who should conduct the ladies and children of the shooting party to the Hill Station of Kasauli, near Simla,—the Governor-General of India's hot weather retreat,—and this duty fell to my lot. I was to return immediately to join the men out in the jungles, after conducting the party safely up to the hills. This was accomplished during the next three days, following the departure of my brother and friend.

In the elastic sense of the word, Kasauli is a perfect little summer retreat. Nine miles from Kalka one goes up a straight wall of mountains, 6,500 ft. high, among the sweet scented Himalayan pines that give the air a healthy resinous nip. The peach, the apple, and the apricot are in blossom; and the picturesque little houses—many after the fashion of English cottages—lying on the north side of the mountains, and facing Simla, are gorgeously decorated with the lemon-yellow Banksia and large white roses, creeping and interlacing in amorous riot. The roads are hedged with the Himalayan May-flower, in lavish white bloom, looking like snow drifts propped up on either side; and, pouring out from their clusters of red flowers, perfume and honey for the bee, the beautiful rhododendrons with their dark evergreen foliage, enrich the hill-sides with masses of crimson; one feels the sudden change from the fierce heat below, into a fairy land of soft sunshine and sweetness. Many a Britisher, thrilled with the bounty of nature on these beautiful heights—a white man's country—has wondered when the British people are going to awake and seek expansion on the Himalayas—the most glorious realm of their Empire that overlooks the world.

My obligations are at an end, and I return for my holiday in the jungles. The cars have all gone on ahead and I have to do a night journey by train. The Punjab Mail pulls up at Dhampur, a small wayside station. It stops but two minutes, and I tumble out at 3 a.m., eyes glued with sleep. A bright moon encrusts everything with a pellucid plate of silvery sheen and I shiver with the cold chill in the air. In the pale light, three elephants are standing out like monster iron statues. They are padded and ready. I meet a tall cloaked gentleman—Colonel Mac, on the platform, and we introduce ourselves. Both of us are guests on the shoot and have thirty miles to accomplish on the elephants to Buxar Camp, where the party is awaiting us in the lower hills. We are in the Bijnor district, reputed for big game.

"Topping night! let us start at once," remarks Colonel Mac.

We climb up on top of our elephants without delay, and start off with our rifles and lunch baskets, leaving our baggage and servants to follow up behind in carts. We have travelled seven miles, and it is beginning to get light. Suddenly, reddening the dull, ashen horizon in the east, a big round crest emerges, of faded orange hue; and, as if dimmed with age, and resentful of its enforced obedience to perpetual motion, the great Orb of day rises slowly and sullenly. It hangs over the plain, and the distant outline of the purple hills is shot with ruby. A delightful breeze springs up, and the ripening wheat crops for miles around, shimmer in long waves, like a golden sea swept by a sudden gust.

We are approaching the land of game. A hare runs out from under the trunks of the elephants; and the grey and the beautiful black partridge, are calling lustily in every direction. We cross a river bed and put up a sounder of wild pig; and further on, many a herd of black buck. We cannot wait to shoot, and hurry on. We have breakfast at 11 o'clock and drag out the rest of the hot afternoon journey, arriving for the night at the Kaligarh Forest Bungalow, the headquarters of the Kaligarh Forest range. We have come twenty-two miles, and are now in the hills. At our feet flows the beautiful Ramanga River, fresh and clear from the higher mountains; and we have a voluptuous dip in its cool, crystal waters, amidst the splashing of huge mahseer.

A lovely, fresh dawn cheers us on the road again winding along the precipitous gorge of the Ramganga, rich in wild scenery. Far down below us, a sambhur stag and hind are wading the waters. Suddenly, a Hanuman black-faced monkey gives an alarm cry. We suspect either a tiger or a panther, and wait silently on the road side, on the brink of a thousand feet fall. The elephant is as steady as a rock, and we can see right over. I am anxious to take a snapshot, and seize my camera instead of the rifle. The monkeys are yelling like maniacs —we are hot on something!

"There, there!" I whisper, "Colonel, your right front! A fine panther is crouched on a rock looking up at us." The Colonel presents his rifle, and I move my camera—but, alas!

I never thought of the sunlight flashing on the nickel of my range finder, and we lost him. The camera would have to be camouflaged in future—it was obvious! A lesson once learnt in the jungles, never to be forgotten! We move on towards Buxar Camp and see the Bungalow in the distance; and travel on, till we are under the high bank on top of which, smoke from the camp fires is curling upwards. The voices of our good host Col. J. K. and Diggs arrest our attention.

"Hallo! you are late, you fellows. Any luck on the way?"

We dismount and join them, and have a very merry breakfast together: Diggs and I move off at once to the river with our rods and tackle, and have a dancing time with the spoon and the fly. A pack of wild dogs chase a sambhur hind down to the river and she takes refuge in deep water. We save her, and shoot a couple of these destructive brutes. Our bag of mahseer fish the first day is 15 lb.

In the afternoon, the four of us go out together on our elephants, to look up two old tiger "kills," taking along a buffalo calf with us to tie in a likely spot for the night. We do our own tracking, and follow up the huge pugs of a very big tiger along a deep nullah; but as dusk is fast approaching, and the ground is impossible in any other light but that of broad day, we return, and tie the calf up at the mouth of the nullah. We hear the tiger roaring in the distance as we return to camp.

After dinner we sit out in the moonlight for "short drinks" and smokes to celebrate our first night in camp, and listen to Diggs, who is a wonderful shikarri with extraordinary instincts in the jungles. The following thrilling account of one of Diggs' tiger experiences in these very jungles, in his own words as much as possible, will help to show how fascinating is "the great sport" in the wild lower hills of the Himalayas that attracts the Britisher, and calls him away from the monotony of his life in the burning plains to face sudden dangers.

Some years ago Diggs and a shikar friend, who was also a reputed sportsman, took leave together to shoot over some special ground which Diggs had in view—"a hotbed for tiger" as he calls it—in a secluded valley known as Patharepani (literally rock of pure water) situated somewhere in that vast tract of Government Forests, covering the lower Himalayas, between the

Hill Stations of Náini Tál and Lansdowne. The formation of the country here is almost an interminable stretch of low hillocks covered with dense forests, and broken up by successive and almost parallel valleys curving down from the higher hills, each contributing its waters to the main valley of the Ramganga River.

For the purpose of this story, I shall refer to his friend as S. P. He was a great shot too, and he and Diggs could print their initials on the target. Two more deadly shots could not have got together to shikar stripes and spots. Their rifles were the 375 and the 400 high velocity; small bores, but they went in for selection shots, such as the head and the neck.

"We were once trying to bring to account an enormous tiger that was terrorising all the cattle stations in the neighbourhood. His pug marks, up the ravines and on the forest roads, were as large as soup plates. We had never seen anything like them before. It was our first visit up a beautiful valley called Patharepani, in a country where we subsequently bagged nine tigers and eleven panthers in two weeks. The ground was quite new to us, and we spent the first few days exploring and tracking. We had four good elephants with us, kindly lent by a Maharaja who was a friend of S. P.'s. Of these, our favourite 'howdah' elephant was a huge big tusker who had been a kedda 'chucker out' in his younger days; and about forty tigers had been shot off his back. His name was Chand Murat (face of the moon) and his mahout's name was Akbar Khan. They were both fine old veterans—the mahout with a flowing white beard, and the elephant with great pointed tusks, like protruding beams enamelled white—both nerveless and fearless, and true to the marrow.

"It is the middle of March—still damp and cold at night in the lower hills—and that romantic hour just before break of day when the stars flicker, which can be more exactly described in a poetic turn :

**Come, Pageant immortal, the diamonds toss gay*
*On thy night robe dismantled, thou usher of day !*
*As if thou, commissioned a moment to light*
*Those firework remnants to signal rent night,*
*Wert sick of delay, and in quick eagerness*
*Dost unfold to creation thy pale nakedness !*

" In this hour of the twinkling dawn, we move silently along on Chand Murat to the mouth of the ravine, where the evening before we had tied up a buffalo calf for this monster tiger.

" ' Hazoor,' says Akbar Khan, in an awe-stricken voice, ' some horrible mishap is about to take place. The Almighty has not given elephants their great brains for nothing ; they can foretell ; and my child, by his peculiar behaviour all last night, has given signs which we mahouts know only too well ! '

" ' Hush ! ' we say to him.

" There is an uncanny feeling in the chill air as we approach the deep, dark ravine almost noiselessly and find the buffalo missing. He has been disembowelled—the rope is broken and the peg torn out of the ground.

" Suddenly, Chand Murat lifts up his trunk and scents the air ; we take the warning, and the mahout quickly guides the elephant behind cover, to allow some wild elephants in front to cross the river bed in which we are standing. A thin mist hangs over the valley ; and a disturbed barking deer is yelling itself hoarse. There is no other sound but the falling of dripping dew, and our caps and coats are wet. We see the big form of the elephants go noiselessly by ; they cross the broad bed and scramble

*Quotation from a poem by the Author, " Dawn in the Himalayas."

JUNGLE BEATERS AND THE THRILL OF THE "HOWDAH"

*By kind permission of*
*The Thomason Engineering College,*
*Roorkie, U.P., India.*

up the opposite bank; a few stones only are rolled down.

"We emerge from our cover, and try to find the drag of the tiger's kill. We hunt about, but can find not the slightest mark of the kill being dragged. Chand Murat is behaving queerly—he has never before shown such signs of restlessness. He now seems disinclined to obey his driver, and crosses the deep gorge of the ravine higher up, reluctantly. We think it most strange, but say nothing to the old mahout.

"'The tiger has shouldered and taken the kill clean away,' whispers S. P.

"At that moment we had climbed up on the top of a small plateau with a low hillock in front of us, not fifty yards distant.

"It is sufficiently light now to see the foresight of our rifles—and I suddenly touch S. P., who pulls up the elephant. I try to point out something that looks like a monstrous form, standing still in deep shadows against the side of the hillock. A great head appears to be gazing down intently at the elephant's legs. S. P. cannot make out the outline nor can he place it, and presses me to fire: but it is his turn, and I refuse.

"Suddenly, there is a movement in the grass; up goes S. P.'s rifle with a flash, and two shots ring out and echo through the still forests, as an enormous tiger gallops over the brow of the hillock. The thudding of his heavy gallop and his colossal size are impressing beyond words, and we try to keep the elephant still, to listen. But, beyond the distant cries of pea-fowl, that yell at every disturbance in the jungle, dead silence follows. We wait twenty minutes, trying to keep Chand Murat steady. S. P. thinks it is a clean miss; but, as no animals round about have given the slightest indication of the tiger's movements, I refuse to believe in a miss or that the tiger has gone. I decide to dismount to see if there is some blood where the tiger was standing and ask S. P. to keep me covered; but he won't hear of my going alone, and we try to get down together.

"But, to our astonishment, the elephant refuses to sit down. The mahout forces him with his iron weapon and he trumpets in a rage. He finally makes a half attempt; and, with the 'howdah' at a steep incline, rolling like a ship, we scramble off and jump to the ground. But our rifles! Akbar Khan cannot hand them down to us—he has lost control of the child! We shout to him in desperation; but for some unaccountable reason, Chand Murat, the staunchest of elephants, turns and bolts in a panic! And—horrors! behind us we hear that heavy thudding gallop again, and we see the huge tiger—having apparently taken the disturbance for a threat, returning over the hillock to fight for dear life. We turn sharply together, armless and helpless, to face the hillock and the savage monster that has crashed down in the grass barely twenty paces in front of us. We have turned just in time to stand shoulder to shoulder and to freeze like statues, though right in the open before him! We know nothing can save us but successful jungle deception—the practice of wild animals—and we do not move a hair's breadth. The brute is so close that we can see the vital blood jerking out of two small holes, high up, well in front of the shoulder, and pouring down his near flank. Terribly wounded through the lungs, he cannot roar; his breathing is like a great pair of rasping bellows. His claws are extended full length, and his tail is lashing furiously. With ears savagely back, his great head moves round alternately—one moment slowly away from us in the direction of the hillock, and the next swiftly and fiercely back to face us again with a ghastly grin and a low guttural threat, followed with a deafening spit like the escape of steam from an engine. These head movements with the terrible snarling and spitting are repeated, until we feel our nerves gradually collapsing. We know that the slightest mistake, or that the rustling of the grass near us for any cause, would mean instant death. Our knees are beginning to feel quaky, but we must hold out—death is the alternative !

"And deception triumphs at last. We see the claws being drawn in, and the head is now steadily facing the hillock. To our left front we suddenly see the welcome form of Chand Murat standing still in the shadows, a hundred yards away. The old experienced mahout is watching us—he has quieted and brought back the elephant—and from our frozen attitude he knows what is wrong and makes no mistake. Suddenly, the great monster lurches up and gallops back over the hillock. Slowly we retreat rearwards, step by step, and the elephant is brought round to meet us. We are on the back of Chand Murat again, and our rifles are grasped in deep gratitude. It seems as though we have passed through an eternity of agony ; but it is still morning, and the golden sunbeams are darting through the trees.

"S. P. and I are around that hillock looking down on the dead tiger. With his paws up and the whites of his eyes showing, the monster is sprawling on the broad of his back. I tell S. P., however, that I do not like his unnatural appearance, and advise him to make certain with another shot ; but he thinks the skin will be spoilt, and we decide to throw some empty cartridge cases to see if there are some signs of life.

"The cases are thrown and we curse our stupidity ! Like a flash of lightning the monster is between the elephant's legs ; we fire two shots but his movements are too rapid. The tiger's great claws tearing the elephant's thighs on the inside of his hind legs, Chand Murat, in terrible agony, trumpets like thunder. He lashes out and whirls round, but cannot get at the tiger to throw him off. Amidst a din, as if hell were let loose, a terrible tussle begins. The howdah is a match-box on an ocean wave! The woodwork and the ropes are creaking ominously, and we are being hurled about and shaken to bits. We try to jump, but it is impossible, and have to trust to luck! Akbar Khan is yelling to the great elephant to use his weight, and directs him, and he begins to sit down on the tiger. We are warned that the elephant may roll and that we must be prepared to jump! But the tiger loosens his mighty grip as he feels the elephant's weight, and lollops back to that hillock. We yell to the mahout to hold Chand Murat steady for a second, to draw a bead on the furious monster panting in front of us; but the elephant bolts again in pain and panic over the low hills—over terrible ground, with a torrent of blood behind him; and we pull up in the valley below from which we came up!

"The whole of this second incident lasted no more than half an hour. Poor Chand Murat was almost disembowelled. We unharnessed him, flinging howdah, pad, ropes, everything to the ground, and walked him slowly back to camp pouring with blood; we could do nothing more, while we followed behind on foot.

"Two hours later, on fresh elephants, we were round that fateful hillock again, and found the dread monster lying for a second time on the broad of his back, again showing the whites of his eyes. We took no more risks and put two bullets into his head simultaneously. He was a magnificent specimen. Lying on the spot, he measured 10 ft. 6 in. from the tip of the nose to the tip of the tail.

"We heard of the death of old Akbar Khan, the mahout, some months afterwards. He must have died of a broken heart; the shock of his child's behaviour, in whom he had implicit faith, must have haunted him and cut short the remaining days of his life. Chand Murat almost succumbed to his wounds too, and it took him several months to recover."

# CHAPTER XIII

## THE TRAIL OF A ROGUE ELEPHANT

As our shooting permit from the Forest Department for the Buxar Forest Range was held for a period of seven days only, we had to make arrangements to work very strenuously to shoot over as much of the best portion of the ground here, as the time allowed. From the previous chapter, it is necessary to recall that our first afternoon was spent in looking up two old tiger kills; and that, after we had tied up the buffalo calf late in the evening, we heard the tiger roaring on our way back to the Forest Bungalow at Buxar—about two and a half miles distant—where we were encamped. The following morning had to be devoted to visiting the place where we had tied up the buffalo calf as bait for this big tiger. We felt fairly confident that we should find the calf had been killed during the night, and we looked forward to the excitement of tracking the kill through the thick jungle to see where the tiger had hidden it, and to have a "machan" (tree ambush) fixed up over the carcass. It is much more satisfactory to conduct the tracking of wild animals oneself rather than leave such important operations to the Indian shikarri, as a great number of sportsmen are inclined to do.

We had arranged over night to send out, very early in the morning, two of our trained elephants to a certain old wooden bridge over a hill stream—a Forest Department, cold weather "make-shift"—within about a quarter of a mile of the ravine at the mouth of which the calf had been left. The elephants were to await the arrival of our car. Where jungle cart tracks can be negotiated—provided the circumstances allow of a car being used—not only is time saved, but one arrives on the ground much fresher, owing to the conservation of energy which should always be considered on strenuous undertakings.

We selected the Standard, with its good reliable engine, as likely to give us the least trouble, and started off immediately after early breakfast. On reaching the old wooden bridge we found the two elephants *non est.* This was puzzling and annoying too, as we had sent on our rifles on the elephants, in charge of two shikarri orderlies. The elephants' tracks were clearly there, and we could not understand what had happened. No time, however, could be wasted—neither could we call out for fear of disturbing the tiger—and, leaving the car near the bridge, the four of us proceeded, empty-handed on foot, to look for the calf. We stalked round the foot of densely wooded hillocks—the jungle appearing quiet and undisturbed—and arrived at the spot, only to find to our great disappointment that the buffalo calf had not been touched, and was grazing quite unconcernedly. We examined the ground all round the calf, and up the dark-looking ravine, and found to our surprise huge, fresh tiger tracks. It was apparent that the monster had been round, and had had a look at the calf, but had refused the bait for some reason. This was another puzzle. Diggs believed the tiger had a natural kill somewhere close by, and was not in need of further mutton for the time being. But we could see no vultures hovering about as an indication of this, and gave up this second puzzle for the present, bringing away the buffalo calf with the intention of replacing him with another calf in the afternoon.

We got back to the bridge as quickly as possible, and found the car quite safe and undamaged by mischievous wild elephants. We had taken the precaution to camouflage it as much as possible with broken branches. We got the buffalo calf inside the car after some difficulty, and before starting the engine on our return to camp, we examined our elephants' tracks all round. On one side of the bridge, down the nullah, we came upon enormous tracks of a wild tusker, and concluded it was the rogue elephant against whom we had been warned by the Forest Department ranger. This accounted presumably for the absence of our elephants we had sent on ahead in the early hours of the morning. We were not surprised on returning to camp to find our elephants there. The mahouts and the two orderlies, who had carried our rifles, reported that on reaching the bridge, the rogue elephant had suddenly emerged from the jungle on the right hand side, and had charged down upon them, chasing them back in the direction of camp. They had no alternative but to turn and fly, and had taken refuge in a wood-cutters' camp about two miles away, where the tusker was driven off by a crowd of the lumbermen. We had just missed the whole occurrence.

The enormous tiger we were after was worth any risk, and we were determined to try our luck again and bait a second time. We started off after lunch on two fresh elephants, having decided to leave our cars in safety in camp. The second buffalo calf gave us considerable trouble on the way, as he refused to go and had to be dragged along, but we reached the tying-up spot eventually. The rogue tusker was nowhere in evidence, and we hoped that he had taken up his quarters in some other feeding ground after the chase that morning.

It is late in the evening before we are able to return to camp again, after tying up the second buffalo, and dusk has already set in. In front of us, in the pale gloaming, the fantastic ink-black summits of the distant mountains, deepening the faint rose-tint glow in the west, stand out sharply against the sky, as if silhouetted there: while below, on the ground before us, a cold damp swamp through which we are passing, stretches out to lose its far length in the gathering dusk; and, across the swamp, over the tall wiry reeds and grass, a low mist draping the near giant trees, hangs in long whitish grey bands, above which, far on either side of us, the dark forests rise and fall like gigantic wave crests, tossing their shadowy spray over the low hills. Down the forest fire-line or roadway, about twelve feet broad, leading like a vista under the arched bands of mist, the two elephants are walking quietly abreast.

Suddenly we stop to listen! Through the chill dusky gloom, and the solemn stillness of the forests, comes the roar of the wandering tiger like the distant boom of a big gun, rolling up its last pent-up volume in a climax of deep sound that seems to shake the very ground, and, in scattered diffusion, dies away into the creeping darkness beyond us.

We talk quietly and comment. How the poor sambhur and the spotted deer in the forest must quake in fear at those dreaded sounds, that begin in the high staccato of the tabby cat's "mee-ow" and gather in depth and volume till they roll by the stricken creatures in a clap of thunder!

Roar follows roar; our elephants are getting restless and are beginning to beat their trunks on the ground: they do not like it. They are in a hurry to get home to their comfortable camp fires and their evening meal of baked flour cakes. As the last roar dies away and complete silence follows, we move leisurely on again, full of high expectancy of what the next few days have in store for us. As a rule, when a shoot is over, and the journey back to camp is commenced, all jungle ceremonies are waived; and we are not particularly careful as we saunter along on the pads of the elephants with our legs dangling down, smoking and chatting gaily, with the black outline of the mountains facing us, and the damp mist wetting our caps and shoulders.

"That tiger should kill to-night!—a monster it should be that can roar like that!" remarks Col. Mac.

"Yes," says Diggs, "he is a big tiger—but there is no certainty of his killing tied up buffs."

And, while the latter and Col. J. K. are explaining to Col. Mac and myself, how frequently, during the last few years, the tigers about here had been missed over kills by various shooting parties; and that as a natural result it was impossible to depend upon their killing, or their usually regular habits of returning to kills during daylight at certain marked intervals—which was accepted as a rule of thumb in places where tigers were less disturbed—our elephants suddenly stop on the road of their own accord, without any authority from or suggestion on the part of the mahouts.

And now, as if we were in close proximity to some of their tribe, they begin to lift their trunks high up in the air—now stretching them out full length in front, and now twisting them round from side to side, with the snouts raised up like the hood of a cobra. We keep perfectly still meanwhile, and peer anxiously in the dusky light all round us, trying to catch a glimpse, or to hear the faintest rustle amongst the high reeds towering up on either side of the fire-line almost over our heads: but we can neither see nor hear anything, and decide to hurry along as fast as possible. Diggs is saying that a wild elephant might be standing quite still, within fifteen paces of us, in all the surrounding high stuff, without our being any the wiser. He and Col. Mac are leading the way and follow the fire-line round a sharp turn that brings us into the middle of the swamp. Suddenly, we hear Diggs —who is watching ahead, close behind the driver, stopping his elephant abruptly : and our elephant behind, that is blind in the left eye, nearly bumps into his.

"Back if you can quietly!" we hear him say.

But it is too late! A loud trumpet ahead of us, and sharp shrill cries like squeaking wheels, come down from every part of the swamp, and we find to our horror that we have rushed into a big herd of wild elephants, that have come out either to graze in the swamp, or to cross over to the other side. There is a general commotion; and through the rapidly increasing gloom, we can just make out huge moving forms, and can hear the trampling down of reeds and the splashing of water.

In amongst a wild herd of elephants—even if the tuskers happen to be quiet or in a good humour, and there is no immediate danger to be encountered by an attack from them—there is always the fear of a sudden stampede; which is serious enough in the daytime, but made a thousand times worse in a dusky light or in the dark. Elephants are curious animals; brave as lions in the presence of real danger, and as timid as, and ready to jump like young girls at nothing worse than mice. There are, perhaps, no other animals more liable to panic, for the most trifling cause conceivable; and a mahout must be a man of tact and of considerable resources in order to be able to handle various situations.

The position was made worse by the fact that our two elephants were in reality baggage animals, used for marching purposes only, and could not be depended upon as staunch "shikar" elephants. We had made use of them that afternoon in order to rest our trained elephants for a shoot involving hard work the following day. Beyond the high roads, these two baggage elephants had no experience of the jungles, nor had they ever seen any members of their race in a wild state before. With such material to handle, in the delicate situation which we were suddenly called upon to face, we were on the horns of a dilemma; for no course of action could be decided upon with the slightest degree of confidence: whatever could be done, depended upon the nerves of these two elephants and their behaviour under restraint. We had, moreover, foolishly come out without shotguns and lanterns—which are usually a part of the equipment, particularly in the afternoons, for fear of delays and darkness, and sometimes unavoidable contact with the lord of the forest, who understands no other law but that of boundless freedom, and no other right but that the forests are his, and that man is no more than an impertinent intruder. The lantern is a safeguard at night, as elephants object to fires and lights; and, in order to drive them away, a shotgun is least expensive—rifle cartridges being too precious to waste on shots which are banged off in the air!

But to proceed with the adventure:

There is not a moment to be lost in deciding upon something to be done; for, not fifty paces in front of us, crashing down high reeds at the spot from which he emerges, out walks an enormous tusker, on to the middle of the fire-line. He is standing broad-side on, and we can see his great curved tusks—protruding many feet beyond his trunk, gleaming white in the dusk. We feel, under the circumstances, that we should be much safer on foot; but our daring to create a disturbance in front of this mammoth, by making our elephants sit down in order to slip off, would be courting a horrible death. Something must take place; and we are only thinking of how we can avoid a collision, or escape with as little injury to ourselves and to our valuable elephants, as possible, if the tusker should take it into his head to charge at such close quarters. Our elephants had been very kindly lent by a Maharaja friend, and we could not be too careful of them.

Suddenly, the wild tusker turns round and faces us abruptly, and our hearts are in our mouths! His huge massive head, covering our direct front, looms up—almost twice our height, like a hideous nightmare. His great ears, that seemed to be flapping good-naturedly like big, palm-leaf fans a moment ago, before he turned, are now drawn back close to the sides of his head and are quite motionless; the attitude betokens surprise and annoyance, and the brute looks terribly fierce; but, he is standing still in that position like a gigantic statue, and not a sound now comes from the surrounding swamp. It seems as if the rest of the herd had taken their cue from their master of ceremonies; for all the members have frozen into great silent figures, which look like black patches, only just distinguishable where the grass and reeds are short.

For fear of a disastrous stampede in the dark, we dare not fire off a single, rifle shot in the air. We should be bowled over like ninepins, and, along with our two elephants, very probably crushed to death. There are forty to fifty elephants in the herd. In the circumstances, it is safer to keep from firing unless all other manœuvres fail, and it must be resorted to in the last extremity. Moreover, there is a Government fine of Rs. 500 for shooting a wild tusker; unless it can be proved that life was endangered, but in the *copia verborum* of the elaborate Forest regulations, this safety valve is so congested with "red-tape," that it is a thousand times more preferable to take a considerable risk rather than fire upon a rogue elephant—the resulting trouble being endless!

Unfortunately the wild herd is on the leeward of us, and though we are trusting to the on-coming darkness to screen our conspicuous figures on the backs of our elephants, yet we are aware that the tusker must be conscious of the presence of men. Our own untrained elephants are keeping so remarkably still, that it makes matters more uncanny. Something is wròng with them —although the mahouts are leaning forward and, with their wrists well outwards, have the points of their iron weapons pressed against the foreheads of the elephants.

With one hand on the ropes, and with the other grasping each his rifle, we are watching the terrible tusker before us, intently, fascinated, unconscious of what may happen! We seem to have naturally frozen in harmony with everything around us, and it seems like a dream. Suddenly the tusker takes a step forward, and we hear the bolt of Diggs' rifle being pressed home with as little noise as possible: Col. Mac just behind him on the leading elephant is trying to follow his example. We, behind on our elephant, look to our rifles as well. Diggs turns his head slowly and repeats again quickly: "Back—back!" We whisper to our mahout who tries hard, but he cannot move our elephant. We press him, and he tries silently again and again, but, for all that the mahout's efforts can avail, the elephant might be dead in his standing position. The huge wild tusker halts to survey us, as if doubtful; and at that instant, we see Diggs and Col. Mac experiencing a weird shock. Their pad suddenly begins to shake from side to side and they look all round to see if the ground is quaking! The shaking gets worse and worse; and they are holding on the ropes for all they are worth, for they realise—and we whisper to them, that their elephant in front is trembling dreadfully, and that it would be an easy matter for her to shake them off.

"That elephant is 'terror-stricken'—both these elephants will collapse on the ground presently. We can do nothing!" whispers our mahout: "Allah! Allah!" he says *sotto voce*. He whimpers something under his breath about our time having come, while we are egging him on to try to prevent the terrible calamity he predicts, but the man is a wretched pessimist.

"Look out!" I exclaim quietly to Col. J. K.

Our elephant immediately follows the example of the leading one and begins to tremble like an aspen leaf—the sensation is a horrible one. The hind-quarters of our elephants are now sinking and I am going down behind—the leading elephant is also collapsing to the ground. It is awful. The mahouts seem powerless and can get neither of them to stir, either to the right or left, or backwards. Though we should be followed, to get our elephants to bolt back the way we came is the only possibility of escape; but this is out of the question. They are stricken with terror at the sight of the tusker looming up twice their size, who is now beginning to take halting steps forward—and—horror! We can see his trunk like the bole of a tree, rising straight up over his head for a moment; and now it comes down like a twisting python and begins to fold into his huge mouth! We are dimly conscious, with our two elephants trembling frantically in a half-sitting posture, that the folding of the trunk is preparatory to a charge! In the deathly stillness, we can hear our hearts beating like a pump engine; but, at this terrible moment of crisis, suddenly—quite close to our left at the edge of the forest, the deep, sharp bay of a sambhur stag and the shrill cry of a hind, ring out in a spasm together, and vibrate through the forest. Their hot alarm cries are kept up furiously, stinging our already strained nerves and shooting through the brain. What this new development can mean is beyond our benumbed state to realise instantly. Diggs is looking hard in the direction, hanging on to the back of his elephant at an angle of 45 degrees. If the tusker were to charge at this instant, his elephant would receive the impact full in the chest, and she would be hurled on the top of us. The idea is ghastly ! But the wild tusker, too, is taken by surprise and hesitates for a moment or more, apparently to recover.

The scene is terribly impressing. But it is suddenly changed by a crashing sound through the thick undergrowth where the spur of a low hill juts down into the swamp, and we realise that the sambhur are rushing madly away, bellowing hard till their alarm cries die in the distance. Awful silence again prevails for the space of some seconds. And now, as the tusker moves forward for the expected charge, our two elephants in fear are almost falling to the ground—Mercy ! Diggs' rifle is up to his shoulder, and we are on the point of jumping—anywhere—into the high reeds where we should disappear like ants in a cornfield ! I throw my camera forward into the reeds, where it goes down with a faint rustle—and, we are trying to slip down holding our rifles, when—Heavens ! The bowels of the earth are opening out ! Next to us, from the spur of the forest jutting out just behind the tusker, a deafening roar crashes upon us with such detonating suddenness, that its very impact is felt, and, along with the breath, every muscle of the body is suspended with the shock. The lofty trees round about seem to shake—and then, but for the fire-flies that fall through the darkness like tiny green sparks from an explosion, everything in a moment seems turned to stone ! But, before another roar follows, stupor awakes. We become conscious of a heave up—lucky that we were holding the ropes firmly—and we see, for the shake of a second, the enormous form of that terrible tusker swinging round, and we hear him rushing towards the spur with a crash through the reeds, back in the direction from which he first emerged ; and we know no more beyond the fact that we have flown by the spot where he was standing ; and that we are flying on the backs of our elephants through the darkness, now down the fire-line and now through the swamp, as never John Gilpin flew on the back of his horse down the streets of London Town.

Maddened with frantic terror, screaming in the weirdest fashion, and racing alongside of other huge moving forms all shrieking in wild confusion—with the pea-fowl joining in, half daft with anxiety !—our elephants, who were spurred into action by the terrific shock of the roar, are bolting blindly, dementedly—leaving behind them the stampede of the wild elephants—the roars of the tiger, and the trumpet blasts of the infuriated tusker that had threatened us, and who—apparently—had turned from us to dispute the unceremonious entry of his tribe's foe, into the sacred recess of their quiet grazing ground.

Holding on by the skin of our teeth, we race over a wide river bed spiked with rough ragged boulders, and —on the other side—up a hill on to higher ground, where the forest road curves and broadens out, and leads direct to camp about another mile distant. We have travelled nearly one mile in five minutes, and can see the scattered camp fires of Buxar glowing in front of us. Our elephants, completely exhausted, slow down, and, still trembling in every limb, finally stop. We are all out of breath, and so shaken, that we cannot help trembling ourselves. But for the bright stars that are flashing in the clear heavens, like jewels suspended over our heads, it is almost pitch dark ; and, in the darkness, we make ourselves comfortable once again on the pads of our elephants, and light the soothing cigarette. We can hardly realise the whole occurrence, and say nothing for a while. We are silently thanking our stars for the lucky escape, while listening to the disturbance still going on in the distance! The short intervals, between the tiger's breaths and his far echoing roars, resound with that angry tusker's terrific peals that sweep through the forests like the spasmodic gusts of an unsettled cyclone, and end, as each wave of sound dies away, in the higher octaves of a wind, shrieking round the masts of a doomed ship! Though our poor elephants are shivering and shaking, and keep turning round continually in that direction, so terrible to them—as if they had at last plucked up a little courage to show fight—they are glad of the rest. Though too dark to see, the plateau upon which we are standing, in the middle of the road, is an immense grassy plain, with clumps of trees dotted about, and with the far hills rising up all round us, like a vast amphitheatre. It is all much too interesting to leave; as the din of the disturbance is still being carried down to our ears—though less frequent, and diminishing in violence, till, presently, it ceases altogether. Col. Mac strikes a match to glance at his watch, and reminds us that it is past eight o'clock! Our dallyings here have taken the best part of an hour.

"My word!" said Diggs, "we've missed being hurled into eternity by a hair's breadth! I don't think I have the heart to shoot that tiger now, even though he may turn out to be a record!"

"Talk about confusion worse confounded! Nothing could be in it with that little show!—the worst experience I have ever had in the jungles," said Col. J. K.

"Allah! Allah-ho-Akbar!" (God—God is great!) added the mahouts in dramatic tones.

I suddenly remembered my camera, and told them that

I had dropped it; this made us all think of various odds and ends, and we hunted on top of the pads, and found that our cartridge bags, sola-topees, two big coats, a blanket, and Col. Mac's brandy flask in a leather case, had all been dropped. These things could not be easily replaced in the jungles and were a serious loss.

"Not that we should have had any use for the brandy, had that tusker's charge come off!" laughed the Colonel.

"No, and I certainly don't think we had better risk going back for the things now; nor had we better remain here any longer—tuskers are vindictive by nature, and have a nasty little habit of following one's tracks up; particularly a solitary tusker, which I think our monster is—in which case he should not have been with the herd!" added Diggs, upon whom we looked as infallible in all matters pertaining to jungle law. We found we had a few rifle cartridges apiece in our pockets, and instructed the mahouts to hurry home.

We were about to move off again, when we suddenly heard the huge branch of a tree being smashed about three hundred yards behind us. This was too much for our nerves: even Diggs told the mahouts to induce their elephants to bolt again; we did not relish the idea of another repetition of physical insensibility on the part of the elephants! But, again to our dismay, the wretched creatures would not, or could not, move: they had stopped trembling, and now for some unaccountable reason—the tusker not being near enough to give them cause—they commenced their tricks in a relapse of terror which threatened to be as bad as the last experience. We instantly loaded our rifles and prepared to fire in the direction of the broken branch. We knew that that horrible tusker might emerge suddenly out of the darkness at any point, and carry home a charge. There was no hesitation this time. We pulled our triggers, and a volley that seemed to sound terrifically loud in the darkness of the quiet night, crashed out in a blaze of fire. This sudden explosion had the desired effect again on our elephants. They first spun round in the direction of the unseen foe, and then back again facing camp, and bolted a second time, with their trunks up in the air and their tails stiffened straight out, parallel to the ground! Some wild pig, disturbed, rushed across the road in front of the elephants, and the rustle of the grass added impetus to the speed at which we shot along. Holding on to the ropes and to our rifles, our muscles were strained to the utmost, and our fingers by this time were quite sore. At last, we flew through a cattle station—a few hundred yards beyond which lay camp. Diggs, remembering the road, called out to us to duck our heads; which we did just in time, as some low hanging boughs swept over us.

The forest bungalow surrounded with bright lights, now began to show through the darkness—but our hearts leapt up again in great anxiety! We suddenly recollected that a flimsy wooden bridge, hardly strong enough to bear the weight of a horse, spanned a deep broad nullah between us and the bungalow. We were now but a few yards away from this death trap. Zounds—mercy on us! what were our elephants going to do in this pitch darkness? The mahouts saw the danger, and applied all possible methods to stop the bolting, but failed. Suddenly, the leading elephant swerved with a shriek, missed the bridge by half a yard, and dashed through the nullah and up the opposite side, as if it had been a garden walk in broad daylight. Our elephant followed suit; and in a few more moments we had broken through the Government wire fencing round the bungalow compound and were landed safely within. We had considerable trouble however in dismounting, as our elephants' nerves were thoroughly upset, and nothing could now induce them to sit down—a new demonstration of fear, quite the opposite to their exhibition in the jungles!

"Were you fellows nervous about that bridge?" inquired Diggs.

A few whiskies and sodas had put us right, and we were comfortably laughing and smoking in arm-chairs after an excellent dinner, decked out in our soothing "pyjamas."

"There was nothing to fear," he emphasised. "There is no creature so sensitive of its weight and so sure-footed as an elephant; even in the maddest frenzy they never make a mistake; you can always be certain of that one thing! Whether memory or instinct, it is difficult to say, but they always know a dangerous spot, and always just avoid it, whether in the light or in the dark."

"Well—look here, Diggs, before we retire, for goodness' sake explain what happened this evening," said Colonel Mac; "was it the same tiger we heard before, that arrived upon the scene in time to save us? The more I think of it, the more marvellous our escape seems; and I cannot make head or tail of it. It all seems jumbled up like a hideous nightmare!"

"Yes—come along Diggs, let us hear what you make of it," we added.

"Well," he said, "to begin with, it was exactly the same tiger we first heard roaring. Those were the full deep roars of disappointment and vexation; and they usually indicate a change of hunting ground. He has been up that particular valley the last ten days; and, we happened to strike the very time—late in the evening—when he was moving off. Either he missed seeing our buffalo bait, or refused it; and, unless it is killed by some other tiger, we shall find it untouched to-morrow morning. He will probably travel eight or ten miles to-night, and we shall hear of his depredations in some other place. The tiger here change their grounds as the droves of cattle move about. As these are easier to kill, their chief game is cattle. They fall back on sambhur and other deer in the forest as occasion makes necessary, and treat them, in a general way, as reserve food—unless, of course, deer come in their way, and a "kill" happens to be an easy one; or unless they desire a change of diet, when they will stalk sambhur for preference.

"Now, we know that most animals in the evening leave the high forests, and gradually make their way out to open country, where they spend the night in various hunting and grazing grounds, returning to cover in the early hours of the morning. All carnivora on the move, after dusk, are very particular as a rule to make use of sandy river beds, roads and paths, owing to the comfortable travelling, which suits their soft pads. When we first heard our heroic benefactor, grousing in his stentorian delivery, he was about half a mile away, coming down some other nullah, on to the fire-line. When we came to a standstill, in among the herd of wild elephants, he must have been walking along the road behind us, having caught us up (as they travel fast) and, suddenly, seeing our elephants standing still before him, he waited for us to get a move on, and to see what we were about. Tiger, like the whole of the feline species, are predisposed to curiosity; and he must have been watching our movements; and then, later on, he must have slunk round into the forest to our left—probably with the intention of getting in front of us, on to the fire-line again—when he came upon the sambhur unexpectedly and began to stalk them. We were at this moment in the terrible position before the wild tusker; when the tiger made his rush, and missed the sambhur, which took him close behind the tusker. Then, in another fit of disappointment, the tiger opened out his lungs and gave tongue; which caused the stampede, changing the whole situation and saving, very probably, our lives.

"At such close quarters, a stampede was in reality our greatest fear. This prevented our firing; and, when the tusker suddenly emerged, I had hoped he would mistake us for members of the herd and pass quickly on. With good trained elephants, we should have got quietly out of the place—or at any rate, at a distance safer to fire. We should have had trouble in any case with that tusker. He is a solitary brute, and firing in the air would have had but temporary effect upon him!"

We retired soon after, and slept that night as we had never slept before.

# CHAPTER XIV

## A TIGER AND AN EARTHQUAKE

*Like duck upon the wing, a sudden breeze,*
*That springs up frightened on the sun-baked plain*
*And starts the black buck, darts down through the trees——*
*As if its terror were such mortal pain——*
*To linger in diversion were no ease——*
*And flutters past, a tiny hurricane——*
*That breath of warning that foreshadows doom,*
*When Nature is disturbed and wears her gloom.*

*Now seems as if the bowels of the Earth,*
*Are growling with the hunger of some beast*
*Of heathen fable, whose incarnate mirth*
*The Demon lust of Belial might have leased*
*To haunt the realms of Pluto, and show worth*
*To drown the gurgles at some doomed souls' feast.*
*The Earth gives tongue, and through its depths unbound*
*Like a tiger's roar rolls down th' uncanny sound.*

*Then shakes the Earth—as if this planet grazing*
*Some mighty meteor hurled through endless space,*
*Disturbs eternity and works amazing*
*That, for a second stopped, might leave no trace*
*Of our whole constellation, while erasing*
*A hundred more, and yet some more displace.*
*So wrought Heaven's work and far dependent forces,*
*The planets dare not linger in their courses.*

*Extract from a poem, "The adventures of Lady Fane O'Donoghue," by the author.

THE voices of my companions came through the open door and woke me up with a start. As I tried to sit up in bed and recall the events of the previous evening, it seemed as though I had been asleep but ten minutes! Colonel J. K. and I were occupying a room together in the Buxar Forest Bungalow that had a large uncurtained bow-window opening on the east side. Through the bare panes of glass, like a dull rainbow with the faintest suggestion of purple and orange, some weak rays tried to penetrate into the room and light up the dim corners, with an apologetic effect for day that made me glance outside quickly. Clouds hung heavily over the east, and the sun seemed all but obliterated. I pulled out my watch hurriedly and found that it was nearly six o'clock! Jumping out of bed, and putting on my big coat quickly, I greeted the others who were making an inspection of the cars and directing their cleaning.

"Hallo, so here you are!" said Col. J. K. opening out the sparking plugs of his car and showing one of the jungle men how to clean them in petrol. "Thought we'd let you have an orthodox Europe morning after yesterday's elephant nightmare!"

With that lightness of heart one always feels in the real jungles of India, as if one were treading upon enchanted ground, we took our seats at the "chota hazarie" table with appetites not to be ashamed of, and chaffed each other over the experience we had of the wild tusker and the elephant herd, and our own bolting elephants.

"The pea-fowl took the cake—joining in with their wretched chorus from the top of their safe perches on the trees!" said Col. J. K.: "They simply yelled to each other from one end of the forest to the other, as if they were trying to make head or tail of the embroglio. Most amusing birds with their inquisitiveness!" he added: "Every animal's trouble—in fact every kind of disturbance in the forest, seems to be a personal affair of these feathered creatures!"

"Rather!" said Diggs. "The jungles could not do without them. I have even seen them actually taking parts—which often occurs when they are with monkeys."

One must be in the jungle "know," as it were, to understand the different cries of birds and beasts; and to appreciate certain causes which are ordinarily not intelligible, and which give rise to all the commotion among the various animals, so frequently heard in the jungles, and passed without notice by such "sportsmen" as come out for blood only—who take no intelligent interest in Natural History.

It looked very much like rain and we remarked on the gathering clouds. In the north, looming up in front of us, across the wide Buxar valley that rises on either bank of the Ramganga—forming an immense flat plateau covered abundantly with long grass, range upon range of luxuriantly clad mountains receding in graceful symmetry, rise higher and higher, till the furthest peaks are lost in the slow drifting clouds; and, encircling the plateau, on the east, west and south, the lower ranges, brilliantly decked out with the stately sal and other magnificent trees of antiquity, fringe the sky-line around, and catch the eye with the flame of the forest conspicuous in gorgeous patches of crimson; as if some resisting sunset had blushed madder and madder, and, washed by the night, had stained the canopy of the hills, with their emerald crests and dark green slopes, in fantastic disorder. The plateau is big enough to hold a station like Dehra Dun and would make an excellent cantonment for troops.

"What about the things we dropped last night, and the buffalo?" I inquired. "I hope my camera will be found all right, and that it is not damaged," I said, feeling anxious about it.

" The buffalo-men and my two shikarries have not returned yet," said Col J. K. " I expect them back any moment now."

" The camera must be suspended safely between those thick reeds, I should imagine," said the Colonel ; " and the men will bring it back none the worse for the night airing," he added.

" I hope so ! " I said.

" We just want a good shower or two of rain, to wet the dry grass and leaves sufficiently to help our elephants to stalk along without making a sound—it would be ideal ! " remarked Diggs, as he glanced up at the clouds.

" Quite ! " said the Colonel.

" To save time," suggested the Colonel, " let us anticipate that the buffalo has been killed, and draw lots for the lucky one to sit up this afternoon ! If there is no kill," he added, " let us all go out together and, with our elephants, beat up the Ramganga Valley where it narrows five or six miles from here, as proposed by Diggs."

" My word ! " said the latter, " one of us is destined to-day to—to another—some kind of interesting experience for a certainty ! I wonder to whose lot the ' Zal-Zill Sote ' is going to fall ! "

" The what ? " we asked. " Whatever do you mean ? " we exclaimed quite seriously.

Col. J. K. had just written down the word " tiger " on a slip of paper, and had ordered his trusted factotum—who was well trained in these little " shikar " jobs—to prepare several other similar blank slips, roll them into balls, and hand the hat round.

" Oh ! the ' Zal-Zilla ' or, commonly known by the natives here—among the cattle folk, timber merchants and wood cutters—as the ' Zal-Zill Sote ' ! ' Zil-Zilla ' is an Arabic word meaning 'tremor,' and 'sote' as you know means 'valley.' The valley of tremors!"

"Holy horrors!" one exclaimed—"you are a Job's comforter."

"Yes, that's the valley where we tied up the buffalo last night," continued Diggs. "It is an uncanny valley, I must own. I know it well," he went on, "and, though I am not superstitious, something remarkable always takes place up that valley with its hundred nullahs running down, and broken up as it is into dangerous basins, deep dark gorges and ravines. The hillocks all seem tossed about as if they were continually being shaken. The whole valley seems to be lying upon an unsubstantial crust, consisting of soft shale and unsolidified sandy strata that seem to fall away with a breath of wind. Landslips in the dry, hot weather are common up there, for no apparent cause. Of all my jungle experiences, the worst one I have ever had was up that valley sixteen or seventeen years ago—I think it was—during that terrible Dharamsala earthquake in the Punjab, that was felt in every corner of India," he said. "Though the valley is covered with bamboos and beautiful timber—which help to keep the place firm—there are no wild elephants from a certain point upwards which is a consolation. They don't like this valley of tremors! The herd we met last evening were well down below in the swamp; the men we are expecting with news of the buffalo will have tracked the herd, and will tell us the direction they have taken—I only hope they have had the sense to track that tusker. We must avoid him at all costs!" he concluded.

"By Jove!" said Col. J. K., as the hat came round and we all dipped our hands into it, "what uncanny prospects!"

"Well!" said Diggs, "as the Indians who have

business up in this wild country wisely remark: 'the jungles are the jungles, and one must be prepared for surprise dangers!'"

We opened our rolls of paper—but all four drew blanks. We dipped again, and unrolled our balls with feverish excitement.

"My word!" said Diggs with a smile, "here it is! I can never get away from this 'Zal-Zill Sote'! I only hope I can bag that tiger."

At my request, Diggs agreed to take me along with my camera, for any snapshots which the opportunity might offer. In the meantime it was decided, if the buffalo were killed, that Colonel J. K. and Colonel Mac should shoot up the Ramganga Valley; and that, after doing a shoot up the "Zal-Zill Sote," Diggs and I were to return to the bungalow for lunch; and, in the afternoon, we were to proceed again to sit up over the kill. Having to go further away, Colonel J. K. and the Colonel were to take lunch out with them. And so, fixing up this programme on a hypothetical basis, we tackled Diggs about his experiences:

"Now, tell us," we said, "while we are awaiting the return of the shikarries—about that experience of yours up this terrible 'Zal-Zill Sote,' so long ago as the Dharamsala earthquake!"

"Right oh!" he said, and began the following story, lighting up a cigarette every now and then, to relieve his feelings.

"My word," he said, "never can I forget it! Being here on the very spot again, brings every detail back to memory. It was the beginning of March—either the 4th or the 6th day of the month—the evening before that dreadful earthquake, that, on this very veranda, I was trying to persuade the Forest Officer to come and sit up with me on a 'machan' the whole of the night. We were having afternoon tea together, and the elephant—a steady old shikarri called 'Moti kali,'—ready equipped was standing in front of us waiting to take me out. The Forest Officer was a friend of mine, and always addressed me as 'my dear fellow'; and I can almost hear him arguing with me, that night shooting was no catch, and a useless waste of energy. I agreed, but said there were occasions when it was necessary.

"The fact was that a huge tiger—known as the 'langra shere,' or lame tiger, who, judging from his tracks, was apparently damaged on the right front leg—probably the result of a bad shot from somebody's rifle—had played hide and seek with us for over ten days. From Nature's great armoury, various weapons of self-defence are dealt out to suit the peculiarities of all her creatures. The physical prowess he had partly lost, was made good out of all proportion, in a cunning development of brain that nearly beat all my records! I tried every stratagem that long experience had put in my way, but he evaded me day and night, and yet ate his kill. We had merely succeeded in bribing him with half a dozen expensive young buffaloes to remain in the valley. We had gloated that very morning over his huge pugs in the bed of the river; and I, at any rate, had determined to sit up the whole of that night over a kill which he had dragged far up the valley, and had carefully covered over with high grass, that was pressed down over it.

"The Forest Officer wished me good luck, and, with some sandwiches, a bottle of water and a bottle of cold tea, with a quilt to spread on the 'machan,' a pillow with a khaki cover, a blanket, my rifle, and my big coat, I started off on Moti Kali about half-past five in the evening. I took a forest peon along with me to see the place, and to return with the elephant. It was necessary, going along, to give the mahout and the peon careful instructions, as they had to call for me at six the following morning, and the spot where the kill was dragged could only be reached through many winding and dangerous ways. The 'machan' had been fixed up during the day on a sal tree which I had personally selected.

"Daylight is beginning to fade as we reach the swamp. I am not poetical by nature; but, suddenly, fascinated with the view in front of me, I actually stop the elephant to look.

"Close over my head it seems, streaking with pale silvery grey the semi-circle of dark towering peaks linked together in concave elegance, like the inside of a bowl —as if the jagged rim were falling over—a huge, round white moon, edged with a suggestion of faint lemon, hesitates for a moment half screened between two bare heads, and then it dances over the arrow-headed summits like a suddenly animated queen of immortal beauty, conscious only of the soft splendour she splashes over the sombre hills, and the dark, undulating canopy of the forest below, lying, like an inclined plane, with its farthest border uppermost, and glinting from end to end of the expansive valley. At the apex of the swamp, and down on either side, fringing the scene below in striking perspective, the nearest trees with their straight giant boles, stand out boldly like a vast assemblage of pale grey ghosts; and, from out the masses of timber, the dark ravines—that run down through the canopy of the forest like black zig-zag lines —open out their wide mouths and emit their white trickling waterfalls that are caught by silvery beams as they emerge into uncovered spaces like dancing 'will-o'-the-wisps'; and, at the feet of my elephant, the points of the flat wiry reeds are flashing like countless cavalry swords, erect at the carry.

"What a night of splendour! I am struck at the early

brilliancy of the moon, for she has stolen a march on day; the jungle fowl and the pea-fowl, crowing and calling lustily, are only just flapping their wings on the ground preparatory to flying up to their roosts on the trees. A couple of pheasants, with a startled cry, dart over our heads and flop into some hanging creepers. And the animals seem restless; for now, as we move forward, from all directions come the plaintive cries of herds of cheetal like the sweet tones of innumerable bells penetrating into the silvery night; while the shrill bays of sambhur, with deeper bells from the stags, echo far in striking discord. Passing through the swamp, we put up a barking deer suddenly on the fire-line, and it rushes through some small reeds with short sharp barks—while far under the hills to our right, another is keeping up a continuous hoarse bark of some imagined fear; for the indications of the approach of carnivora, that these sweet little deer give by their alarm cries, are very uncertain.

"'Ahrush Ka chand!'—the moon of the Seventh Heavens!' says the mahout; who, like all brothers of his profession, is a devout son of the Prophet. 'It was a moon that shone on earth like this,' he adds, 'when Mahomed passed to Heaven.'

"And now we are at the mouth of a deep, wide ravine, and I begin to climb up the left side, and to pick my way through the dense undergrowth and under the overhanging boughs, zig-zagging up the Valley of Tremors. Everything somehow seems unnatural as the elephant moves along at a snail's pace, feeling his way very carefully over the dangerous ground; the mahout stops him every now and then to be guided by the bright patches of moonlight as I give the direction; even the natives with me, under their breath, remark on the unnatural appearance and condition of the restless jungle alive with calling deer, and the ever alert pea-fowl that sleep with one eye open!

"Up, and higher up, we crawl till at last I recognise the tree, and mark the 'machan' swung up on two light boughs about twenty-five feet from the ground. I believe in a commanding view; but the usual height for a 'machan' is about seven or eight feet from the ground. I now direct the elephant right under the high tree and stand up on the pad. Being a good climber, I have no difficulty in wrapping my arms and legs round the bare trunk, and shuffle up some five feet before being able to reach the lowest branch. My things are now handed up, and the peon climbs after me to help me on to the 'machan.' I now lay the quilt down, and, with my heavy ulster on, for it is distinctly cold, I settle myself for the night.

"'Cigarette, Hazoor?' asks the mahout as he turns the elephant to go. I throw down a couple for the mahout and the peon, giving them strict injunctions in regard to the way out. They warn me that to go after a lame tiger is a very bad omen as it means the challenging of fate and that I must be very careful; and then, 'salaaming' me profoundly, they move off quickly as if anxious to get out of the weird but beautiful place.

"And now I am left alone in the deepest recess of the lonely jungles, to the glory of a dazzling night! But there is something in the whole surroundings that I do not like; some inexplicable dread seizes me, and my nerves are jumpy. I have never had the feeling before in like situations; and, as I hear the mahout's voice in the distance, scolding his elephant, and, through the still night the thud, thud, of the flat part of his iron weapon resounding on the elephant's head, I am seized with an uncontrollable longing to recall them while they are still within earshot. We had a particular kind of whoop, understood among us in the jungles, and I actually gave the coo; and, startled at my own voice, followed suddenly by the baying of sambhur, I wait for the reply; but it is apparently not heard; and, listening to the sambhur's bays, which may perhaps mean the approach of the tiger, I change my mind and decide to remain.

" The sambhur stop calling, and there is deathly silence for a space; not a leaf is stirring. I glance at my wristlet and see that it is a quarter to ten. I am on a hill-side, and, not two hundred yards behind me, two bare brows of rock and shale glint over my head. From on top of the hill, a crevice about twelve feet broad and five feet deep runs down past my eastern front, then curves round abruptly and crosses my direct front scarcely twenty paces ahead. There, at the edge of the cleft, straight down in front of me, lies the carcass of the buffalo hidden in long shining grass, half-eaten since early morning. The tiger may make his appearance at any time after midnight, but I do not expect to see him before morning.

" I am overlooking the whole valley, and there, stretching far before my vision in wave upon wave—wherever the moonbeams are caught on the smooth surface of the leaves and broken and deflected into a network of crystal rays—I see the canopy of the forest beneath me, a heaving sea of silvery fire, alive with the flickering of phosphorescent gems, as the innumerable fire-flies twirl about, dipping into the forest spray, and rising again to flash over the moonbeams. And what a sight above! Rising higher and higher, the moon seems to be knocking in front of me against the low-hanging stars—which, as if on myriads of pendulums, seem to be set in motion, swinging and flashing in ruby, gold and emerald, till there appears to be no space in the heavens, but immortal transplendency!

"I close my eyes to rest them, and open them again; I cannot sleep, the night is too beautiful! Far up in the north, the dark peaks of the higher Himalayas tower up into the gorgeous sky; and, over a solitary peak, a star shoots down, and falls on the top of that dark head, leaving a momentary comet behind which bursts into fragments like a fancy rocket, and melts into space. On such a night as this, to sleep would be a sin, and it is impossible to keep one's thoughts from soaring to the sublime. I think of a visit once to the Pindre Glacier; and then my thoughts dwell again on the mighty heights of Kinchinjunga, and Mount Everest, in the Eastern Himalayas.

**Eternal patience looms there on thy crest*
*From which stars fall—O mighty Everest;*
*Like a great giant in the calm repose*
*Of earth's vast contemplation, wrapt in those*
*High astral solitudes—yearning for sound*
*Of earth's far oceans, and to stillness bound.*

"And then again, my thoughts are reaching that acme of sublimity, depicted to impress the mind with the idea of height—a hyperbole!"

**Merged deep the frozen silence of thy heights*
*Where Time's confused with Patience, and the nights*
*With filt'ring shades of spheres lost—where each day*
*Sees every comet passing on its way.*

"Suddenly, a soft rustling in the grass at the back, awakes me from my dreams. Slowly I pick up my loaded rifle lying by my side. I am shivering with excitement, for I have waited long and patiently for this

*Lines from a poem, "Mount Everest," by the author.

Elephants enjoying their morning scrub

A saber-toothed "terror" of jungle villages, shot by the late Col. J. K. Knowles

monster tiger! Nearer and nearer comes the silken friction of the grass, and presently, something stands beneath me in the shadow of my tree. I glance at my watch; it is half-past three in the morning!

"Breathlessly I wait. Can he be suspicious of my presence? Suddenly, a big jet black thing, with long thick hair, shuffles out into the moonlight before me, and begins to snuff rudely in the air. 'My word!' I say to myself, 'Blinkety blank; a clumsy old Himalayan sloth!' He is a fine big he bear, and, as I think, a mere passer-by. But no. He moves straight to a big ant-hill to my left, and deliberately squats on his haunches to paw it down. The dinner of these beasts seems to last all night, as they move from one end of a valley to the other; he soon exposes the ants, and sits down to his 'white bait' tit-bit, making a humming sound as if someone were gargling! Every now and then he sneezes, lurches sideways, and lifts up a big paw and shakes it, evidently to get the ants off that have got into some soft part! I can almost see his black claws in the bright light. It is not Teddy that I want, however, but the lame tiger; so the old bear keeps me amused for some time, till the droning sound that emanates from him makes me doze, and I begin to find myself nodding—nodding! I cannot keep awake, and gradually fall into a reclining position with my head against the bole of the tree and my right hand on my rifle, lying across the 'machan'—and then everything appears a blank.

"But, suddenly, there is a grey dusky light, and something big comes out of the dark forest: it is the bear again in the form of a dragon with long black hair. He is standing below my 'machan' in front; and horrors, the long neck begins to elongate! The hideous head struggling to lift, pulls the neck out like India rubber! Higher and higher rises that awful head, till it is on a level with the 'machan'! My limbs are now almost paralysed with fear as the dragon spits at me like a venomous snake, with a long tongue shooting in and out! My elephant is standing close by, but the mahout is looking the other way. I try to scream, but I cannot! I have lost my voice, and can only gasp out in a whisper, 'mahout—mahout.' Suddenly, the brute opens a huge gaping mouth, and an unpleasantly gritty gust of wind blows in my face, and, with a piercing yell,—'ma—hout!—' I start up to hear a terrified sambhur bellowing hard, quite close to my left in the dense jungle. I hear the sound of a single stone displaced, and my heart sinks. The lame tiger has heard my voice and has gone! He must have been coming on to the kill at the very moment I yelled, and my only opportunity is lost. The leaves of my tree are still rattling with that awful breath of my dream; and, with my rifle ready on my lap, I look anxiously round, while the sambhur are still baying in a frenzy. I can hear them beating their front legs on the ground—the alarm could not be hotter—and I know my lame friend must be near them somewhere.

"But what can have happened? There is no bear eating white ants, and sucking his paw—no beautiful night! My watch shows a quarter to six, and instead of a bright dawn after such a perfect night I see ominous clouds in the east hanging over the frowning brows of the hills, and a sombre light, like a dismal monsoon morning, making the distant mountains and the forest all round look black and gloomy. The air is close and uncomfortably depressing, and the mosquitoes that seemed to have been enchanted away by the moonlight, are now most aggressive. Suddenly, a swift clammy gust of wind rustles by and whirls over the high rocks over my head, leaving in its wake an upheaval of fine gritty dust, like the warm whirlwind of an express train dashing by at full speed. Hardly has this gust passed, when, breaking through the jungle at headlong speed, the frightened sambhur dash away in terror, bellowing as they go. I can hear the crashing through the undergrowth a long distance till it dies away. Terrible silence then follows—not a sound—everything as still as death, and then—what is it? I look round. A low murmuring sound like deep guttural thunder, seems to be travelling under the hills from the west; and then again, a few seconds of awful depressing silence. Suddenly, the grass in front of me heaves up and the tiger's kill moves; and, at that very instant that my tree—too—shakes violently, a rush and a deafening roar nearly paralyse me. To my breathless astonishment, while I am clinging to the tree with my 'machan' at all angles, I see the lame tiger in a furious rage out before me from somewhere, to protect his kill. His hair stands, bristling up on his arched back. He has apparently been crouching by, watching his kill, and now actually thinks that somebody or something is pulling it away. Being heaved about on top of the tree, to get in a shot is out of the question; and, to my terrible disappointment, I see the monster with his ears savagely back, standing over the carcass broadside on, trying to balance himself: he suddenly falls; and then, with a terrific roar, he lurches up, and gallops back into the cover again, just next to me, but out of sight the very moment that the shaking stops.

"I am trying to recover from my surprise—trying to understand the meaning of it all, and to settle myself on the 'machan' once again, hoping that my lame friend will show himself a second time. Suddenly, from the direction of his cover, I hear a low thrilling note like an organ, violently sustained and menacing, and I know that the tiger is watching angrily. I move my head slowly round but can see nothing. I dare not shift my seat in the 'machan,' for fear of making a noise and giving away my position; for it is usual for a tiger—not being a man-eater—to make off the moment he suspects somebody's presence. I find that my sola-topee and bottles have fallen to the ground below; and my big coat, which I had taken off owing to the sultriness, is hanging on a lower branch below me. I also find that the ropes, holding my 'machan' have been loosened dangerously. I am beginning to feel most insecure on the tree; and, while the low growl is continuing threateningly, I look up in front and glance round.

"The surprise of the shaking, and the unexpected appearance of the tiger, has been so great that I have so far realised nothing, but suddenly again that oppressive gritty breath of wind, as if it were some deadly warning, darts down through the dark forest and makes the foliage all round me rattle like bones knocking—and, merciful Heaven! it is again immediately followed by that terrible murmur through the ground which increases to an echoing crash, as if the sound of some thundering avalanche far away were being carried down through the bowels of the earth! And, just as the cause of the last shaking dawns on me, I see the dark mountains in front of me, breathing like great upheaving breasts, and then comes a shaking that throws me into a panic! The kill distinctly lifts up—rolling over this time—and out comes the furious tiger again with a thunderous roar and seizes the kill desperately. He and his kill seem to be rolling, mixed up together on the ground, and, horror upon horror! my 'machan' is giving way! I am clutching the tree and my rifle in grim desperation when, suddenly, the ropes burst, and the string-laced bed hangs and swings in the air. Down falls the balance of my things, carrying my heavy ulster with them, sprawling on the ground. The great lame tiger lifts his head at the noise, sees the falling things, and then on to my ulster and quilt he comes in a terrible rage, spitting and giving tongue in short gasps, and stumbling over the shaking ground. And now, with thundering roars, he is tearing my things to shreds. At this terrible moment I hear big stones rattling down the hill-side behind me, and I look up. There to my unspeakable horror, I see the bare hill brows almost knocking against each other—swaying like the heads of drunken men! What if those mighty boulders should be hurled down on the top of me? I am passing through an agony of indescribable mental terror, and am almost unconscious of the tiger roaring and tearing beneath my tree. I can feel myself falling, and my loaded rifle is slipping from my grasp! It seems to be a Herculean task to grip even for dear life! Another moment of the hurling about, and I must fall. Merciful Heaven! I am giddy and feeling sick, dazed for a moment, as when a flying express with a grating noise comes suddenly to an abrupt stand. My eyes are fixed on the ground as the shaking stops, as suddenly as it came, and I see the tiger lurch backwards, and I hear him growling as he limps off again, panting like a pair of great bellows.

"Save for a few stones still rattling down the hill-side, there is complete silence again—even the tiger's low menacing growl from his hidden place has stopped! I raise my head slowly and try to look round; everything appears to be topsy-turvy. The trees seem to be bending in all directions, and their foliage looks inside out, like the ruffled feathers of a bird.

"The sky is looking a bilious grey—the deadly colour of pea soup; and there is a misty haze in the atmosphere, as if storms in the plains below had blown up all the dust. All the animals and birds now seem to be in a most abnormal state of restlessness. The jungle is alive with frightened calls and cries; and sounds of rustling through the grass, and the crashing of undergrowth come from every direction, as if all the creatures, disturbed, were rushing about from place to place, hunting for shelter from some impending disaster. The pea-fowl, jungle fowl, and the college pheasant are on the wing, darting backwards and forwards across the valley and shooting by my tree in their gorgeous plumage.

"I notice, for the first time, that my tree is bent slightly forward, and realise that it is the result of the earthquake shocks. I have thought of slipping down to look for some open flat ground for safety, but the presence of the ferocious lame tiger makes the attempt far too risky, and I decide to cling to the tree whatever happens.

"Suddenly, within fifteen paces to my left, without the stir of a blade of grass or the crackle of a dry leaf being heard, the huge monster appears—as if by magic—and stalks out to his kill. My rifle is already loaded, and I rise from my clinging position across a thick branch and shuffle round slowly inch by inch. How my heart leaps with excitement! The tiger is taking his time to stalk, so slow and gradual that the movement is barely perceptible. He is giving me an exhibition of that wonderful soft tread, the power of which is possessed only by his species. In trembling anxiety I am waiting for the beautiful striped brute to take but a few more paces forward to give me a clear, unhampered shot, when, suddenly, that ghastly rumbling, intensified in volume and duration, sends a terrorising warning through the jungles for the third time. The tiger halts to listen. With his ears cocked forward, and fierce whiskers streaming away on either side of his wide panting nostrils, his great handsome head lifts in noble defiance, and turns slowly to the right and then to the left; and now he is gazing steadily in front of him far over his kill as if in lofty meditation! The picture is magnificent! But I cannot wait another moment, and try to shuffle still further to my left. At last, in an awkward position, I twist my body round and raise my rifle! But a sway comes, and my bead is moving now up and now down. I have not a second to delay and pull the trigger! Scarcely has the flame darted from my barrel when a terrific roar from the tiger is drowned by a tremendous crash at my back, and my tree heaves backward and forward and throws me clinging to a lower branch. I see the tiger hurled up on to his hind legs, and then he plunges forward blindly and, dragging his kill with him, stumbles into the crevice in front, with gasping roars as if he were wounded.

"And from high up on top of the hill those bare jagged rocks are thundering down on either side of me, leaping past my heaving tree. They bound over the crevice, over the spot where the tiger stumbled in, crashing far down into the valley. Great falling trees all round me, bound and rebound on the ground. Everything appears to be moving downwards! The spot where I am is like an island between mighty rivers of rolling shale—the hill has given way! I have fixed my rifle round the bole of the tree, which gives me the only support possible, and I cling for dear life with my legs wrapped round a branch lower down. In between the terrible din of falling earth and crashing boulders, the furious roars of the tiger can be heard in the cleft below. While I am swinging in all directions feeling giddy and sick, I glance up toward the hill in mortal terror! There a centre piece of towering rock and earth, that has so far stood, is bending—mighty horrors! I see it coming, toppling over, like a tower of child's bricks, with a boom as if ten thousand big guns together were bursting their metal! I am now lost in a dense fog of fearful dust, and feel my tree going slowly. I do not know where, and do not know whether it is the tree or I that am falling until, suddenly, I hear the top branches above me gently bumping the ground. I can hardly credit my good fortune, though the vibration of the timber sends a nerve-racking jar through me. But next moment the dust rising below me—as if it came from just under my body, stretched out on the top of the tree trunk—makes me realise my awful situation! My tree is lying across the crevice like a bridge, and I am stretched on the top of that uncanny intermedium, looking down into the dark cavernous space close below me, where the savage lame tiger lies wounded.

"About two paces to my left, there is a slight bend in the crevice, and, as I gaze down, and my eyes get accustomed to the semi-darkness, I see the tiger's great forearm and paws—his head is just hidden round the bend, and I can feel the monster's hot breath as he roars; and the stench from below is suffocating. The crevice beyond him, and beyond me to the right, is choked up with debris of the landslip. Should he make the attempt, the tiger could easily scramble up to the surface, practically brushing past me; and, however still I may be at such close quarters, it is not likely that I should escape from being torn into shreds like my ulster. Though it is dangerous to move a hair's breadth, the thought of this drives me to make some desperate attempt to save my life.

"I know that there are cartridges in the chamber of my rifle; which—lying across the opposite side of the trunk—hangs beneath me, while, my arms being around the trunk from on top, I am grasping the weapon on either side. In these circumstances, my movements must be quick and sudden. I could not move slowly on the rough bark of the tree without making a noise! I must swing my rifle up suddenly, click the bolt home, and shift back two feet so as to see round the bend, and face the tiger for a clear shot. It would be fatal to adopt any half measures.

"I prepare for the desperate moment! And then I suddenly swing up the rifle that crashes against something, and throw myself up into a position astride the trunk of the tree, with my legs dangling down. But out comes the terrible lame tiger with a ghastly spit and a roar! He does not see me for an instant, as I am just above him; and that instant saves my life! My bolt is home with a rattling noise, and with the muzzle of my rifle almost against his huge head, I pull the trigger! . . . I found my way back to camp here on foot, about ten o'clock that same morning, in a bedraggled state. There was no sign of the elephant to meet me. I found that the Forest Officer had narrowly escaped with his life, as the old thatched bungalow had half collapsed—by the earthquake—while he was in bed. We had to erect tents; and, after he heard about my terrible experience and saw the state I was in, he put me to bed with a strong brandy peg. He told me afterwards that everyone in camp had seen the landslip and never expected to pick me up alive. My elephant had been sent out in the early morning to fetch me back; but the party had lost their way, and returned late that afternoon, the mahout and the peon relating a dreadful adventure.

"Following my instructions and having the peon with him, the Forest Officer very kindly went out in the afternoon with an elephant, and five or six men, and brought back the magnificent lame tiger which measured over ten feet. I felt myself rewarded for all I had been through to get him."

## CHAPTER XV

### SAVED FROM A ROGUE ELEPHANT

DIGGS had just finished telling us the story of his thrilling experience in the valley of tremors, during the night just before that dreadful Dharamsala earthquake, when the shikarries and buffalo men arrived with all the things we had dropped off the backs of our bolting elephants, the evening previously, while we were escaping from the wild tusker. We were, I may recall, fortunate enough to get out of the stampede of wild elephants without coming to serious grief.

It was a little past eight in the morning and we were still sitting round the " chota hazarie " table in the front veranda of the Buxar Forest Bungalow, when the shikarri men came up very excitedly and told us that the tiger had killed the young buffalo and had dragged it up the ravine —some three hundred yards from the spot where we had tied it up—and that he had covered up the kill most carefully. They informed us at the same time that the tusker had taken up his quarters close to the swamp, and that they had just had a narrow escape, as he had charged out at them unexpectedly from behind some thick bamboo clumps, where he was standing quietly, apparently waiting an opportunity to attack anybody who passed along the forest line. They said that he was exceptionally big, and appeared to be a most dangerous rogue. They found that the rest of the herd had gone in the direction of the main Ramganga Valley, where Colonel J. K. and Colonel

Mac had decided to shoot in the event of the buffalo being killed.

While the men were thus reporting the result of their reconnaissance, up came two Government Forest Guards, decked out in green turbans and khaki uniforms, to inform us of the appearance of the tusker in the vicinity of the camp. These guards are generally supposed to warn shooting parties and travellers of dangerous rogues (and man-eating tigers, if any) if the whereabouts of such animals are known to them. The shikarries, in presenting us with our things, suddenly handed a lump of muddy-looking pulp to Col. J. K., with broad grins on their faces. " Take care," said Colonel Mac, with a smile, " it might be a bomb ! "

We tried to open the wet and sticky stuff, and found a piece of khaki cloth stuck in the centre. It seemed to be a puzzle and we dropped it on the ground. We immediately began to overhaul our things to see what was missing. The overcoats were all wet and mud-stained. Colonel Mac grabbed his flask, and I my precious camera, which I was delighted to find had not been damaged. We each took our sola-topees, wet with the dew.

" But where is my hat ? " said Diggs, quite concerned.

There was a roar of laughter as we pointed to the mess on the ground. The shikarries enjoyed the joke and held their sides.

" The tusker seems to have picked your honour's belongings out," said the head buffalo man to Diggs ; " for he must have danced upon your honour's sola-topee ; we found this pulp buried in the slush at the edge of the fire-line ! "

Diggs began to examine it closely.

" It is my sola-hat with the khaki cover right enough," said Diggs ; " but no tusker has danced upon it. Look at this ! " he said.

We all looked down and examined the spot on the pulp. There to our surprise, neatly impressed upon flat pieces of damp clay adhering to the crushed sola, were many half-pug marks of the tiger, and indents made by his claws, which none of us had noticed. The shikarries applauded Diggs, and said there was no shikarri in all the world like himself.

"The pug marks of the hind leg, too," said Diggs. "Do you know what happened?" he inquired.

"Not the faintest idea," we said.

"Well," he went on, "I'll just explain. The pulp is the shape of a roly-poly pudding. It has been rolled in the slush under one of the tiger's hind legs. What happened was that the tiger and the tusker must have come into contact when the latter rushed towards the spot where the tiger roared so close to us. My hat fell at the edge of the swamp, practically in a line with the animals. In a fight between a tiger and an elephant, the latter is forced to back, which he does, swinging from side to side, as the tiger's frontal attacks are made with the object of getting in between the elephant's legs, from one side or the other; or, inducing the elephant to turn and expose his rump, when stripes would be on the top of him like a flash of lightning. The tiger must have made the tusker back to the fire-line, beyond my sola-topee, which brought the former directly on the top of it, and, in his movements of attack, the tiger crushed up the hat as you see it. It must have come under his hind legs, as the tiger darted backwards and forwards, rolling up the pulp like a pudding. Had our elephants last evening remained calm and steady, we should have witnessed something of the fight in the dark. The terrible din which we heard gave evidence of it. It would have been a wonderful experience—one not to be had in a thousand lifetimes of man!" concluded Diggs, with a sigh.

"By Jove!" said Colonel Mac, "you have conclusively proved that there was a fight after all; and I almost regret now that we lost the opportunity. But what will you do for a sola-hat?" he concluded.

"I have a couple of spare ones," said Diggs, as he retrieved his khaki cover. "One learns by experience never to come out on these shoots without half a dozen sola-topees," he said, smiling.

We then called up our elephant drivers to give them orders for the day. Colonel J. K. arranged to put a fine staunch female elephant called Piari (Sweetheart) at the disposal of Diggs and myself; the former having won the toss for the tiger's kill, as previously related, we were booked for the valley of tremors and the more dangerous pursuit, and it was necessary to have an elephant on which we could depend.

After a consultation with our shikarries, who had just brought news of the kill and the rogue elephant, Diggs and I decided to approach the spot where the kill was situated from another direction, so as to avoid the first two miles of going along the whole length of the swamp; which locality seemed to be haunted by the rogue elephant. We could not, however, get away from the swamp, from whichever direction we approached the spot which had to be visited. We immediately called up and dispatched Piari, the elephant, along with the shikarri and a fine old buffalo-man (a herdsman who looked after our young buffaloes and supervised the tying up of "buffs" and goats for tigers and panthers) with instructions to proceed along a certain circuitous route—about double the distance round—and to await us at a certain bend of the Ramganga River, near the huts of some wood-cutters. Up to this point we could take a car, and we got the Ford in readiness. We allowed the elephant and the shikarries—accompanied by two coolies carrying a "machan" and ropes—two hours to reach the spot indicated, before Diggs and I made a start. Meanwhile, Colonel J. K. and Colonel Mac, who were to spend the day beating through the Forests higher up the Ramganga River, sent on the four remaining elephants, with the rest of the shikarries, to another place indicated by them for their shoot. It was after 10 o'clock in the morning that we finally made a start in our respective cars. Colonel J. K. and Colonel Mac went off in the Standard with a substantial "tiffin" basket, while Diggs and I left in the Ford, with some biscuits in our pockets and a couple of bottles of water, as we expected to return to camp for lunch.

Down the main forest drive it was fairly easy going for the Ford, and Diggs and I reached the spot at the bend of the river, glad to find that our elephant Piari, the shikarries and the "machan" (to tie up over the tiger's kill) had all arrived safely. We left the Ford on the roadside in charge of one of the coolies, and started off on the elephant in the direction of the swamp, followed by the shikarri, buffalo-man, "machan" and ropes. We took the usual precaution to screen the car as completely as possible, with branches of trees, which we cut down for the purpose, and told the coolie in charge he was to be on the look-out for wild elephants, which he was to scare away, if they approached the car, by drumming on an empty tin which we gave him. He climbed up a large tree with wide-spreading branches, close to the car, and was left comfortably in charge until our return.

The clouds which still hung heavily overhead kept off the sun, but made it hot and close. There was not a breath of air stirring. We had made a careful mental note of the exact spot where our men had last seen the tusker that morning; and, as we began to approach the swamp, we stopped the elephant and discussed the probable position of the tusker with the shikarri and the buffalo-man. The tusker was heading north when last seen; but we thought it advisable to see his tracks and satisfy ourselves as to the direction he had taken; for, not only had we to avoid him while entering the valley of tremors, but we had to think of our return journey; and then again our afternoon trip back over the same ground to sit up over the tiger's kill.

We get off the elephant's back and direct the mahout to hide Piari behind the ridge of a hill nearby, while we proceed on foot with the men. We examine the bed of the river between our position and the swamp, but find no tracks. We now walk down the fire-line through the centre of the swamp, where we find the reeds crushed down in every direction. It is the spot where the stampede had taken place the evening before. We next cross over to the north side of the swamp, and begin to examine the ground along the edge of the forest; and here we find the tusker's fresh tracks leading into dense jungle.

Being anxious not to be disturbed by him during our morning shoot, we decide to follow up his tracks, and plan, if we should come upon him within half a mile, to fire some shots over his head to drive him still further away. We find the stalking most difficult, as the grass and leaves are as dry as tinder, and the slightest movement makes a noise. There has apparently been no dew during the night, owing to the clouds. Moving along very slowly in single file—Diggs leading—and keeping our eyes and ears wide open, we have scarcely covered about a quarter of a mile up hill and down dale when, just ahead of us, in a small valley, we hear some bamboos being broken. We stop to listen! The breaking stops at the same instant, and there is immediately dead silence! We are on the top of a small round hill, and each of us has taken the precaution to place himself behind a tall sal tree (the *Shorea Robusta*). We are, unfortunately, not close enough to the hill-side to look down and get a view of the valley.

Suddenly, a little below the edge of the hill, a solitary jungle cock flies up with a frightened cackle and disappears through the trees. Almost the very next instant, to our sudden and terrible astonishment, without any other warning save the jungle cock, up looms the monstrous form of the tusker, as silently as if it were a great shadow and nothing more! He has suddenly appeared before us without even the crackle of a dry leaf. On the top of the hill, not thirty paces in front of us, he stands with his ears forward, as if he were trying to catch the slightest sound: his trunk is curled up from the ground; his gigantic ivory tusks, curved like great white bows, seem to project half the distance across to our position. With the base of the tusks as thick almost as a man's thigh inside his mouth, his huge jaws bulge on either side of his broad head, intensifying the frightfulness of his appearance. We have to glance furtively—high up—to catch the glimpse of his great expansive forehead, rising over our heads like a formidable-looking boulder that might at any moment be hurled on the top of us! The monster stands at least twelve feet high from the ground, and the spectacle is terrorising.

Being so close, we realise that if he makes a sudden rush he is certain to catch one of us, even though we should fire off at him or try to run. The leaves of the trees are hanging listlessly, and there is not a movement in the dense undergrowth and grass around us—not a breath of air stirs! So dreadful is the stillness that a pin might be heard to drop on the ground; we fail for this reason to understand how the brute could have got so sudden a clue to our presence, or what possible sense could have incited him to stalk up to our position with such deliberate care, as there is no breeze to carry the slightest suspicion. The shikarries had told us a moment ago that he was a desperate and a most cunning criminal; but this acute and extraordinary intuition that he had displayed has thrown us completely off our guard. We stand behind our trees, freezing in momentary panic. We know that, here again, our lives depend upon calmness and keeping quite still, and we dare scarcely breathe!

Suddenly the awful silence is broken by that diabolical Koel, or hot-weather bird, that begins his discordant tuning on a tree just over our heads, just as the great stealthy criminal takes two silent steps forward and puts out his trunk to smell! His red gleaming eyes, like little balls of fire, are fixed on our trees, as if he were gloating over his find. At this agonising moment that terrible bird startles the forest with his maddening cry—"Brain-fever, brain-fever, brain-fever!" The last notes, echoing through the stillness in a screeching crescendo, aggravate the tusker, who comes deliberately forward now, feeling all round the trees nearest to him with his outstretched trunk.

It is a living nightmare! He seems so near now that, for the first time, we notice great clots of congealed blood and strips of flesh hanging down his trunk, where deep marks of long gashes, still bleeding, are quite prominent. It flashes through me how right Diggs was when he said that the tiger—during that memorable evening of the elephant stampede—had come actually into contact with him. Those terrible marks that make his appearance more savage than ever are the result of the battle and the tiger's punishing claws. We realise now, with redoubled anxiety, that we are not only dealing with a bad rogue elephant, but a wounded one. Diggs, from behind his tree in front of the shikarries and myself, glances quickly in our direction, trying to make us understand with his eyes that we must make a bolt for it and dodge this ghastly, blood-thirsty demon among the trees, firing the moment that we are released a few paces from our imprisoned position.

My knees feel weak, as if I were only just convalescing after a long illness. There goes the snout of his trunk but a few paces from Diggs' tree. The latter takes a step rearwards, and I am ready to shove off in the dash for life after him when, at that momentous second—that terrible moment when Fate and Decision seem to meet as twin brothers linked arm-in-arm—we hear a crash through the undergrowth at our back and to our unspeakable horror, we see the half-naked figure of a man suddenly darting past our trees right in front of the tusker! It looks as if the thing in human form, whatever it might be, has suddenly gone mad. It appears that he is going to throw himself at the feet of the tusker. But no! With strange yells he dances but five paces in front of the brute, as if to tantalise him; and then, as the monster in a paroxysm of fury turns on him with a terrific roar, as if a bomb were exploding, the agile figure skips to one side and dashes off in the direction of the valley from which the big elephant so silently emerged. The brute swings round as instantly and crashes after the poor wretch at a pace that would give even a champion athlete but a poor chance of escape in a straight run.

But this gives us the longed-for opportunity. Our rifles are instantly levelled, and a volley bursts close over the monster's back. He hesitates a moment—we see the human figure gliding round in our direction again—and then, as another volley from our rifles (mine a heavy 500-577) crashes over him, the bullets whizzing a few inches over his head and ears, the great elephant dives down the valley from where he came. We follow up the attack, while the shikarri runs up with a spare gun. From the brow of the hill we see that huge tusker crashing through the valley, and we fire volley after volley till the animal climbs the opposite hill and disappears the other side. We wait a few moments till we hear a distant trumpet, and we know then that the brute has gone.

"Where is that brain-fever bird?" I exclaimed, as I took the gun from the shikarri.

"By Jove!" burst out Diggs, as he sat down and mopped his brow.

Then who should suddenly appear before us but that half-naked figure, with a happy smile on his face; and the object of his running in front of the elephant dawned upon us, the second we recognised our faithful buffalo-man!

"By Jove!" said Diggs. "The pluck of the man!"

I confessed I was bewildered at the time and did not recognise him. We both shook hands with that middle-aged Mahomedan with his round, closely-cut beard, while the shikarri embraced him tenderly. They were both Mahomedans of the sect known as "Sheikhs," who prevail in the Bijnor District. The man saved our lives—or the life of at least one of us! He deliberately acted as he did, to draw away the attention of the tusker and to give us the opportunity to fire, without running too great a risk at such close quarters. We rewarded the man handsomely afterwards for his unparalleled pluck in this field of shikar and his priceless services.

# CHAPTER XVI

## A TRAGIC STAKE: THE CHAMPIONS OF ISLAM

HESITATING no longer, after our narrow escape from the rogue tusker, we hurried off to Piari our elephant whom, along with her mahout, we had left well screened in good cover on the other side of the swamp, as previously related. We found them quite safe, to our great relief, and awaiting our return patiently. We did not tell the mahout about our recent terrible experience with the tusker, as it would have made him unnecessarily nervous of being left alone in the jungles, the necessity of which might arise at any moment. We knew that, around their camp fires at night, after their evening meal, the adventures of the day would be discussed. We then proceeded to skirt the swamp on the opposite side, after we had placed the shikarri on top of a tree at the edge of the forest, facing the swamp and the jungle into which we had followed the tusker. We gave him a strong whistle to blow, in order to warn us if the tusker should come out again; and, with strict instructions to remain on the tree till we called for him again and to keep a sharp look-out, we proceeded up to the ravine where the buffalo had been killed by the tiger as reported by our men. We took our faithful buffalo-man upon the elephant; which now made four on her back with the driver. The coolies with the "machan" followed on foot.

We arrive at last at the mouth of the ravine. The buffalo-man points down to the tiger's tracks—they are huge! He then points in the direction in which they followed the drag. We give the coolies orders where to remain, and to come up when we whoop, and we begin to follow the drag. The elephant scrambles up over difficult ground, until, about three hundred yards from the spot where we left the coolies, we stop before the kill, hidden right down in the ravine, which opens out into a wide, deep valley densely covered with trees and undergrowth. Diggs looks round and selects a good tree. We then give the whoop, and wait twenty minutes for the coolies. It takes half an hour to tie up the "machan," which Diggs attends to personally. We felt anxious about our Ford car, which we had left on the roadside in charge of a coolie, but hoped later on, if we should be delayed, to send a message to camp ordering one of the chauffeurs to take it back.

"We shall now leave this place undisturbed for the afternoon," says Diggs, "and spend the rest of the morning stalking through those ravines to our left. I do not expect the tiger to be out before four in the afternoon," he adds.

But he has scarcely said this when sudden alarm calls of sambhur higher up the valley, ring out loud and clear! We discuss the situation, when suddenly some black-faced monkeys begin their snorting cries where the sambhur are bellowing, and the valley becomes a Bedlam with the yells of frightened animals. We can hear the monkeys jumping among the trees and coughing excitedly—the warning could not be hotter!

"Those good old 'Hanumans' never tell a lie," whispers Diggs. "The tiger is up there for a certainty."

We decide to take the opportunity that offers, rather than sit up over the kill in the afternoon—even though there is the risk of frightening the tiger away for good and all, if we do not get him at once. Our faithful friend, the buffalo-man, is now one too many on the elephant's back—he would be in the way for quick movements—so we post him up on the "machan," over the kill, to keep watch and report what happens. And now we begin to stalk the tiger. We feel a few drops of rain as we turn the elephant's head round, and begin our stalk up the ravine to get in amongst the sambhur, and under the trees of the coughing monkeys. Diggs points up in the direction of the rugged tops of a steep hill overhanging the valley, and informs me that his adventure during the Dharamsala earthquake took place just across a ridge to our left, at the head of the next valley. The hills overlooking that valley have no rugged tops, and look scooped out, as if landslips had left their marks of devastation, and filled up the valley beneath, which has almost been raised to a low plateau. We stop the elephant for a moment, and Diggs points to a dark-looking streak, coming down zigzag from between the rounded tops of two hills. It looks as if it had been completely eliminated in many places.

"That is the crevice I spoke of this morning. I was sitting up on the 'machan,' right away there, just this side of it, where it turned and crossed my direct front," he says. "It was there that my tree was pressed down by the slip behind, when it came gradually to the ground on top of that lame tiger in the crevice—a marvellous escape!"

It is an unusually still morning. Suddenly, on the foliage and broad sal leaves up the winding valley all round us, comes the surprising loud pitter-patter, pit-pat of big drops of rain, falling in lines straight down like a beaded curtain of pearls. There is a delicate feeling of freshness as the leaves of the trees are washed to brighter green, and a sweet smell—as of newly turned turf—rises from the dry, hard ground mantled with deep humus, as the nectar of the sky touches it and causes it to exhale. How softly and silently the huge elephant is treading! Now standing like a statue, as the mahout gently lifts up an overhanging branch in the way and passes it on, and we carry it over our heads and pass it behind, as the elephant takes a step forward: now she turns to the left, now to the right, as Diggs from behind directs the driver by silent touches on one arm or the other, and we approach the coughing Hanuman monkeys nearer and nearer—as stealthily, as if our big elephant were an accomplished thief. We suddenly distinguish the moving forms of the sambhur. They are looking straight down into the deep empty nullah, paved with great boulders and hidden with the drapery of dry ferns, and the dense foliage of undergrowth which runs down the centre of the valley—the bed of a roaring torrent in the monsoons! So agitated are the sambhur that they hardly notice the presence of our elephant. They are beating their front legs on the ground in a threatening manner, and looking down into the nullah, baying in short, loud gasps. We move on and on, cautiously, step by step. We are among them now, they are on all sides, within twenty paces of us! Another fifty yards ahead are the monkeys. Some of them are looking down into the nullah from the overhanging boughs of the trees; and, strange, some on the other side of the trees, are looking down over a gradually rising bank which opens out higher up to our right, and extends to a bare ridge covered with short, dry grass. The monkeys have not stopped coughing for an instant, and are choking themselves with excitement. Some see us and jump about on the trees, but it is evident that they dare not drop on to the ground, and run off to trees further away, as is usually their custom, when they behold the strange sight of human beings on the top of an elephant, in their jungle home. They are accustomed to see wild elephants and are friendly towards them, but the sudden apparition of such an appalling spectacle that we must make in their eyes, must be, to say the least, most inexplicable and dumbfounding from their standpoint.

We cross the densely covered nullah very slowly, in broad view of the yelling animals; and, how wonderfully our trained elephant stalks! She understands the art perfectly and knows the game we are on. That she has smelt the presence of stripes cannot for a moment be doubtful; for we ourselves now get that nauseous whiff of the feline tribe that we are all so well acquainted with at the Zoo. We are standing still on the right bank of the nullah, with the herd of sambhur in front of us on the opposite side; there are some seven or eight animals keeping up a deafening chorus. We are as still as if we were sitting on the top of a great boulder. The only time our elephant moves is when she changes the great weight of her body from one leg to the other, and then the movement for rest is scarcely perceptible. Her trunk hangs down, so still and straight, that it might be the bole of a tree. We are straining our eyes in the direction that the animals are looking in, but cannot see anything like stripes. The passing moments are extremely exciting. Diggs is beginning to think that it might be a panther, as, with their spotted coats, they are most difficult to spy.

Suddenly, a magnificent stag walks close up to the nullah, and sniffs the air with extended nostrils. It is out of season for sambhur, but, in any case, being after tiger, we should never dream of shooting at anything else. The rain is now falling steadily, and everything around us is dripping—water is running down in streams off the stag's smooth, thick coat. He now raises his beautiful head, with the tips of his antlers gleaming white, and stops baying, staring at our elephant and shaking his horns! The monkeys are persistent in their coughing—they, above all animals, never lie! But where can stripes be? Somewhere close to us, but where? It is a puzzle!

Suddenly, rattling some stones, something rushes out of the nullah, and we catch glimpses of a red patch through the thick entangled growth, running straight up the wooded valley towards the open ridge above; at the same time, the herd of sambhur turn round and bolt off in the opposite direction; apparently the cause of their alarm is disclosed, and they are satisfied! We immediately cross towards the moving object, under the monkeys that are still coughing furiously, and move up on a level with the bare ridge, which we immediately command. We hear the animal coming up; it is apparently going to cross over the ridge, and our rifles are ready. Diggs is in front and sees the animal first. In a second his rifle goes up, but comes down as quickly:

"What now?" he whispers, exasperated, as he tells me to peep over his shoulder.

A poor little wounded, barking deer staggers along in front of us, then stops and sits down in pain. Blood is trickling down its neck; and, as it turns its sad reproachful eyes up in our direction, we can see two fang punctures on either side of the neck, just below the jaw bone. It struggles up again, and we see that one of its front legs, high up near the shoulder, is broken. It makes an attempt at a rush again, but falls to the ground. We look up at the monkeys still coughing, more agitated than ever before! Some are still looking down at the nullah, while the others are standing up on the branches on their hind legs, trying to peep over the other side of the ridge, as it seems.

Behind the low-sweeping bough of a big tree with large leaves—beautifully screened—our elephant is standing like a rock; the pad is slightly raised above the level of the bare flat ridge, and we wait patiently, in full command of the position, to discover the meaning of this jungle tragedy. A tiger would not trouble to kill so small an animal; or, if it did, a mere touch of his huge paw would be sufficient to despatch it, and it would disappear, bones and all, in a mouthful or two; yet, this poor little wounded thing, in the vicinity of a tiger's kill, must be treated with the greatest suspicion. The monkeys are telling us plainly enough that they can see a tiger or two, and we are getting more and more puzzled.

"Extraordinary," whispers Diggs. "The dead buffalo down in the nullah is a tiger's kill all right, and yet there is this little barking deer staggering along, that has been wounded, but a few moments back, by something much smaller than a tiger."

While watching the barking deer from our excellent position, we try to solve the problem in low whispers. On the bare ridge in front of us, the little deer suddenly sits down, unable to proceed further owing to its wounds. We are beginning to think that the culprit of this tragedy must be a hyæna—the most cruel and clumsiest of brutes that mauls its prey—but the fact that monkeys do not, with rare exceptions, give the alarm cry at sight of a hyæna, puts this possibility out of mind. A panther is also out of the question, as the dainty, feline tribe kill cleanly and mercifully, with the neck grip, or the sledge-hammer stroke.

Suddenly, the monkeys on top of the trees, coughing more lustily than ever, gaze up and down the nullah, seeming to divide in their watch. Those looking down, are more noisy in their alarm cry, than the other half of their numbers gazing up the ravine. This is still more puzzling, as it denotes the presence of more than one animal that has caused the agitation—one apparently stalking across the ravine on top of the hill, and the other crossing below. The monkeys are terribly disturbed, and begin to dance about on top of the branches. The excitement becomes intense, as we hear down below us, a slight crackling sound at the back of the elephant. Our eyes are strained in every direction, while the good old beast under us, knowing that something imminent is about to happen, stands like a rock.

Diggs touches my arm, and I glance up the ridge where he is looking anxiously. Under the cover of some fine waving grass, we see something of a dark red colour moving along stealthily. It looks like a large jungle cat, and almost seems to melt away against the reddish brown background of a clump of leaves soaked by the recent shower of rain. At this very instant, a low " mee-awl " comes from below, at the back of our elephant, and we glance down simultaneously. To our surprise we see another cat standing about twenty paces below our position. It has apparently just come up from the deep nullah that we had negotiated a few moments ago. We glance at the little barking deer to our right front, still sitting down in its pain, and moving its small head about restlessly, with terror in its large, beautiful, pathetic eyes.

" Tiger cubs," whispers Diggs in my ear. " Watch," he repeats ; " here is something worth studying. The cubs are apparently learning how to kill, and the tigress must be hiding somewhere close by, watching their practice attempts, and keeping an eye on our elephant. She has probably wounded this little barking deer to make the lessons of attack easier for her cubs."

We had not long to wait to be fortunate eye-witnesses of a wonderfully interesting tragedy. How stealthily and daintily the little cubs are stalking up to the barking deer. It seems as if, in each hesitating movement, they are trying to recall the particulars of every stalking lesson previously learnt, from the time they were but a few weeks old. Now they have attained the age of from four to five months; and no detail to be observed in the fine art of moving noiselessly, of crouching and taking cover, and of passing only through such stuff calculated to give the best effect to protective colouration, escapes their attention.

Slowly they approach the object of their pursuit; the cub on the top side of the ridge arriving first, apparently at a given spot, where he crouches cleverly between two small rocks, and seems to disappear. He is undoubtedly waiting for the other cub to come up. On the lower side of the ridge there is some scanty dry grass about a foot high, through which the second cub is stalking. The sight is most fascinating. More careful even than the smaller cat species, not a blade of grass shakes as he glides. He might be some indistinct shadow, the material substance of which is suspended over our heads.

The two cubs are now on either side of their prey; the one above being a little further off, while his confederate below has come up to within ten to twelve paces, without giving the little barking deer the slightest alarm. The latter cub crouches quietly, and is as well hidden as his resourceful accomplice between the small rocks above.

In the tiger's habits of attack, the sudden self-restraint practised, when the approach has been made successfully enough to complete the *coup de grâce*, if the rush be followed up at once, is an extraordinary and inexplicable feature. Even though the tiger may be suffering from the pangs of hunger, he will often abstain from killing immediately, provided the game has been so ensnared as to make escape impossible.

We mark this inherent instinct showing itself in the cubs before us. It is not cruelty alone that induces this habit, but a deeper purpose underlying the fiendish delight of torturing the victim prior to the feed. The cubs, though unaware of our presence, have, of course, seen our elephant; and although they are probably by this time accustomed to wild elephants, the tactics of our domesticated beast are strange to them. There is no animal so suspicious as a tiger, whose hard-won kill is often stolen by a lurking enemy; and, if there is any such fear present, he will abide his time before completing the attack and dragging away his kill, lest some evil-eye should mark its hiding place.

The experienced mahout understands the slight touch given to his arm by Diggs, and he allows his elephant to graze about carelessly, as if it were a wild one.

The cubs are now watching the elephant's legs in the grass and undergrowth with the greatest anxiety; and some fifteen minutes elapse before we notice that our new tactics have allayed all suspicion, and have put them at their ease.

Soon begins a series of attacks that prove only too plainly, that though the cubs are merely practising for a time, the wounded deer has been put in their way, with sufficient energy left to demand considerable skill on the part of the cubs before they can hope finally to attain their prize. How cleverly the lesson has been thought out by the mother!

The cub on the lower side of the ridge moves forward again, and sneaks up to within a few paces of the trembling deer, while the mate above is watching intently. The cub, now within such close range, suddenly takes a bold step forward; but the panic-stricken deer, as if by instinct, dashes up the ridge before the cub has shown himself. But the agility of the cat family is wonderful. As quick as lightning the cub races side by side, and we suddenly see a lurch forward with a little paw stretching out, and descending on the head of the deer with, as it seems, a playful slap. The deer rushes on a few paces, and then sits down again, almost beside the other cub hidden in the rocks above, while the attacking party immediately retires into some cover and is lost to sight.

The sledge-hammer stroke on the gallop has been practised. This is one method of killing, that the tiger and the panther adopt when the game has been scared, and these carnivora have to secure what they can on the run. It is a difficult stroke, but the full-grown tiger's paw comes down with so unerring and terrific a slap, that the victim at full gallop rolls over stunned, as if shot with a rifle, and seldom rises again. This sledge-hammer stroke is also used when a dangerous horned or tusked animal, such as a sambhur stag or a formidable wild boar, is being attacked. It is obviously safer for the tiger to take such game on the run.

It is the next cub's turn now, and he pursues exactly the same tactics; alarming the deer sufficiently to make it run, racing alongside, and coming down with the sledge-hammer stroke, as the cub's gallop suddenly terminates in the final effort of a spring.

For a short space of time, the cubs actually let their prey rest, and then take up the practice again, driving the wounded deer from one to another. Often, at the critical moment, the deer dodges, and the pretended slap misses its mark. Whenever this occurs, a low growl of annoyance is emitted by the attacking tiger cub, who curls himself up in some cover, and wags his tail furiously.

Suddenly, the attack is changed for a new practice. Each cub now in turn plays hide and seek with the deer, to get an opportunity for the neck grip. It is the nape seizure from on top, and, the moment the grip has been correctly obtained, the deer is released. It is essential that the game should be at a standstill for this method of killing, as this grip cannot be obtained on the move. It demands very clever stalking up to a distance of a few paces of the victim; before the rush is made.

The next practice is the throat grip from underneath; and again the deer is raced and dodged up and down the ridge, until this grip has been successfully made by each of the two cubs.

The last two grips are the more common ways the tiger and the panther have of killing their prey; the throat grip from on top, and the throat grip from underneath. In the former method, when the tiger springs on his prey from on top, he grips the animal by the nape of the neck, closing his fangs like a bull-dog, and, at the same instant, slewing his body round so as to give an added purchase to the wrench, which either breaks the neckbone, or dislocates the spinal cord. In the under-grip, the neck of the prey must be thin enough to permit of the grip being made successfully in this manner. It is what the panther usually does, as the animals he kills are much smaller game. It is an absolutely exploded idea, that, after a tiger has killed his prey, he sucks the animal's blood. Nor is it true of the panther. They do no such thing. These carnivora sit down and gloat over their kill, and shake the neck again, as the common house cat deals with a mouse, if any signs of life are shown.

Both the nape and under-the-neck grip are not actually in the throat, but high up under the jaw bones, where the two main side arteries are immediately severed. Mahomedan shikarries often call the tiger and the panther the "champions of Islam"; since the peculiar habit of these animals, in touching only such meat that has been freely bled by their own slaughter—the quick and clean severance of the arteries—is so closely allied to the religious doctrines of Mahomedans; who touch no flesh unless the animal's throat has been cut in the orthodox fashion by one of the faithful, and the arteries similarly severed for the free flowing of blood. This act is called "Zabah," which means throat-cutting; and when the act is being performed, the Mahomedan cries out "Bismillah"—Allah ho Akbar (in the name of God—the great, great God!)

It is a wonderful instance of savage instinct and the ethics of civilisation, so far removed from each other in moral status, coinciding in a special method of killing, with the common object of observing the principles of Hygiene, to which each—quite apart from custom—is unconsciously led to conform.

During the practice of the cubs, and the bold, open performance to which they have treated us—their spectators—the coughing and snorting of the monkeys has continued unabated. A rest now seems to be the order of the programme. The cubs seem to have taken cover, for they are nowhere visible; and the deer is lying up at the edge of the ridge, on the far side, down which another nullah runs.

We bring the elephant up, grazing leisurely, on to the top of the ridge, and take cover behind a thick bamboo clump. At this instant, we hear a deep, low, threatening growl that comes from below, and we know at once that the tigress is hidden in this nullah, and intends to dispute our further advance. We keep perfectly still behind our fortunate cover, and watch further proceedings, hoping to get a shot at the mother of the cubs in a few moments, should she dare to show herself.

Suddenly the cubs call to each other, and the mother answers in a deep gurgle. We can now catch a glimpse of the mother's big head as she stalks up from the nullah and puts herself also, into a commanding position—though beautifully screened from full view—to apparently direct proceedings. It is breathlessly interesting and exciting, and we let the chance of shooting her go, as the study in Natural History is much more desirable.

Next instant we see a cub stalking up to the deer again : there is a sudden rush—and it looks like business this time. The exhausted deer is seized by the neck ; there is a swinging twist, as the cub lurches his body round, and the little barking deer lies stretched out, kicking in its death agony. The other cub now comes up with an envious snarl; but an angry, warning growl from the watching mother makes him retreat quickly.

The cub that killed is on the carcass. And now begins the disembowelling process to clean the kill. What a wonderful sight it is ! The cub rolls the small carcass on to its back ; and, holding it down, with the left front paw pressed firmly on its chest, he raises his right paw a little above the white stomach of the carcass, lying upwards. The claws are opened out to their full extent, and gleam in the sun like a bunch of little sharp knives ; the next instant they come down with quick strokes, and the stomach is ripped open from top to bottom. A growl comes from the mother at this moment ; and the cub, as if in unswerving obedience, steps back with his hind legs, and works his two front paws sharply on the slit carcass, in much the same way as a dog acts when he digs a hole. The cleaning process is going on ; and soon we see that everything is perfectly removed. Nothing is left but the solid mutton, with the head, neck and four legs. The cub now walks round his kill, seizes it on one side, between the neck and the shoulder, and begins to drag it down the ridge, into the nullah below, moving backwards with marvellous agility. In a few moments the kill and the cub have disappeared, and not a sound is heard.

Diggs turns the elephant quickly, and we stalk, crawling along the edge of the ridge, moving downhill, and parallel to the nullah. But there is no sign of the tigress and her cubs ; they seem to have melted away with the kill. We know that the tiger drags a distance away, to hide his mutton from vultures and other thieves, who depend upon him for their livelihood, and we return to the place of the tragedy to follow up the cub's drag.

But at this moment, we hear the distant warning whistle of the peon posted on the tree far down below, and know that the rogue tusker has returned. We decide not to follow up the cub's drag, but to return to the buffalo kill, pick up the buffalo-man, whom we left sitting on the "machan," and to spend the day in another valley, on the other side of this kill, until the afternoon, when it will be time to sit up and watch over the buffalo calf's carcass. We feel certain now that there is a whole family of tigers ; and it would be advisable not to disturb them further at this early hour, as it is the big tiger that killed the buffalo, which Diggs is anxious to bag. The tigress and her cubs will probably keep away, as it is obvious that the mother is hunting with her young.

We reach the "machan," and hurry away in the direction where we intend to pass the afternoon—safe from the savage tusker, up the valley of tremors ! We part from the buffalo-man, ordering him to go away quietly to the peon on the tree, and to despatch him to camp to fetch our lunch out. Colonel J. K.'s great factotum, we knew, would be ready to oblige ; he was fired with *shikar, and would undoubtedly conduct the luncheon party personally to the spot. We also instructed the buffalo-man to send word to one of the two chauffeurs left in camp, to proceed to the spot down the main forest line, and to take the Ford car—which, it will be remembered, we had left on the road at a certain bend of the Ramganga River, in charge of a coolie—back to camp,

*"Shikar" means hunting and shooting.

as there was now no chance of our being able to return to lunch, and it was impossible to tell what time of night would see us back in camp.

After giving the buffalo-man strict orders not to blow his powerful whistle under any circumstances, after three o'clock in the afternoon, lest the big tiger should be disturbed on his way out to the kill, we get off Piari's back—to give the elephant a rest—and patiently await the events to follow. The alarm cries of the monkeys have completely ceased, and the jungle is wrapt in silence—save for an occasional peacock that yells out the hour of the day from some high tree perch!

WHERE THE ELEPHANT DWINDLES IN SIZE

THE AUTHOR'S WIFE AND BROTHER, MR. E. D. KNOWLES, ON "SHAMGAJ" A TIGER-FIGHTER

# CHAPTER XVII

## SECRETS OF THE JUNGLE : BEHIND THE STAGE

IT will be recalled from the preceding story that, after our adventure with the rogue tusker—when we had to all intents and purposes driven him away—we posted a peon up a tree with a whistle to warn us in case the elephant should take it into his head to return in our direction; and the reader will remember that, after our experience with the tiger cubs a little later, Diggs and I were about to return to camp for lunch—as we had plenty of time before the tiger was due on its kill—when we heard the alarm of the whistle and decided to remain where we were, up the valley of tremors—the safest place from the tusker. We despatched our faithful buffalo-man to the peon on the tree, instructing him to arm himself with the whistle, and to keep a close watch over the rogue elephant's movements. The peon meanwhile was to proceed to camp with two messages; one to the chauffeur to fetch the Ford car back from the place where it was left on the roadside, in charge of a coolie—the chauffeur having to walk a distance of five miles; the second message was to be delivered to Colonel J. K.'s "chief factotum" to send out our lunch. We knew that the latter would manage it somehow. He was the typical stamp of that smart regimental production, who is always present at all big camps, and without whose resourceful "bravadoisms" no shikar would be possible. The peon was to show one of the* "kits," or the mighty factotum himself, the way

*"Kit;" abbreviation of "Kitmudgar;" table servant.

through the forest—about a mile and a half distant, with strict injunctions to dodge the tusker and to produce our lunch safely at all costs, with at least four unbroken bottles of beer, at the exact spot where we were waiting!

Our message as to the details of lunch—after half an hour's explanation—being enthusiastically delivered, we finally impressed upon our brave buffalo-man that, under no circumstances was the whistle to be sounded after three o'clock in the afternoon; as, from that time to dusk would be the great time of watch, during which no disturbance must take place in the jungles to embarrass our quiet vigil, and the tiger's unsuspecting peace of mind.

However dangerous the presence of the rogue tusker might be, Diggs announced that, though he desired to conceive no previous intention—which always meant bad luck—he did not wish to run any unnecessary risk of losing stripes, whom he had won at the lot drawing that morning. Though still roaming in the freedom of his jungle home, the tiger was, up to the time of sunset—undisputedly—Diggs' private and personal property, by all the formidable unwritten laws and time-honoured traditions of aristocratic shikar!

We had meanwhile made ourselves as comfortable as possible in our wet clothes, while the mahout had relieved Piari the elephant of her heavy wet pad, and astride her naked back, had taken her up a cool adjoining ravine to lunch on fresh young bamboo shoots that hung temptingly and gracefully around. How we envied the elephant at home in a beautiful valley with plenty to eat and drink, while we were as badly off as her mahout, languishing with hunger! How blissfully our thoughts lingered on the possibility of lunch—to be washed down with a bottle of cool beer, as we listened to the departing footsteps of the faithful, who had so recently saved our lives. But we were obliged to possess our souls with patience; and, though we discussed the advisability of practising strict teetotalism in the jungles, we felt that a little departure would be warrantable after the nerve-racking experience we had been through, in the early hours of the morning, with the Lord of the Jungles, who was apparently suffering from hurt dignity. It was possibly the mauling the tiger—of the previous evening's adventure—had given him, which mishap the rogue tusker seemed bent upon connecting in some mysterious manner with us, judging from the persistent way in which he was dogging our footsteps.

We soon found that the biscuits we had brought in our pockets were soaked with the rain that had fallen in the forenoon, and were uneatable. And now, as a hot wind sprang up suddenly, as it seemed from nowhere, we ensconced ourselves in a shady nook, and fell back on the amusement of feeding the jungle squirrels on the mess from out of our pockets, trying to relieve the presently, increasing pangs of hunger, with the wonderfully accommodating cigarette. That tobacco has actually the power of some nourishment in the absence of food, is not to be gainsaid: if it be imagination, in any case, it satisfies the body to an extent which means a great deal under straitened circumstances. It is a provision of nature, that the mind should support the body directly, through the influencing power of the imagination; as well as indirectly as it does, through the medium of devising ways and means of sustenance.

It must have been two hours that we passed impatiently, hearing nothing but the wind shrieking through the bending and creaking timbers of the forest, and the breaking of bamboos up the valley, which our elephant seemed to be enjoying, as the midday sun at last began to swing round slowly to the west. Every creature, but the large squirrels we had been feeding, seemed to be at rest, indulging in the afternoon siesta of their jungle home. We had gradually disrobed ourselves of our wet kit, drying our clothes in the sun, and had dressed again, feeling as comfortable with the result as it was possible to feel, without the necessary ballast contained in the long-looked-for tiffin basket; which we had counted upon to make our enforced dalliance in the jungles as near a paradise as possible. We had given up all hope of seeing the froth of good, pilsiner beer that afternoon, and had contented ourselves with a sip of cold water—running fresh and clear over the rocks in the valley—when we heard the jungle cock announcing the afternoon, with a familiar crow that rang through the valley, and which was instantly responded to by numerous others of these feathered timekeepers, till the jungle world seemed to be suddenly transformed into an immense, poultry yard. It seems proverbial that most sportsmen seldom or never burden themselves with a watch, but trust to the movements and calls of birds and animals, and the prehistoric means of telling the time by the position of the sun, and by shadows of various objects on the ground. These crude ways develop the powers of observation and help to sharpen natural instinct—without which accomplishments, among many others, a shikarri might just as well retire gracefully, before being obliged to do so with a nervous breakdown, or a broken limb, or as the result of a final exit below ground.

"Time to be moving," said Diggs, as he gave the jungle whoop for the elephant to come up. "We must hurry up and get into our 'machan.'"

I immediately commenced to examine my camera, and was thankful for the excellent leather case in which it reposed, which saved it from the inclemency of the weather. Inside was a spacious note-book which I laid bare on the ground with a pencil attached.

"What in the name of worthy Shakes the cow driver, have you brought out all this vast paraphernalia for?" demanded Diggs.

"This," I replied, hugging the camera, "is for a snap-shot of your tiger; and that," pointing to the note-book, "is the parchment upon which my instantaneous poem is to be impressed, as the whole scene lies before me."

"Anything else?" inquired Diggs. "You authors are nothing if you are not premature—always counting your chickens before they are hatched. I consented to the camera in a weak moment," he went on, "but the note-book!—We might, just as well, return to camp straight-way and recline in arm-chairs as shoot the tiger, if that's your little game! One can't expect to draw a tiger by 'lot' every day—and then lose him for the sake of an instantaneous—how much!—did you say?"

"Poem," I jerked out.

"Damn!" said Diggs.

"Don't be pessimistic," I reproved *sotto voce*. "Why should you lose the tiger, my dear fellow?"

"It is the worst possible luck that you are courting," he grumbled. "I've had experience before of coming out in the jungles too prepared—it always ends in a fiasco!"

"Why should it? That's pure imagination," I said.

"No imagination about it," he said seriously. "I've proved it to my satisfaction anyhow! There are certain things in this life that, if they are at all predetermined, immediately work by contrarieties. The old adage: 'Man proposes but the Almighty disposes,' was not handed down to us for nothing. Nature works in ways inexplicable to us so far," he continued, "and, often carries out this law to the letter; and in the jungles, by some unknown law of universal intelligence (which we shall never know until the animals can explain themselves), Nature awakens this latent, prognostic instinct of the lower creatures, when a preconceived intention connected with them, is working in the brain of man, for any purpose whatsoever."

The mahout had come up, and was busy saddling the elephant with her pad; while the dead "Katra" (young buffalo) lay a few hundred yards farther up the ravine, over which the comfortable "machan," which Diggs had fixed up, swung from a high sal tree.

"You are touching upon metaphysics," I quizzed. "You don't surely believe that animals receive a kind of supernatural warning, otherwise it would be fruitless shikarring!"

"I laid stress," he said, "on preconceived intention. I believe that wonderful things exist and are possible in nature; that all animals are perfect clairvoyants, with a far greater second sight—ruled by some inherent principle of a truth of which we haven't the barest notion—than ever man was possessed with. And, that great force or truth, might be some part of the fourth dimension that scientists imagine they have got a clue to!"

"But," I said, as I felt myself becoming serious, "you come into the jungle with the intention of shooting!"

"Yes; and that's precisely the reason why there is such a lot of bad luck as it is called. Go into the jungles without a gun—with absolutely innocent intention, and you'll see a whole menagerie! It happens every time. Take the novice; tiger will walk out and stare at him! He has really no intention, but an imagined one, as his nerves are far too untrained, and he would rather not see anything uglier than himself."

"My dear fellow!" I expostulated, as I felt the truth of all this, and was beginning to feel uncanny; but I was determined to cling to the intention of my camera and note-book.

Diggs seemed to be fully wound up—I was sorry I took out the unfortunate note-book to see if everything was in readiness. We mounted the elephant and proceeded to the " machan," while he still held forth in subdued tones.

" There is no ' preconceived intention ' if you act on the sudden spur of the moment, and shoot an animal," he said ; " provided, prior to the act, your mind was honestly free of any kind of intention. In such a case, there would be no suspicion previously set adrift—which you can sometimes almost feel in the very air—to directly strike the intelligence of the particular animal or animals through the medium of the theological forces at work in inherent nature—which those creatures, living nearest to nature are alone susceptible of, and can understand."

" What about primitive man then ? " I queried ; " he must have been superior to us, in knowing more about these mystical forces than we do ! "

" Man's mentality," he said, " for some set purpose, has always been differently constituted. Reason with him takes first place—it is the first sight, with result that the powers of his second sense have been proportionately suppressed. With the animals, it is just the opposite. What we call instinct, has in it something deeper. I could give you innumerable instances of uncanny cleverness, that Ghost Bull, for instance."

" Can you say that you are always without intention in the jungles ? " I asked.

" As a rule, I never come into the jungles without first genuinely trying to disabuse my mind of intention. Experience has taught me," continued Diggs, " that it is really the only way if you wish to see or to get anything worthy a trophy. But remember, it must be at the same time, a matter of complete unconcern to you whether you get anything or not."

"Surely," I said vehemently, "this is deception!"

"No!" he exclaimed emphatically, "there is no self-deception if the mind is really honest in endeavouring to practise what it believes; but it is a matter of very great training to be able to free your mind of all intention, as you can well understand. You must acquire the new taste of innocently enjoying nature, in all its beauty and avenues of thought, without the savage passion for taking life. I confess to you," he went on, "that, at the present moment, my mind is most guilty. I have never had such a strong desire to bag a tiger before; and, though I have been trying hard to fight against it, and to put my mind into an absolutely neutral state—as to whether I get a tiger or not—I find that I cannot shake off intention. In consequence, I do not believe that either you or I shall get a shot at this tiger this afternoon; certainly not off the 'machan!' Mark my words that something will happen to prevent it."

"It does not matter then," I said, "whether I make a display of all my paraphernalia on the 'machan' or not?"

"Well," he almost sighed, "in reality—as matters stand, I am quite unconcerned about it. I have tried to impress you with my belief—that's all! You are at liberty to do what you like. Had I been able to get myself into any 'jungle humour,' as I call it—honestly free of any previous intention against this tiger—I should have objected, but merely on principle!"

"The principle of preparedness I suppose," I said; "but what about arming yourself with rifle and cartridges, as you must on every occasion that you go out," I added.

"If you can train your mind and acquire the true jungle

humour," he replied, "you would honestly take your rifle for self-protection only. When in that humour, I could no more tell you what I should do if I came face to face with a tiger, than fly. I might let him go or shoot him on the spur of the moment. I have often let a tiger, panther, and a beautiful sambhur stag go," he said. "You must be prepared to do this, for the sake of the training, or make no attempt to try to acquire the secrets of shikar craft!"

I thought of the great reputation Diggs had, as the luckiest man alive in the jungles; and how people in a shooting party with him, would even toss for the bare chance of sitting on his elephant during a hunt.

But it is not all luck with Diggs. He has always been a very keen naturalist, and his knowledge of animals —including birds and fish, is exceptionally remarkable. Nobody could have a more interesting companion in the Indian jungles, whatever might be the pursuit—provided it is good honest sport, giving an animal every chance of escape—even including carnivora, unless an exceptionally large and mischievous tiger or panther is the object of the hunt.

The alarm cries of wild animals and of all the many birds one meets with in the jungles, are distinctly different from their ordinary calls, and this is, in itself, a very great science and study. To be able to detect every sound one hears—and even to place the animal correctly, is a matter of a life-time's study and experience—not merely the superficial experience gained by shooting parties, however frequently they may have indulged in big-game hunting—but the hard experience won by the naturalist after many years of almost inexhaustible patience and hard labour, with heart and mind thirsting after knowledge of the life and habits of, what man denominates, the "lower creatures." Real "jungle craft" cannot be obtained by the mere desire to shoot. There would be some hope of a " shooter " learning a few lessons—with his mind bending in the right direction, to be entitled to the name of " shikarri "—if he could for instance, let the chance of shooting a record stag or a tiger deliberately go, for the sake of making some observation pertaining to natural history, if the occasion afforded such a lesson. There are a very few "sportsmen," indeed, who would make such a sacrifice unhesitatingly, for the sake of some information, however small, to advance man's present knowledge of wild animal life; but India has seen a few such sportsmen, and one is Diggs. There is no alarm cry in the jungles which he cannot place and correctly interpret, with the result that—as will be readily understood—he can follow up and get into quick touch with the quiet movements of animals, the presence of which would be wholly unknown to the ordinary sportsman passing by. Many have been the instances in which Diggs has opened the eyes of "sportsmen"—in wonder and astonishment—which have led to the immediate bag of a tiger or a panther, in search of which days and weeks of promiscuous and fruitless driving have been wasted, with seldom or never such a thing as a thrilling adventure being experienced. Adventures in the jungles, and great occasions for study, can, to a greater or lesser extent, always be found, if " jungle craft " (assuming a thorough knowledge of the subject) is put into practice, and the sportsman is bent more upon observation and discovery, carrying his rifle merely as a weapon of defence.

I took in enough food for thought to last out the quiet watch that followed on the " machan," after the interesting argument with Diggs, on the subject of the " Prognostic Instinct " of the lower animals, as related above.

# CHAPTER XVIII

## AN ILL-FATED KILL

AS related in the previous chapter, " Secrets of the Jungle: Behind the Stage," Diggs and I moved off to our silent watch over the tiger's kill, which, it will be remembered, we had tracked up the valley of tremors. It will also be recalled that we had sent a message to camp for our lunch to be brought out to us, owing to the return of the rogue tusker in the vicinity of the swamp below; as also, a message to one of our chauffeurs to walk down the main forest line, a distance of about five miles, to fetch back the Ford car which we had left in that direction, on the roadside. It was planned that we should return to camp in the evening—which would probably be at a late hour—on our elephant, Piari.

" The jungle seems remarkably quiet," said Diggs at last, after we had sat patiently on the " machan " for nearly three hours. " I am afraid there is nothing doing," he said. " Pack up your camera and note-book."

I glanced about and concluded it was at least 6 o'clock in the evening, and we had taken up our watch at about three in the afternoon.

" I told you," he continued, " all that preparation of yours would end in a fiasco. We have drawn a complete blank, and had now better call up the elephant, as I am afraid this fine tiger has deserted his kill and has gone. He must have been somewhat close by this morning, when we moved about under those yelling monkeys, watching the performance of the tiger cubs, and the tiger has been scared away. I am not sorry," concluded Diggs, "for what has happened to-day; for I should much rather have witnessed the wonderful lesson the tigress gave her cubs than to have bagged this big tiger. We must just tie up for him again—to-morrow night, allowing this place a rest for twenty-four hours."

We waited an hour for the elephant to come up after Diggs had blown his jungle whistle, but, as we could hear no sound of any movement in the jungle, nor the usual solemn tread of the elephant indicating its approach, we began to fear that something had gone wrong, and immediately suspected that the rogue tusker had come out again and had cut off our relief party. We blew the whistle now several times and whooped again and again, but only the dread silence of the jungles followed each distant echo as it died away.

It was getting quite dusk, and we knew that darkness would follow on quickly: there was no time to be lost in consequence in deciding what to do. We had had nothing to eat all day, and had given up all hope of seeing Colonel J. K.'s factotum with our lunch basket, owing to the rogue elephant's obstruction—we could see no other cause for the failure of our shikarries to obey the call of the whistle—and did not think it worth while to spend the night on the "machan."

"We must walk back to camp," said Diggs, "making a B-line over that hill to the south of our position, and so strike the main forest line at the bend of the Ramganga River, where we left our Ford car. We must hurry," he added, "as the moon will rise late to-night, and we must get over the worst part of the jungle before complete darkness blots out all sense of direction."

Owing to Diggs' fancy for a high "machan"—the object being a commanding view, we found great difficulty in descending the tree and getting our rifles down safely. This accomplished, we began to pick our way through the high grass and dense undergrowth without delay. It was bad going in the dwindling light with the many deep and dangerous ravines and small nullahs to cross, before we hoped to reach the foot of the hill Diggs had indicated. We accomplished this however, in as good time as possible, and reached the brow of the hill without any serious mishap. The scramble through the dark jungle on foot was full of anxiety, as we might at any moment have stumbled over a bear in the darkness, or a wild boar, or found ourselves suddenly in among wild elephants again. The dread, too, of suddenly meeting the rogue tusker, after we had left the valley of tremors was a constant nightmare.

From the top of the spur of the hill, on to which we had climbed, we tried to peer through the darkness which had by now completely set in. By the aid of the " Big Bear " and the two pointer stars, we fixed the north star, and were about to scramble down the opposite side of the spur, feeling our way down by grasping the tree trunks, when suddenly we saw the faint glimmer of two lanterns, and heard cautious treading through the forest. We immediately kept still to watch and see who these people were : as the wild jungles of the Himalayan Terai and of the lower hills, are a great harbour for dacoits who plunder in the plains below, and take refuge in the deep recesses of these forests, evading the police and escaping out of British Territory when tracked down. They are usually hardened criminals and are armed to the teeth. Diggs and I got our rifles in readiness, in case of an unpleasant encounter with desperadoes, as we intended to challenge them, and awaited the approach of the party.

But, suddenly, as they came up close to the foot of the hill, we heard to our relief the mahout speaking to his elephant and recognised the voice of our buffalo-man who seemed to be leading the way. They were apparently a relief party, who had come out in search of us.

We called out to them, and a few moments later we learnt what had happened that afternoon, during the time Diggs and I were seated on the "machan." It was a fresh elephant with another driver that had been sent out with the party of men.

The rogue elephant had returned, and, crossing the swamp, came straight in the direction of the tree on which our buffalo-man was seated with the whistle, and where our elephant, Piari, was resting and awaiting our summons. They had to move off quickly, and went straight back to camp as the tusker seemed to be following in their tracks. They fortunately met Colonel J. K.'s factotum and our lunch carriers on the way, and took them back to camp. Colonel J. K. had sent out a brandy flask with some sandwiches, which revived our spirits, and it was not long before we were out on to the main forest road where we found the Ford car awaiting us. From this point we were in camp within half an hour and glad to find that Colonel J. K. and Colonel Mac had returned safely after an adventurous day. They had both missed a fine male panther under extraordinary circumstances, but had brought back with them some rich discoveries of fresh ground and tiger haunts.

The next three days were spent tracking tiger and tying up young buffaloes but "bad luck" seemed to be dogging all our efforts. It was not till the fourth morning after Diggs' tiger kill, that two tiger kills were reported: one up the higher reaches of the Ramganga River which Colonel J. K. and Colonel Mac had explored, and the other kill was up the valley of tremors—Diggs' old tiger! This gave Diggs and myself another chance in the old place, as Colonel J. K. and Colonel Mac elected to sit up over the kill on their ground, up the Ramganga River.

The rogue elephant was reported to be still in the locality of the swamp, just below the valley of tremors, but Diggs and I were determined this time to avoid the tusker and get our tiger. We took lunch out with us on this occasion—Colonel J. K.'s factotum being allowed to go with us to serve the lunch, as he begged very hard to be permitted to go out on, at least, one shoot.

We started off at ten in the morning, as we intended to have lunch in the jungles at about twelve o'clock and sit up in the " machan " from two o'clock in the afternoon; the report gave every promise of the tiger's returning to his kill, early.

We again took a circuitous route round to the valley of tremors and halted in a safe place for lunch; but again we were destined to forgo this necessary meal. On arriving within half a mile of the tiger's kill, we heard such hot alarm cries all round, that we decided to sit up on the " machan " at once. It was necessary again to guard the swamp, and we again sent our trustworthy buffalo-man down there to climb up a tree on the look out for the tusker. We were obliged to send Colonel J. K.'s factotum with him; as also the lunch basket and the two carriers.

We are at length safely on the top of the " machan " (trying for this big tiger a second time) with the hot sun directly overhead, and hear Piari, the elephant's retreating heavy tread, as the mahout guides her away from the place. We had given the mahout orders to take Piari straight back to camp for fear of her being molested by the rogue tusker, and to return for us at six o'clock in the evening by the circuitous route.

We make ourselves comfortable on the " machan," and I get my camera in readiness again, with my note-book lying by my side. Diggs is not too pleased with this paraphernalia, as he called it, and shows his displeasure as he did on the previous occasion.

Nowhere perhaps is the force of the wind felt so much as in the valleys of the lower hills, when it does blow. It has blown fairly violently all the morning—as a result of dust storms in the plains, and we still feel the fine gritty dust whipping our cheeks. Rather than abate, the wind commences to swoop down upon us with a velocity that causes us to glance at each other in alarm! We are at least fifteen feet off the ground and do not relish the idea of our "machan" giving way. The branches upon which it is lashed swing in a terrifying manner. As each gust, after an ominous lull, bursts down upon us, we are obliged to clasp the main trunk of the tree to keep ourselves from being swept off.

Suddenly, from a distant ridge to our right, we hear the deep bay of a sambhur stag, followed immediately by the quick sharp alarm calls of some hinds. Diggs looks at me significantly and we make an attempt to readjust ourselves in the "machan": but the task appears to be easier suggested than done. The wind has uprooted some trees behind us with a crash, and several branches wrenched from their trunks are being whirled up over the tree tops. As the "machan" is heaved up violently and dashed down again, we feel as if nothing can save us from following the debris up the terrific whirlwind, and we sit tight expecting an ugly fate. But, suddenly, the storm dies away and a deadly calm follows!

We put ourselves into position and look round anxiously. Not a leaf is stirring: and once again—now through the deathly stillness, the ringing bays of the sambhur echo from ridge to ridge, and we listen to the trembling cries of the hinds, till a sudden stampede through the jungle indicates that some dangerous animal is close to them. Breaking through the undergrowth on the high hill slopes to our right front, some of the sambhur are visible for a moment as they plunge out of sight. The tiger is apparently moving rapidly on to his kill!

About fifteen minutes elapse without another disturbing sound, when we suddenly hear something at the back of us, and dare not move our heads to glance behind. There, below our " machan " is a soft rustling—as if a passing silken gown were shaking a few blades of dry grass, and our nerves creep! But the next moment, the gentle flutter dies into the dreadful silence, and we breathe again as we discover that it was just the suggestion of a breeze. A single leaf flutters over our heads and rattles uncannily.

To the right of us, masses of entangled cane and high reeds in flower, droop over a deep recess, through which a starved stream—some fifty paces beyond the hill—is lost to view as it trickles down the winding ravine. We expect the tiger to follow the water down from the cane brake, and to sneak up to the hill in front of Diggs from under the high bank of the ravine.

And, suddenly, across the ravine to our right front, a terrible crash at the left edge of the cane brake makes our nerves jump again, as we wonder what the disturbance can be! Diggs' rifle goes up mechanically, and my camera shakes in my hands. But, the next instant, a large peacock, with gorgeous tail in full plumage, shrieks and flaps up, winging its way heavily over the ruffled canopy of the forest to some fresh haunts. We feel as if we could hurl a few epithets of rude reproach at him, and at all the ancestors of the annoying pea-fowl family!

The leaves of all the forest trees and undergrowth are twisted round, showing a sickly whitish grey instead of the bright green of Spring, and the massive foliage everywhere hangs listlessly. And again that awful stillness settles down—that frightens the novice!

Scarcely has our attention been drawn from the peacock when we hear the cawing of a crow. He is apparently following some carnivora to discover its kill. We feel certain it is the tiger! The crow swoops down from the adjacent hill-side, and, circling over our heads, alights on a tree in front of us, facing the very spot from which the peacock flew up.

To the left of the brake an open glen covered with short grass, stretches across our immediate front, till it is lost, low down in the valley. Diggs is sitting to my left, directly facing the tiger's kill which lies below the cane brake, with the ravine intervening. Suddenly, close to the place at the left edge of the brake from which the peacock rose—which spot the crow has marked and is watching diligently—there is a piercing bark, and a dash through the thicket! I look at Diggs, in surprise as he almost starts; but he is immediately steady again as a little barking deer rushes out, and bolts at headlong speed across the glen in front of us, jerking its bark out in terror! We are now interested in the crow and the cane brake only; suddenly the crow turns and looks down the ravine! It is very dense there and we can see nothing. Some moments pass in intense excitement! But—suddenly, what is it, just at the very back of our "machan"? The sudden powerful respiration of deep breathing like a draught of air, makes us conscious of the tiger! He has stalked round from the ravine and is at the back of us—underneath our "machan"! We sit as still as mice; but alas, we suddenly hear the quick agitated panting of suspicion—and then, stillness reigns!

But the brake? The crow has again turned round to face it, and our hearts sink with disappointment. We have not set eyes on the tiger yet, and he is going back! What can the matter be? But the crow is gazing at the cane brake again, intently.

It is a last gust of wind, as it seems from its diminished velocity, that suddenly sweeps over the valley and dies in the distance, where some mountain foliage heaves. With a grating noise, the giant creepers—as they rub against the tree trunks round which they are coiled—swing back to their strangling embraces; and all nature, instantly motionless—as if the observance of graveyard silence had been suddenly understood in some inscrutable manner—weighs down with an oppression, till every branch seems to overhang, with a relentless threat to suffocate the trespasser, who dares to lay a claim to an iota of space and air.

Into the depths of the forest gloom, the shadows creep; and the shadows grow deeper, where, at the left edge of the brake—on the right hand and wrong side of Diggs—the high grass slowly and imperceptibly cleaves; and it stands cleft for a moment, while the spot suddenly dazzles in livid stripes of black and gold—where the rays of the fast dropping sun play phantastically through the leafy boughs. We sit lost in admiration!

Hardly visible in its movements, and as soft as gossamer, a huge paw falls outside the clump of grass; and there, following immediately, comes slowly into view a great massive head of gorgeous fur, with streaming white whiskers. A magnificent mane hanging from the neck, appears almost to drag its length on the ground! The next moment, the monster cattle thief emerges into full view, with his huge body trailing on the short grass—about forty paces across the ravine. What a sight for the gods! And he stalks, this magnificent creature! Blending with the sunbeams that fall upon him, his head and shoulders might be an optical delusion—some freak! Perhaps some metamorphic boulders that, posed like a statue, are streaked with light and seem to move. Now a decayed log surrounded by dry leaves several inches thick, lies across the pathway of this monarch, as he moves forward almost invisibly—proud, grand, serene! He is in the open glen; completely exposed, heading away from the kill, down in the direction of the valley! What can be the matter? His position is safe—is he conscious of it to judge by his careless ease? Diggs dare not shift his position for a shot, as the tiger's eyes are everywhere and the movement would be instantly seen. He may return to the ravine, or cross Diggs' direct front, and no risk can be run of losing him.

He stands a moment now, before the log, with head turned towards his kill, and his tail drooping gracefully like a painted bow. Suddenly, his body lurches over to the far side, and the near front paw is raised high over the log. It is brought down softly on the other side, barely resting on top of the leaves. With the great shoulders still at the lurch, the paw is pressed down with increasing weight—so gradually, that it reaches "terra firma" without the crackle of a leaf! With thrilling interest we watch each paw in turn being lifted over the log, the great body lurching over, now one side and now the other: the head is persistently turned in our direction!

My eyes drop for a moment—the tiger is suddenly across the log—but where? There was just the suggestion of a big patch of something striped in black and red, darting over the open glen! It might have been a few departing rays of the setting sun. I am conscious of Diggs' slow shifting. His rifle is imperceptibly raised, and the muzzle is gradually coming round, to the right, across my near front. I follow the direction with my eyes; and there, at the edge of the high tree forest across the glen, behind a delicate screen of high grass, the monster stands—seen yet not seen! He is gazing in the direction of his kill with head bent low, sniffing in deep suspicion again as if some dreadful mystery hung there! Diggs' rifle has come round. He has given up all hope apparently, and is going to wait no longer! The mosquitoes are vicious at this moment, singing round our ears and stinging unmercifully. The rifle is now steady. I expect each instant to feel the warmth of the flash, as Diggs' 375 high velocity echoes through the solemn stillness. It will be a deadly head shot, I know!

But what now? Diggs is gasping for breath and choking! He suddenly coughs and there is a stir! He utters a "Damn" as I bend back, and he swings quickly further to the right, to follow the disappearing striped shadow—and the silence is more intense!

A little later a sambhur and his mate call—what jeers of bitterest fate! A disturbed jungle cock quite close to us, is still cackling furiously. Suddenly the tiger gives tongue, and, like thunder, his roars come rolling down the hill-side. We listen to his raging disappointment, till the roars grow fainter and fainter in the distance, and cease altogether with the last flicker of sunlight!

"Are you not going to whoop for the elephant?" I said. Diggs was lost in deep thought.

"He took care to give one no chance," said Diggs. "I at least expected him to cross my direct front after that beautiful exhibition of stalking. His suspicion from the commencement, and the precaution he took by coming round at the back to prospect, was most uncanny. I have never experienced anything more tantalising, and then to get a mosquito into my throat!"

"What extraordinary bad luck," I added, "and such a magnificent tiger too!"

"Why in the world didn't you fire," said Diggs, "when you found I couldn't?"

"I had my camera in my lap and dared not change it for the rifle, for fear of spoiling your shot," I explained. "It was your tiger you know! Besides, who on earth would have expected mosquitoes to make such a sudden and murderous attack upon you, as to prevent your firing."

"Well," said Diggs, as he blew a powerful whistle, "there's no use lamenting now—he's gone! Had it not been for that paraphernalia of yours, you might have been able to fire when you found I couldn't."

"To think that such a thing could be possible," I said, in a pleading tone. "The mosquitoes attacked me too, and I couldn't even press the button of my camera for the opportunity the tiger offered at the log!"

"I told you," Diggs said, "that something would happen: anything is possible in the jungles, and 'luck' is merely a byword for a science about which we know nothing. But I've learnt something new about mosquitoes," he said. "They apparently know how to befriend tigers, or I should have dropped that beauty in his tracks!"

The mahout came up with the elephant, and we found the buffalo-man with him. The latter told us that there had been great trouble with the tusker; that the two coolies conveying our lunch, and the great factotum himself, had spent the afternoon on top of trees: that there was nothing left of our lunch basket and box of beer, as the tusker had danced upon both of them. The factotum and coolies had made a B-line back to camp, on the first opportunity that offered.

Dusk came on rapidly as we took a direction for camp, hugging the hills that comprised the valley of tremors, so as to avoid any risk of meeting the blood-thirsty tusker. We moved as quietly as possible, and waited for the cover of darkness before emerging into the open broad river bed, beyond which the light of camp shone to our immense relief.

"What luck?" shouted Col. J. K., as he and Col. Mac seated in the front veranda of the Forest Bungalow, greeted our arrival.

Diggs said nothing. I merely pointed to him and said: "Wind him up and he'll tell you!"

Drinks were brought up—but no whiskies and sodas could drive away the vision of that beautiful tiger stalking. The story was unfolded, during the telling of which there was keen interest shown by the hearers. The factotum stood by respectfully, with a rag round his head instead of the swell turban he usually wore and, at the finish of our account, he gave his own experience, vowing vengeance on the tusker and the tiger; and remarking that the loss of his gold laced turban, that had cost Rs. 35 in Delhi, at the shop where the Lord Sahib's servants bought their things, did not matter; as he knew of course that the gallant "Hazoors," before whom he dared to open his mouth, would amply compensate him, by bringing to account that bold thief, the tusker, and giving to him (the factotum) a brand new turban!

Colonel J. K. and Colonel Mac, after hearing our story, suddenly took Diggs and myself round the corner of the Forest Bungalow where our eyes fell upon a big striped thing being skinned, with a group of camp servants and followers sitting round, watching the operations.

"Our bag up the Ramganga Valley!" exclaimed Colonel J. K. "This fine tigress fell to a well-placed shot behind the shoulder by Colonel Mac. We have been luckier than you to-day. We bagged this tigress under a family of calling 'Langoors' (the black-faced Hanuman monkey), while on the way to her kill for which we had set out. She was apparently bound for her kill too, as she was travelling in the right direction when we heard the monkeys giving the alarm cry, and we intercepted her."

## CHAPTER XIX

### THE WINGED MONARCH OF THE HIMALAYAS

THE same evening that the big tiger was lost up the valley of tremors, through misfortune, or the clairvoyance of animals (whatever it was) so strongly advocated by Diggs, the four of us sat down to an early dinner with prospects of exciting shikar the next day, which Diggs had promised.

As previously related, Colonel J. K. and Colonel Mac had prospected new ground up the Ramganga River, where they had hunted when Diggs and I were negotiating the tiger—that apparently had an understanding with the mosquito race—but Diggs said that this new ground was just the bare fringe of the more distant place to which he would take us. He knew the country well, and had been giving us such thrilling accounts of another valley up the source of the Ramganga, which he called the "sportsman's delight," that, notwithstanding the long distance into the higher ranges of the Himalayas—some fifteen miles away—we decided to put the whole of the following day at the disposal of Diggs, for all round shikar—fishing, shooting, and nesting! Diggs was death on obtaining the rare eggs of the great ring-tail fish eagle of the Himalayas; and we were anxious to see the home of this vicious bird about which he spoke so keenly.

A shooting permit for each range is granted for fifteen days only; and as Colonel Mac and I had joined the party late, there were only five days remaining, to make the most of the forest range comprising Buxar, before moving on to another part of the Forest Division.

Now that the big tiger of the valley of tremors seemed to be altogether lost—as it was no use tying buffaloes up for him again in the old place, frightened as he had been off his kill—we heard extraordinary accounts from the forest guards of a very big tiger that periodically hunted, most cleverly, a few miles in the opposite direction of our camp; which new locality was about ten miles distant from the valley of tremors. Diggs believed that this big tiger and the one we tried to negotiate up the valley of tremors, were one and the same animal. We were determined to track him again in this other hunting ground of his, as soon as time and opportunity permitted.

But about the shoot the next day. From careful inquiries and Diggs' previous experience of the new ground we were going to visit, it was impossible to do any part of the journey by motor car. The road was but a mere pathway, barely fit for a bullock cart, traversing very precipitous ground. Owing to a breakdown in our transport arrangements for supplies—the nearest railway station being about forty miles away—we were obliged to put a car at the disposal of Colonel J. K.'s factotum for a few days, who was to arrange to bring out immediately, all our food stuff and soda water that was lying twenty-five miles out at a small village. We had very little bread left in camp, and had been gradually acquiring a taste for unleavened bread or the Indian hand-baked cake. This is made from dry flour sprinkled with water until sufficiently moist to be kneaded into soft dough. It is then flattened out into a round shape of the size of a half plate. The dough plates are then baked over a hot oven. With the ground husk of the wheat left in the flour, these cakes are extraordinarily palatable, and more nourishing than the white man's white bread, with all the best ingredients removed.

In such cases of sudden transport urgency on shooting tours, when supplies run short or come to grief through some mishap, a car is invaluable—not only for convenience, but for something that spells greater importance—health! The maintaining of good fresh food and soda water—in places where the water is often contaminated—is essential. We gave the Ford car over for this service, and accommodated the chauffeur with a gun and some cartridges to frighten away wild elephants, and for his "general protection"; which phrase usually includes—as it seems traditionally understood—the poaching of (many) an occasional pea-fowl or jungle fowl roosting after sunset, in or out of season—to which it is customary for the "Sahib" in power to close his illustrious eyes in view of the praise that will be showered upon him, when that aspiring Mahomedan servant, be he valet, chauffeur, or general factotum, is enjoying his delightful dinner of "curry and rice," made from the said (or many such) poached game bird or birds; to which, in his unprejudiced opinion, his white Master—holding the duality of sex in the palm of his left hand, in the attributes of both, "mother and father"—pays foolish homage and gives undue and unseeming protection; since "Allah" made all bird life to be eaten by his faithful, irrespective of species, sex or season. And so—sad to relate—it comes about, that all the sweet little cooing doves one hears on one's first arrival in camp, suddenly disappear, in the face of the severest warning—even down to the drastic measure of the immediate "sack"—whoever the culprit might be that is caught in the act. But, once out of camp many things happen unknown to the unsuspecting Sahib or Sahibs; which, should the "mother and father" be fortunate or foolish enough to discover and to institute inquiries, transform the entire camp life from an organisation of noise and confusion—with little doing and much speaking, the programme for each day—into magical taciturnity, bringing into relief each character—from the most important to the humblest servant or " hanger-on "—as an angelically treading man of few words, with a countenance of such sublime innocence, that the " mother and father " being the thorough sportsman that he is—chastises himself for allowing his mentality to sink so low as to harbour the barest suspicion of evil against his Asiatic cousin.

And so it all passes away as if nothing had ever occurred ; but, should the noble " mother and father," many days later, smoking his pipe in a spirit of calm and perfect good humour, allude impersonally to a certain state of things not apparent before ; for which it might be possible to find a cause, or remember perhaps some personal loss (of quite a serious character) about which a few questions might be suggested to the sweeper, the lowest down the social ladder, it is then that the (" mother and father ") is struck with the splendid address on immaculate virtue immediately delivered in good classical " Urdu "—which lends itself to musical rhetoric, on the conclusion of which some listener at the door coughs ; after which the learned factotum, the mouthpiece of virtue, coughs, and the " Hazoor " (mother and father) himself coughs, and lights again his pipe of satisfaction, thinking of his next tiger kill, or what he might see in the jungles the next day; and it all passes away ! And the factotum leaves the Hazoor's presence with not even a smile on his wooden face ; for is he not—the factotum—used to it all ? All he does is to reprimand a distant loud " belch " at the Forest Bungalow well—the satisfaction of a parched carter, perhaps, indulging in a bucket full of cool water—in case it might disturb the "mother and father" in his deep contemplation.

But to continue this adventure. The cars being unserviceable for the next day's expedition, it was arranged that we should take out all the five elephants in camp, including the two timid baggage ones, and leave Buxar punctually at three o'clock in the morning, which would bring us into the vicinity of the grandest "mahseer" fishing to be had in India (as Diggs pronounced) at about eight in the morning, allowing five hours for the slow journey.

While at dinner, Colonel Mac and Colonel J. K. related their adventures during the day. Colonel J. K. had bagged a fine male panther, and Colonel Mac a couple of cheetal stags, one of which measured 36½ inches which is very good for spotted deer. The panther was wounded in a running shot, and had taken cover in a small ravine, out of which they found that they could not drive him. Placing Colonel Mac up at the head of the nullah, some two hundred yards in front, Colonel J. K. forced his elephant in at the lower end, and proceeded to drive out the panther; but it was not realised that the nullah narrowed as it went up, and before the elephant had gone thirty paces, she suddenly got fastened up between two steep rocky sides—her cumbrous pad helping to transfix her. She could go neither forward nor back and became panic-stricken; elephants being most liable to panic, sometimes for no apparent cause! Colonel J. K. was on the horns of a dilemma, and could not expect any immediate help from Colonel Mac, who was hidden away in thick jungle, round two or three bends of the nullah. The elephant trumpeted in terror, and the panther roared in pain and anger; so that together—as Colonel Mac said, they made such a din that they startled the jungles for miles around. Finally the panther, having no means of escape, leapt on the poor elephant's trunk, but Colonel J. K. despatched him before he could do much damage. The elephant escaped with a few scratches down her trunk. Before they could extricate her, however, they were obliged to cut the ropes of the pad and unharness her.

We soon tumbled into bed; but had to tumble out again, as it seemed almost immediately—so sound is one's sleep in the life-giving jungles!

Colonel J. K.'s wonderful factotum had arranged everything, and we sat down to "chota hazarie" outside, under a waning moon which hung like a flicker of a broken gas globule over the dark hills and forests. It was distinctly cold, and we were glad of our big coats at this early hour.

" It is half-past two—half an hour too early! Thanks to your indefectible jack-of-all-trades," said Diggs to Colonel J. K.

The ways of a regimental factotum—if he happens to be both smart and unconscionable, are unimpeachable indeed! Him the " Sahib " may gently admonish with stick or blakey-capped boot, but he sleeps not—though he eats a lot (and the whisky sometimes has a queer taste of ditch water). But his eyes sparkle with fiendish glee at the first crow from the feathered " cutlets " in the chicken outhouse; for then he is avenged! He will witness his Sahib's tortuous wriggles in bed as he calls him, shakes him, and commands him to open his eyes; and he smiles all the time in fatherly affection! He is worth every penny of his high salary for the delicious cup of tea or coffee alone, and crisp toast, which he will produce at any hour of the morning. He knows it is good; for he has sampled it—and has even tested it upon his wife and family before it has passed the lips of his master —his Hazoor of all the Hazoors in the universe.

Mounting our elephants immediately after "chota hazarie"—wrapped up in our heavy coats, we took a road leading directly north, and were soon moving along as fast as we could travel in the cool of the morning. We had to suit the pace of the men on foot carrying lanterns. A lantern in front, one behind, and another in the centre of the procession, were carefully arranged by Diggs as a necessary precaution against wild elephants. We had to think of the dangerous tusker who was sure to be out of the heavy jungle at night, roaming about the open plains that broke the continuity of the forests in many places. These plains, like small prairies, are densely covered with high grass—as dry and inflammable as touchwood during the hot weather, and are usually full of wild animals at night.

We have travelled about five miles. Far in the direction of camp, the last cry of the jackal pack can just faintly be heard. It is not often that these jungle policemen inhabit the wildest parts, as they are not accustomed to wander far from man. It is the darkest hour just before dawn, and the moon is dropping behind the inky-black hills. Suddenly Diggs pulls up his leading elephant, and the mahouts whisper that there is a herd of wild elephants on ahead. We can see nothing in front, but at once surround the timid baggage elephants to prevent their getting into a panic. There is not even the sound of breaking branches; but our own elephants know only too well, and warn us by putting forward their trunks and scenting the air. "Jungli Hati!" The whisper of those two dread words, heard suddenly in the lonely forests—and in the cold chill of early dawn, makes the blood in one's veins freeze for the moment!

We suddenly hear a soft rustling in the grass to our left front, as we are all huddled together in the middle of the road. The rustling stops; comes on again—as if some animal were hesitating to proceed—and then stops within thirty paces of our elephants. The grass is very high there, and we can see nothing. We are ready with our rifles and guns, in case of a sudden rush by a tusker; or it may be a tiger, obstructed in his rapid move, going back to the forests before daylight overtakes him!

The loud crackling of the grass now continues right up to the edge of the road in front of us, and suddenly, a big black object appears, and stands still in the middle of the forest line. We strain our eyes through the tinge of grey lifting the darkness slightly, but cannot make the animal out. It does not appear afraid of lights, and even seems to turn to face us.

"If it is a bear, it's a jolly big one," whispers Colonel J. K.

The next instant, to our sudden surprise, we hear a giggle from Diggs and Colonel Mac, in which the mahouts join quite audibly. Diggs edges his elephant close up to us with the whispered information that it is only a baby elephant, about four months old, that has apparently lost its mother and the herd.

Diggs hurries us on the journey; as he explains that the wild herd of elephants have been scattered through a panic, owing to some unforeseen occurrence, and it would not be safe to delay in the vicinity. He thinks there are very likely other young ones close by, that have been left behind for the time; and tells us that it is our dangerous friend, the rogue tusker, that has come up this side and is undoubtedly giving the elephants a bad time, particularly if there happen to be no bulls of the herd near by to protect them. In such cases, he has known mothers being forcibly separated from their young for two or three days.

As we pass the spot on the forest line, the baby elephant lifts his little trunk up, in the manner of his "grown-ups," and squeaks, as he rushes past into the grass on the right-hand side. But the little fellow, much to the discomfiture of the two baggage elephants, persists in following us for a long way. He cannot understand the elephants not calling to him, in order to hug him; all elephants are very kindly disposed towards the young of the herd. As the lights are put out at the first peep of dawn, the baby following behind gets bolder, and we have actually got to stop frequently to drive him away.

Our elephants are moving fast, and we reach the encampment of some woodcutters, unmolested by any dangerous wild elephants. Here Diggs announces that we have come ten miles, and have another five miles to accomplish.

At last we begin to enter the higher ranges of the mighty Himalayas; and the refreshing change in the atmosphere, as the cooler mountain air braces every nerve, thrills us with the joy of a new life. We are at an altitude of nearly six thousand feet; having risen two thousand feet fairly abruptly, and leaving far down below us the high sal forest. And now, decked in the cool fresh verdure of Spring, and throbbing with the pulse of radiant animation, the new flora of a new world as it were, bursts upon us, and grows more and more fascinating as we proceed upwards.

Winding along the now narrow forest road overlooking the high rough banks of the beautiful Ramganga River, we are beginning to approach the enchanting valley—judging from Diggs' eager exclamations of delight—with the wonders of which he has thrilled our souls. He and Col. Mac are on the leading elephant, some fifty or sixty paces on ahead. With the delicious sound of rushing water ringing in our ears, we turn a sharp corner, and come suddenly face to face with a deep zigzag mountain gorge which seems to ascend in broad steps of massive flat boulders, smoothed by the ever-tumbling water-falls into a marvellous bed of what appears to be some rare white and grey patent flooring, which would be a credit to the art of the greatest engineering genius! Something that strikes the mind after the fashion of glazed granite, exquisitely cut out in larger squares, with the parallel, longitudinal and horizontal lines, inlaid with streaks of felspar in a translucent crystalline composition to a width of several inches, in almost perfect homogeneity. We were as keen on the mineralogical aspect of this striking water bed, so high up towards the source of the river, as on other pursuits, but Diggs' enthusiasm would permit of no dallying. He was eager to show us the home of the great ring-tail fish eagle of the mountains, and to initiate us into the grand sport of "mahseer" fishing.

How wonderfully nerveless such great creatures as elephants appear to be on top of heights! Colonel J. K. and I clung hard to the ropes on top of the pad on our elephant. Our legs hung over the precipitous river banks, that, with the swaying motion of the elephant, felt quite as unpleasant as it would feel dangling one's legs down into space from on top of the wing of an aeroplane!

Suddenly, the forest road again turns abruptly along less steep hill-slopes, richly clad with the "chier" pine and the drooping oak of the Himalayas, leaving the picturesque gorge to our right. At this spot Diggs stops the elephant and bids us dismount. He explains that we must now proceed along a narrow footpath, too steep for the elephants to climb; and with instruction to the mahouts to graze and water the elephants here, we arrange our rods and tackle, while Diggs shows us a neat book-case containing all the different gorgeous flies used for fly-fishing. We are surprised at his great knowledge of the subject, as he describes in detail the peculiar habits of each fly, laying stress on the particular time of the day when each kind must be used; and then he shows us another case of nickel-plated spoons of various sizes, and coaches us up in all there is to be known in the use of the spoon.

Looking down on the sparkling waterfalls, we are standing on the edge of the precipitous gorge, watching the deep blue pools with the shoals of "mahseer" swimming on the surface, and the shadows of protruding rocks thrown here and there from the rugged banks above. We see many a spray followed by streaks of silver, as big "mahseer" dash about after minnows; and then, in a quieter pool lower down, Diggs points to rise after rise, as from the distance we see specks skimming the surface—specks that are held in an instant! We are told they are the "Ross-Scott" flies; and a specimen of this lovely fly is shown to us.

We are ready now to start along the winding footpath, which skirts the gorge over steep rocks, accompanied by our buffalo-man and Colonel J. K.'s factotum in charge of three coolies carrying our sports' baggage; including two large "tiffin" baskets to see us through the day. How our mouths water to try our luck at once with the spoon and the fly in the delightful gorge below us, but we have promised Diggs to see him through on his nesting expedition first, the morning being the time when the nest of the fierce eagle is vacated; and, as he has explained, it is only on rare expeditions like this that the opportunity offers to obtain the unapproachable eggs he so urgently needs, to complete his and Colonel Mac's valuable collection!

It is eight o'clock in the morning, and we are well on the way, struggling up the giddy footpath. To our disappointment, the clouds are gathering overhead in dense black masses, obliterating the sun one moment, and the next, permitting the welcome orb to shine through, like a crimson flood dipping on an angry sea, with its broken beams crowning the wave crests in myriads of flickering halos.

"I am going," said Diggs, "to take you into the realms of wonder—into the hidden kingdom of the autocratic hawks and the first cousin of the extinct halcyon—the sportsman's land of golden dreams, to show you something that you have never seen before, and will probably never again experience!"

To be so *outre*, in giving vent to his feelings in descriptive language, was something quite new to Diggs' character. We had learnt from previous experience his little indiscretions in shikar, which usually sprung surprises on one—of either a grave nature, or something that lifted one to the acme of bliss—and we were prepared for anything—dragons or fairies!

"Nil desperandum," whispered Colonel J. K. to Colonel Mac and myself, as we glanced forward at the dizzy wall of rock across which our path led!

A thousand feet below us rolls the Ramganga. Round a critical corner of the giddy pathway there appears an immensity of space; and the three of us—for Diggs, who appears to have no nerves, walks over the sickening height unconcerned—close our eyes for a moment with our backs turned to the perpendicular drop, which descends into the rushing gorge below, and clutch the wall of rock above us wherever our fingers can desperately grip! We move at a snail's pace over the ledge, which might be a broken step in some attempt to span eternity!

We are round the corner, and, save for the baggage bearers, I bring up the rear. There is a sudden halt!—and the surprised exclamations of rapture in front, invite me to open my eyes gradually. What a sight suddenly lies before us !—we are transported with joy. And the black clouds have just rolled forward.

Below the mountains beyond our ridge, nestling at the foot of lofty cliffs—amidst wild scenery—a charming lake, calm and clear, mirrors for the moment a cloudless sky, and glitters in the morning sunshine !

At Diggs' urgent request, quickly we drop down 500 feet, passing through the narrow outlet of the flow into the gorge below, and stand on the level of the smooth sheet of crystal waters. In front of us at the opposite end, the Ramganga, now a narrow streak of silver, is rushing down from a higher source and feeding the bonny lake ! Deep lagoons to the right and left, run into long narrow openings where the cliffs have parted. Above, from a height of about 300 feet, the bare rock-bound mountain sides are relieved by coned pines, standing up erect like hundreds of candelabra dotted about, and fringing the edges of the lake in reflections of multifarious designs, like a border of dark grey embroidery on a silken surface of pale limpid blue !

"Come," said Diggs, as he led the way half round the lake, stepping on rocks and crawling over boulders, till we stood in a commanding position. "Let us hide here for a short space and watch these multitudes of birds and fish."

Dotted about, some members of the lesser fish hawk tribe, resting on boulders and perched on pines, are pruning their gleaming white and grey plumage : a few still hungry, and quartered in the lagoons of the lake, are struggling like sleuth hounds in search of prey, on tired but persistent wings.

Presently, one bird plunges headlong into the water ; there is a splash, a silvery gleam, and in a few seconds the bird flaps somewhat heavily up with a young "mahseer" in his talons. And then, following in his wake—like vultures waiting and watching—the other hawks, that have collected from every quarter at the moment the successful venture was made, rise, and hovering for a space, suddenly fall on a shoal of fish that has come up to the surface.

Suddenly, in an instant, from nowhere as it seems, a dark form appears; and, choosing his victim from afar, the great ring-tail fish eagle stills his wings and devours in a second, as it were, the space that divides him from his prey! The lesser hawk darts; but an ominous swish of wings over his head, is the tyrannical summons to deliver the prize. In a mighty swoop the Great King Eagle checks his headlong rush, and there, soaring gracefully, prepares to receive his tribute!

In vain his wretched victim grips his dearly won meal hard, and tries to escape, but the winged fury is on him. Dodge, double, and swerve as he will, he cannot shake off his awful pursuer! Once more the relentless rush, but this time the taloned feet are lowered to strike: one blow is enough, and the hawk pauses, dazed for a moment, and drops the fish that falls shimmering in the sunlight. Swift as lightning the great eagle stoops with half-closed wings, overtakes and seizes his ill-gotten meal, before it reaches the water and, with leisurely flight, he wings his way back to his mountain home, looming purple in its vast height against the blue.

Diggs explains, as he points far above our heads, that the usual nesting site selected by this domineering eagle is a commanding ledge on an almost perpendicular cliff, several thousand feet above the lake. Here a large basket shaped nest is placed, strongly made of dry sticks and leaves, in which one or two large, slightly oval, dull white eggs are laid. This family of eagles seldom or never hunts independently for its own food; and yet, the bread winners are very careful not to levy too severe a toll upon the smaller hawks, otherwise, the latter would seek fresh haunts and, in so doing, these eagles would be deprived of their livelihood.

Picture for the moment the lower benches, slanting and narrow, of a rugged cliff towering up to the blue sky with vast colonies of cormorants, armies of terns and razor bills, all breeding at the same appointed time, and it will then perhaps be possible to get some slight idea of the kingdom of waterfowl which the great ring-tail eagle of the Himalayas rules with such tyrannical might. Indeed, the first half hour of our experience of this lord of the cliffs, gave us a never-to-be-forgotten insight into the constant struggle against the various forces of nature, and the forceful instinct to live on others, which is the life of all wild creatures.

On these same cliffs, the peregrines rear their young on the flesh of waterfowl, and the black thief, the mountain raven, has his home. But these birds are, as it were, beggars following in the wake of the King, taking their lessons from this great eagle, the buccaneer of the air, who dominates the whole, and embodies the very spirit of the place in his fierce untamable character.

Up on the giddy height directly above us, Diggs has marked a nest of the great eagle, and decides to tackle the dangerous climb. He asks for a volunteer to accompany him; and as Colonel J. K. and Colonel Mac have not come prepared with climbing shoes, for any such adventurous mountaineering, I consent to go, but not without misgivings in my mind as to my ability to withstand all the dangers involved. At Diggs' suggestion, Colonel Mac and Colonel J. K., agree to follow behind at a certain distance with their shotguns, in order to protect us, as far as possible, from too violent attacks by the huge parent eagles.

Diggs now gets his climbing rope out and binds me round the waist, fastening the other end round himself at a distance of about thirty feet, in the true fashion of a born mountaineer. He tells us that the climb will take about a couple of hours, and after careful instructions to me the four of us begin the ascent. Diggs and I are armed with hooked sticks; but, in addition, the former has a miniature pick-axe swung round his waist, and leads the way.

Up, up, we go, until we are about 200 feet above the lake. Here we find a fairly broad ledge upon which we leave Colonel Mac and Colonel J. K., whilst Diggs and myself begin the terrible climb of another 800 feet up into a lowering cloud.

We ascend by slow degrees, scrutinising every crevice in the rocks, and cutting out steps for our hands and feet, when suddenly, an angry-looking storm that has gathered commences to wreak its fury. We are in an exposed position, but are fortunate enough to have a good grip of some protruding rocks. Diggs pulls the rope up to tighten it between us.

The wind now shrieks and rages, and the rain descends in hissing torrents, which streaks the mountain-sides around the lake with an infinity of tiny channels. We take advantage of every passing lull in the turbulence of the storm, and make as much headway as we can, compatible with safety. On our way up the mighty cliff, we find hollows here and there which have recently been nests, but are now innumerable pools of water, on the surface of which eggs are lying like miniature islets. In one case we find an egg shell broken and the beak of a young bird protruding; it has met death on the threshold of life—drowned before it has actually been born! Other chicks that have been hatched, and are older and stronger, have strayed away from the treacherous hollows, seeking shelter behind tufts of grass. Diggs tries to render such assistance as he can: but the parent birds mistake his intentions, and swoop down, attacking us from all directions: so rapidly is it done that one cannot but marvel at the ease with which they set and manipulate their wings, which at once defies the terrific violence of the storm.

The raven alone dares brave the wrath of the smaller waterfowls, and even plunders their nests with the characteristic cunning of the crow tribe. His usual method of fighting, or rather self-defence, consists in turning on his back in mid-air and presenting his powerful claws, on which his enemy rushes to his own ruin. But even the confidence of the raven in his own prowess, melts before the terrifying onslaught of the peregrine parents, and he achieves by stealth what is denied to him by force. Alighting on the rock within reasonable distance of the nest he has selected, he crawls along, crouching so close to the jagged surface that the attack loses all its sting, and, submitting to repeated buffeting, he philosophically consoles himself with an egg!

Climbing higher and higher, up the dizzy height of the great cliff, unconscious of the danger involved, we approach at last the frightful ledge upon which the great ring-tail eagles have made their spacious nest. Suddenly, before being made aware of it, there is the roar of a huge body rushing through the air, and a great expanse of wing brushes past our heads, vanishing into the lightning-streaked clouds! Thus warned, to go so far and no further, we lift our sticks to be ready for the next attack. Again the male parent bird dashes down in one great swoop and comes straight at us; a powerful hooked beak and piercing eyes; a heavy body lowered with stiff pinions, yet with the resistance of the air; black-taloned feet ready to strike hard, make a dread picture never to be obliterated by time. It is photographed in an instant upon the memory—the monstrous ring-tail eagle of the Himalayas!

Instinctively we flinch as a third attack—this time by both the parent birds together—nearly overbalances us off the ledge upon which we are crouching. Diggs' sola-hat is sent flying off his head by the terrific impact of wings and talons, and dashes up against the upright wall of the ledge. His forehead is bleeding, and it looks as if it were going to be a fight to death. I crawl up hastily close to Diggs; and there, facing the awful precipice, with our legs dangling in space, we sit back to back, each with one arm stretched across to the projecting rocks behind—over the bulky nest—while, with the free arm, we use our sticks in a desperate struggle. We hear the welcome sound of the shotguns down below and know that our companions are witnessing our terrible predicament, and are losing no time in coming to our rescue. Swoop after swoop in rapid succession is beginning to tell on our nerves; it is a question of physical strength and endurance. Our arms are fast tiring in having to flourish our sticks and to strike so constantly. At last, one of the eagles darts down below, and two quick shots ring out, and echo from cliff to cliff. At the same instant, a single eagle comes over our heads again, and carries home a desperate attack. Both our sticks are on him when, within a yard from our faces, he suddenly alters the angle of his wing, and skims over our heads, far out of sight!

We wait for a few moments, but there is no return of either bird. Diggs retrieves his hat, and quickly, but not without difficulty, extracts two eggs out of the huge nest —a kind he has long sought after!

We immediately retrace our steps down the cliff, ready for redoubled attacks at any moment, vowing never to risk our lives again by trespassing on the sacred domains of this King among birds.

Though, on such an adventure, one has moments of fear and resentment when particularly severe blows are dealt, yet one cannot help but respect the bold defence made by those monsters for their offspring, and pay a tribute to the pirate of the air whom the local bird folk prize so highly; notwithstanding the toll he levies, as he is their King, and drives off the marauding golden-headed eagles, protecting the young of all the lesser tribes.

It was fortunate for us that the male eagle was driven off by our companions below, when it dived down to ease its wings and came too near the waiting guns.

## CHAPTER XX

### AN ANGLING ADVENTURE: AND A SWIM FOR LIFE

AFTER our hazardous adventure in scaling the precipitous wall of massive boulders towering up from the lake on the quest of the great ring-tail fish eagle's egg, which the reader will remember from the previously connected narrative, it is a pleasant change and rest to sit down and smoke in a cool shady corner—to listen to the splash of two waterfalls as they come glistening down their rocky course and tumble over the moss-grown cliffs in front of us, into the sparkling mirror of water.

It is midday, and one of the baggage elephants comes up unexpectedly—for we had left the elephants lower down—with our lunch baskets. We hail the buffalo-man, and Colonel J. K.'s factotum, who has a broad grin of welcome for us. The buffalo-man brought the lunch party round a safer way, after parting with us on the dangerous cliffs, and had sent for one of the elephants.

We then clinked glasses and drank to the health of the little fishes in the Ramganga River below the cliffs, while the factotum opened out the sandwiches and hard-boiled eggs.

Second to no experience of delight is the sportsman's joy after a good lunch with shoals of fish gliding by him, in the waters at his feet, asking for their lovely flies. The splashing "mahseer" are leaping all over the lake. Diggs is the first to get his rod ready, and the rest of us follow his lead in great expectations of a grand afternoon devoted to an undisturbed bit of fishing ground that is seldom or never visited.

Diggs throws first, and we stand by to watch for a few moments, the performance of this expert fisherman.

How daintily the Ross-Scott fly skims the surface of the water and leaves a speck, followed by a faint ripple, where it has flicked the transparent sheet in the buzz, as it were, of a second. Again it skims, flicks the water, and has gone! Again it comes, again and again! Once more it comes and seems to hover. Suddenly, there is the slightest splash, and we see the silvery gleam of a large fish—about a five-pounder "mahseer"—as it leaps up with stiff fins and instantly dives. The reel rattles on Diggs' rod—it is a catch!

As the almost invisible line is drawn taut, the point of the rod is bent dangerously low. The reel rattles again, and the line is carried far into deep water. It is pulled now from side to side of the rock-bound corner of the lake as the fish tries every dodge to shake off the deadly hook.

We watched Diggs throwing his Ross-Scott with spell-bound interest; and now we watch his dexterous movements to land a fish too heavy for rod and tackle, which have been manufactured very delicately with the intention of suiting the very commendable instinct of sport inherent in some expert fishermen. To give the gilled inhabitants of the water the best possible chance of escape by the use of delicate rods and lines is as sporting as the use of the small-bore gun which makes shooting appreciably more difficult. The same idea is borne out in the use of the small-bore rifle for big game, which necessitates hitting an animal in a vital spot to get it at all and enforces the best skill in shooting. No sportsman with a small-bore rifle in his hands would select any but a vital spot on an animal; and, being a smaller mark

—the head or neck for instance—there is always the chance of a clean miss and the animal escaping unwounded. To be merciful is the highest ideal of sport, and the selection of the weapon which conduces to art rather than to butchery, should be the first consideration of every sportsman.

Our delight grows keener as we watch the wonderful manœuvring on both sides—Diggs, with the experience of years at his disposal, and the persistent struggling of the big fish with all the cunning devices of its instinct. It is a strong, obstinate "mahseer," and Diggs plays it for a space of ten minutes, guiding it so as to prevent its getting in between the sunken rocks at the edge of the lake. At first sight it appears almost impossible to land so heavy a fish with Diggs' delicate rod and line. The slightest jerk or mistake made in not immediately following the direction the fish takes on each successive rush, would mean the instant snapping of the line; and the fish would live again, to be wiser next time.

We see that the "mahseer" is at last beginning to tire. He comes up to the surface and lies limp, and Diggs begins to draw him in gradually, with the greatest care, ever ready for some unexpected surprise. To land the first catch on a fishing expedition is always a moment of great excitement and, as the fish is trailed in, we are all ready to give a helping hand: the landing net is got ready almost at our feet.

The net is submerged by the buffalo-man, to lift the fish quickly out of the water, when, suddenly, it makes another dash for life and liberty, and carries the line out again some thirty paces into deep water, where one's sight is dazzled by the flashing rays of the sun; for the storm that had added to the danger of the recent climb and the fight with the savage eagles has passed over completely.

"I think the young tit-bit on the line out there, is now *hors de combat*," said Diggs, as he began to wind up the loose thread-like line of gut.

The "mahseer" seemed to be floating on the surface, to judge by the glinting scales on his white flanks that had now come uppermost.

Suddenly, there is a sound as if a terrific hurricane had sprung up unexpectedly, and it seems as if it were swishing through the trees above us in a violent swoop. We look up quickly towards the high cliffs where the pines are standing, to account for the disturbance; but the trees stand erect and motionless.

It is only an instant that our eyes are turned away from the fish and, scarcely has Colonel J. K. exclaimed: "Look out!" when there is an instant splash in the water, and the rod is suddenly jerked out of Diggs' hands. The next moment up rises a big hawk, followed by two or three others, with our fine "mahseer" in his talons.

"My best rod—dash the bird!" cries Diggs.

But it is too late; Diggs' favourite rod dangles down over the centre of the water! Our shotguns are out of reach, as we had put them away for two hours' fishing, which we had hoped to enjoy, never expecting the obstruction of such a disaster!

Scarcely, in our surprise, have we realised the suddenness of this onslaught, when again comes the terrific rush of the sweeping hurricane. It is louder than before, and like a violent tornado on the point of splitting the very rocks. Our hands cover our heads as we flinch instinctively.

"Look!" calls out Diggs.

We look up.

There, once again, we see the monstrous ring-tail fish eagle. The big hawk is in his mighty grip and the greater creature is demanding his toll fiercely. He is undoubtedly enraged; and Diggs thinks it is the same eagle whose mate was driven off in the encounter with us. The distance is out of range for our small 20-bore guns, which we now have in our hands; but we are so fascinated with the spectacle before us that we forget to use them.

There is a momentary struggle; then suddenly the "mahseer" falls from a height of about 200 feet, overtaking in its gathered velocity the falling rod and tackle. But no speed nor distance can put the eagle's prey beyond the reach of his instantaneous swoop. His wings are manipulated to give the desired impetus, and we see this dreaded bird falling, as it were, head foremost in a terrific dive.

The "mahseer" is clutched before it touches the shining surface of the water; but the line is entangled in the huge wings, close to the fine end of the rod, which is carried up again, hanging directly from the body of the eagle, and looking as if it were permanently fixed there. The sight is a weird one, as the eagle soars up into the blue; he makes no attempt to shake off the added encumbrance.

Diggs now points his gun and we back him up with a volley of number three shot to frighten the eagle. This has some effect. The wings are shaken heavily; and, apparently, the line has snapped, for the rod falls and splashes down into the middle of the lake. Feeling completely beaten and annoyed, we fix our gaze upon the great eagle, till he is lost from view over the high cliff. Our first "mahseer," over whose catch we were so keenly interested, and whose delicious fried pieces we were waiting to enjoy, had gone!

"Paid off for your robbery," said Colonel Mac to Diggs.

"What about my rod," said Diggs.

"Yes, what about it," chaffed Colonel J. K.

"Well," said Diggs, "I can't afford to lose that one, certainly, and must retrieve it. Shere Khan, our buffalo-man, has had an attack of ague already this morning, and we could not expect him to go into the cold water. These other coolies are unable to swim."

"I dare not risk it," said Colonel Mac. "You three are the younger—draw lots!"

We did draw lots, and it fell to me. I am fond of swimming, however, and was not sorry. The moment I saw the lake, I had made up my mind to enjoy a swim in its delicious waters, even though it should delay our long journey back to camp. I took my clothes off quickly and dived in. The water was cold but bracing; and, after enjoying a few splashes in the shade of some overhanging rocks, I called for my sola-hat—the midday sun beat down on the water fairly strongly—and struck out for the centre of the lake.

I gradually approached the long dark line in the water that looked like the rod. Directly in front of me I saw what appeared to be a huge fissure in the rocks on the opposite side and about eighty yards distant; curiosity led me to swim nearer and to explore the rocks. I passed the rod lying in the water and swam on.

Across water sound is carried distinctly; and I heard exclamations from the party now and again as bites were obtained. I gathered that Diggs was trying Colonel J. K.'s rod, which he called a barge pole.

Suddenly I heard Diggs' voice distinctly. "Where has he got to?" it said.

I turned round and waved my hand, as I saw them looking towards me. I was too out of breath at the moment to shout anything back. I now looked in front of me and saw a huge dark cave. The water was just lapping inside. I looked to the right and left, and saw that there was no possible way to it, save swimming, for the depth at this point seemed considerable. I came nearer the cave with the intention of resting and found the water getting icy cold! I felt chilled, and some terror, the cause of which I could not explain, seized me, and for a moment threw me into a panic. I was regretting having swum out so far from the place of embarkation, with no landing spot anywhere in front of me within sight. To get a panic on land is bad enough, but when swimming in cold water it is ten thousand times intensified.

What happened immediately after this is difficult to explain clearly. When one is engaged in a desperate struggle for life there is no time to think of the sudden occurrence that was principally the cause: face to face with some inevitable danger, all one can do is to act on the spur of the moment on some instinctive plan of escape, the instant conception of which is impelled by the first law of nature—self-protection!

The cave is pitch black inside, and an unpleasant suffocating smell comes through. My hands are raised to seize the edge of the low entrance floor in order to draw myself up. I am shivering with the cold, and am in urgent need of the moment's rest, on which I have been depending.

I have scarcely drawn my head and shoulders up to sit on the edge of the cave when, without the slightest previous warning of any kind, I am hurled back with a succession of fierce deafening grunts; and suddenly, I find myself in the water again, rolling over and under an enormous inky black creature!

We rise . . . and horrors! A huge black bear, the aggressive Himalayan sloth with his big jaws wide open, is blowing hot steam close into my face. I instantly dive aside, and feel his heavy paw and forearm—that have quickly struck out at me—come down on my back; the force of which, luckily for me, was retarded by the water.

I struggle up for breath, and the brute rises again almost instantly. But now I am facing the back of his shaggy neck and I bring my fist down as hard as I am able on the top of his inflexible head. I dive again as a roar of rage escapes the monster at the effrontery which I have unwittingly offered. He splashes round bobbing up and down like a gigantic, unwieldy ball of long dishevelled black wool.

"Good God! your rifle, Colonel J. K.! At the back of you! Quickly!" Diggs' voice sounds as if it were far away; I can just hear it amid the bear's grunts and the splashing of the water.

They shout to me now to head for the open water—to move away or do something to allow of a shot being fired. But I am utterly exhausted, and my right hand is almost helpless with pain, as the result of striking the bear's hard head. The brute follows me up mercilessly, ploughing through the water in a clumsy but powerful manner. I feel I cannot get away from him and must succumb to the terrible ensuing struggle. To hug him close, so that he cannot use those ghastly claws—that protrude like a raking fork with the points glistening in the sun—is all I can do for the moment; but I cannot delay, and must do something!

I make a last desperate attempt to make room for a shot by swimming on my back parallel to the rock-bound bank. The instant I do this, there is a rifle shot; and never did the smart crack of a modern sporting rifle sound sweeter in my ears!

Not a sound follows—the bear has sunk heavily! Col. J. K.'s deadly shot, I feel certain, has got him in the head. At that moment I feel something touching my shoulder behind, and I turn round to face the plucky buffalo-man who has swum out to my rescue. He knows of a landing place among the nearest rocks, and I am soon ashore and being dried and revived with Col. J. K.'s brandy flask.

During the welcome meal that followed, Diggs explained that he saw a similar case in Náini Tál, when a bear, being harassed by men and dogs, swam across the lake for a short cut; and, as he could not scramble up the steep face of a rock he got into a cave at the edge of the water, where he was shot from a boat.

"Exactly the same thing must have happened sometime early this morning," said Diggs. "This is the season when he-bears fight; and I expect as the result of a beating, this one jumped into the water."

We soon sent for one of the mahouts who could swim; and with the aid of the buffalo-man both the rod and the dead bear—who lay floating on the water—were pushed safely to the bank.

We found the bear had been hit in the head, and congratulated Colonel J. K. on his good shot! Diggs' presumption was also right. There had apparently been a fight as the bear was badly mauled and still bleeding from many wounds. But his head and skin has since been mounted, and it makes a handsome trophy!

CROSSING A CRYSTAL STREAM

"ALLAHOO-DARSAND"—BEAUTIFUL AND DUTIFUL!

# CHAPTER XXI

## TWO MASTERS OF STRATEGY: A BATTLE OF WITS

IT was four o'clock in the afternoon, and but an hour had elapsed since we had turned our backs regretfully upon the enchanting lake in the higher ranges of the hills. After our adventure of the forenoon, and my fight with the bear in the cold waters of the lake, we had sat down to an appetising lunch amid the allurements of romantic scenery and entrancing sport. We were each transported with joy at our individual bag of "mahseer," with the spoon and the fly, and were indulging in further sport enthusiastically when Diggs called time, and we had to pack up our fishing tackle and make our way back to the elephants, on our return journey to Buxar Camp.

We had descended about 2,500 feet, and were beginning to enter the low sal area again, when we began to entertain each other with peculiar shikar incidents and record achievements, to relieve the monotony of the march along the level valley of Buxar. The bear that was bagged was sent on ahead, on one of the spare baggage elephants; and we were marching now in double file, Colonel J. K. and I on a good female elephant and Colonel Mac and Diggs on a fine old tusker. We had a nice bag of twenty pound of fish following behind, all of which had been cleaned out sufficiently to keep for our servants and camp followers.

We jogged along, talking as we got down below the hills, with the pads of our elephants almost touching.

"I was going to tell you," said Diggs, "of an extraordinary ricochet once of a bullet from my rifle, a .375 high velocity. I was sitting up one afternoon over a panther's natural kill—a hind cheetal—to which I had been directed by vultures. The panther stalked out about five o'clock in the evening, but crouched behind some cover, showing just the top part of his head and his two yellow eyes. I waited patiently for about half an hour, but, as he seemed to be quite comfortable, with apparently no intention of moving on to his kill, I decided to take the small mark presented, rather than wait till it was dusk, and fired. I have never yet been able to depend upon a shot with the full blaze of the sun on the fore-sight, and the moment I had pulled the trigger I felt it was a miss. I heard the bullet striking something, and almost at the same moment that the panther leapt up in surprise I heard a double whiz, as it were, of two missiles flying low over the ground past my right front. There were no rocks in front of me to explain a direct rebound of splintered pieces of lead, and there were very few large sal trees about, as I was shooting in a young sapling forest. The panther, of course, disappeared, and there was complete silence for a few moments. Suddenly, well at the back of the 'machan,' on the right side, I saw a patch of high grass shaking, followed by loud rustling, as if something were struggling in violent kicks. I could not make head or tail of this, as it was quite evident that the panther was missed; and, after waiting half an hour until everything was still again, I called up a Gurkha peon whom I had sent back to wait on the forest road. His line of approach was to my left front—the opposite direction to the patch of grass that had been shaking. I slipped down quietly off the 'machan' and met the Gurkha, to whom I explained what had occurred. We were shooting on foot, and had to be careful how we approached the patch of grass. As explained, this spot was to the right of my 'machan,' but well back behind it. We stalked up with the greatest care, my gun at the hip on full cock, and the Gurkha with his deadly knife (the Kukri) gleaming in his right hand. The panther might be lying there wounded, and we had to take every precaution. Well on the alert, we set foot in the patch of grass, when suddenly my companion laughed and rushed forward, picking up a large peacock in full plumage. We found that he had a bullet wound in the body and was hit badly, apparently by one of the ricochets that I had heard.

"How a bullet could come back in almost diametrical opposition to the direction of its original flight, and killed a peacock behind my 'machan' was an extraordinary occurrence, and we went back to try to follow the shot.

"There was only one large decayed sal tree directly behind the position where the panther lay crouched and, embedded in the decayed portion about four feet from off the ground, there lay a large grey flat stone, with a very smooth surface. We dug out this stone, and I have got it still as a record. It is about a foot in length and three or four inches across. The bullet struck the edge of this stone, having apparently ricochetted off the ground. Well to the right and forward of this tree, a sapling was cut; we followed on, examining the other saplings. Well forward again, bringing us into line with the 'machan' on the right-hand side, we found another sapling cut and this last embrasure pointed in the direction of the patch of grass. It was quite apparent that the soft-nose bullet had splintered against the stone in the tree, and a large portion of the bullet ricochetted right round the right front of my 'machan,' taking a final course past me and killing the peacock many yards at my back. Though I have seen and heard of many wonderful ricochets, this one has been the most extraordinary in the whole of my experience so far," concluded Diggs.

" Talking about extraordinary incidents," said Colonel Mac, " I once bagged a hare and a pin-tail duck in the same shot. I had a sitting shot at duck at the edge of a swamp in the cold weather, and picked up a hare that had evidently been feeding on soft grass or been drinking water."

"The record, I think," said Col. J. K., "will have to be granted to my friend Diggs, who once got an ordinary fantail snipe on the wing with an air-gun. Sometime back we were doing a portion of a march in a trap and halted to rest and water the horse on the banks of a cool stream. Diggs always carried about an air-gun; and we walked a little way down the stream to try to get a sitting shot at a teal, three of which had just settled on ahead of us. A snipe suddenly rose with a loud cry, and began a zigzagging flight, when Diggs put up his air-gun and winged the bird ; a fluke, of course, though he did take deliberate aim. He also, once, killed a sparrow by accident on the lawn-tennis court, whilst serving. Quite a chapter could be written," concluded Colonel J. K., " on Diggs' records ; but I suppose it is only the eye-witnesses who would believe in them."

Suddenly, the hooting of a car down the rough road in front of us brought us to attention. We pulled up our elephants, wondering what sudden calamity in camp had given rise to the necessity of a car coming out to meet us. We were fortunately getting on to the better part of the road and the country was now almost flat. There were dense patches of woodland scattered about to our right and left over the grass-swept plain.

Our Standard car ! It suddenly came up and stopped, and out jumped Colonel J. K.'s Mahomedan factotum from the back seat. He and a Mahomedan chauffeur presented themselves and saluted. They explained that, knowing how far we had been, they felt sure that our march back on elephants would be tedious, and they thought they would bring out the car to meet us. This seemed extremely thoughtful of them—though we knew that that rogue, the factotum, occasionally indulged in an evening drive when his master was away—and we began to dismount from off our elephants, pleased at the idea of getting into camp early for a cup of tea.

"Listen!" suddenly said Diggs.

We had emerged from the dense forest; and, dotted about with small patches of jungle, the open prairies now stretched out on either side of the forest line. The sun was beginning to dip in the west, piercing a thick cluster of trees and bamboos, a short distance to our right, with great, slanting beams of crimson. The elephants standing still for a moment or two, we heard to our great joy the agitated snorting of Hanuman monkeys from this near clump of jungle.

"Good!" exclaimed Diggs. "Whose shot shall it be? It is either a tiger or a panther, as our little black-faced men of the jungles never tell a lie when they give that peculiar alarm call."

It was quickly decided that Colonel Mac, who was shortly to leave us, should have the first shot; and Diggs led the way on his elephant at once through the thick grass towards the clump of jungle, with Colonel Mac sitting behind him. Colonel J. K. and I followed.

The spare elephants were ordered to proceed back to camp immediately down the road, making as little noise as possible, while the car was to remain on the spot until we returned. We left the factotum and chauffeur sitting huddled together inside the car, with longer faces than we thought they had. They were apparently sorry they had been quite so considerate in bringing the car out to meet us, as they did not seem to be pleased at the idea of having to wait and shiver all alone on a lonely road in a country full of wild animals. They were severely warned not to touch the hooter, even though the heavens should fall!

We are now at the edge of the dense patch of jungle, in the centre of which some bulky trees—the "Bombax malabaricum" and the beautiful evergreen, the "Engenia Jambulana," tower over our heads. From on top of their spreading branches the monkeys are gazing straight down below and yelling like maniacs. They all appear to be looking down in the one direction—to our left. A broad nullah runs through the middle of the thick clump, and Diggs puts his elephant into this, beckoning us to follow. As we move quietly along, the grass waves over our heads, standing almost as high as the bamboo shoots that are densely packed round the trees on both sides of the nullah.

The air is confined along this low depression, and it is close and muggy. Suddenly, we pass through an unpleasant atmosphere, and the strong fetid odour is almost suffocating. Diggs halts and whispers "tiger." Both the elephants begin to beat their trunks on the ground and to kick the gravel-strewn bed of the dry water-course with their front feet. They begin to show that they do not like the approach; and there is a low, trembling grumble as the experienced mahouts try to enforce obedience, by pressing their spiked iron weapons quietly into the soft, fleshy parts behind the ear.

"*Bahaut bara Shere, Hazoor!*"—a very big tiger—whispers Diggs' driver, as he points to enormous tracks across the nullah, under the trunk of his restless elephant.

Diggs now begins his tactics of dodging the tiger, in order to force a glimpse of him and to get a shot. Guided by the direction in which the monkeys are looking down and snorting, our movements begin. Now in, and now out of the clump our elephants are stalking. Every side we move, the monkeys look down in the opposite direction and call excitedly. As we pass under their very trees, trampling down the dense growth with distracting crashes, they stand on the top of the highest branches and look over and beyond the thicket. It is apparent that every time we take a sudden short cut down the centre of the clump stripes moves quietly outside and skirts round it in the open. Familiar as he is with wild elephants and their ways, he is undoubtedly puzzled at our systematic rounding up of the clump of trees, and is eaten up with curiosity to know what it all means. Leave he never will until he gets some idea of the game that is being carried on. Curiosity is the great failing of all the feline race; and, if ever it was developed in the house cat, it is intensified in the tiger, in whose nature it comprises the principal characteristic of cunning instinct. To see and learn, and yet not be seen, is his whole mental proclivity.

The shadows of evening are beginning to grow deeper, and soon hope will vanish with the setting sun; a delirious game of hide and seek is consequently in rapid progress. The monkeys are bewildered. One moment they jump round to look at us, and then, as suddenly, turn again in another direction to yell at the tiger. They begin to get more and more terrified, as Diggs' clever shikar-craft is brought prominently to bear against the deep cunning of cautious stripes. It is a case of diamond cut diamond, and as interesting as it is exciting. There are innumerable little tunnels in the high grass below us, made by pig and deer, and the tiger moves about in these passages, through which he can catch glimpses of the elephants' moving legs.

Once more Diggs cuts down the centre of the clumps,

allowing the elephants to make as much noise as they like, and then Col. J. K. and I quickly skirt round one side, while he and Col. Mac move rapidly round the other, encircling the entire clump. But this results in failure. The Hanumans tell us distinctly that our friend has moved into the centre, and that those tactics won't do. His movements are so silent that, were it not for the monkeys, it would be impossible to get an idea as to his whereabouts.

Diggs now quickly adopts fresh tactics, and leads the way right outside the patch of jungle. On the north side there is a long narrow strip of tufted grass, with bare ground all round it. We move along unconcernedly to this open spot, some hundred yards away from the clump of trees, and then stop, facing the strip of grass. Diggs now moves the elephants about quickly in the open, turning and twisting them in every direction, as if they were badly in need of exercise. We watch the monkeys intently, and now notice that they are looking to the west of the trees, and calling. It looks as if the tiger were sneaking away, and we whisper our fears to Diggs, but he only smiles, and puts the elephants into a faster pace than ever before. These great sensitive creatures, unused to such manœuvres, soon begin to show an unpleasant inclination to go the whole hog, and bolt, by way of the suggestive exercise that has been forced upon them. Their tails begin to lift parallel to the ground, and their general behaviour is anything but reassuring; the tiger has merely got to roar once, and there would be no holding them! But Diggs, keeping a good tight grip of the ropes himself, advises us to be calm and take it easy, and promises Col. Mac a shot at the tiger, very shortly.

The mahouts are now using their weapons freely on the heads of the elephants, who begin to growl and trumpet, and the jungles re-echo with the terrible row, which seems enough to drive away a hundred tigers! Had it not been for the monkeys still indicating the tiger's presence we should have thought that Diggs had been pulling our legs.

But all this agitation and hubbub is just what Diggs has foreseen and wants. He is fanning the tiger's curiosity to a fever heat; and knows that it is only some such climax that will induce him to leave the thick cover.

Suddenly, from the west side of the clump of trees, we hear the sound of galloping, as if some heavy animal were thudding over the ground, coming in our direction. Violently, the branches of the trees are shaken by the monkeys, and the loud snorting and coughing is deafening. We keep the elephants perfectly still now, in thrilling expectancy, wondering what will happen next! The galloping sound stops abruptly, just opposite us, and the next instant we catch a glimpse of a huge dark looking object, passing swiftly and silently into the strip of grass, out in the open.

Diggs now moves the elephants rapidly—though against their will—straight for the edge of the clump, cutting the animal off in the strip of grass. As we approach the spot, and our elephants begin to stalk, the monkeys get more and more agitated. Diggs and Colonel Mac are leading; and, high upon the elephants' backs, we are soon hidden amidst the drooping foliage of the trees along the edge of the clump.

Now, a few steps forward, and we come to a dead halt! We are now peering down the opposite side of the strip of grass—and suddenly, what a sight confronts our half expectant gaze! The last rays of the setting sun play on an expanse of orange stripes like a deliberate searchlight, throwing the black bands out like layers of coal, until the view is more dazzling than the coat of

Joseph, painted in its many colours. A huge shaggy head, with fierce heavy moustaches, looks boldly in our direction, with ears cocked forward! The great muscular forelegs and paws are stretched out in front of him—from under his white chest that is as conspicuous as a target, and the great gorgeous animal seems to elongate more and more as the eye follows the body. He is lying at ease like an enormous hound, with a big red tongue lolling out, and with an expression of contentment and amusement, as much as to say: "Now, what's the game!" An exceptionally beautiful tail sweeps the grass, and then beats on the ground, flap following flap; like the wilful cat, when it insists on a game of "last touch" with an indignant terrier, and sweeps its tail in mock temper! Our figures on the backs of the elephants are well hidden behind hanging boughs; and, in the absence of the human voice, or any other sound, all is serene as a summer's day. The monster is at home, calm and indifferent; he merely raises his eyes—and fortunately, no higher than the pads—and is satisfied that the elephants are a couple of young eccentric lords of the forest, indulging in some free and easy pastime, of royal dalliance!

But we see no rifle going up—what are they doing in front! Diggs is moving his elephant about cautiously, as if trying to get Colonel Mac a shot. What can it mean, for no painted target could be clearer? Suddenly, Colonel Mac's head bends forward, and something is whispered to Diggs. Instantly the elephant stops, and Diggs' rifle moves vertically upwards, and then comes down slowly.

We hold our breath for the critical second; but scarcely is Diggs' rifle level, when, to our utter amazement we see the gigantic tom cat suddenly rise, and actually lollop across the bare ground, with back highly arched, and tail curled to one side, in front of us and our astonished elephants, as if to induce them into a romp! And the huge tiger flops himself down again, but forty paces in front of Diggs. This is more than the already excited tusker can stand. He folds his trunk in his mouth, and, with head down, prepares to charge. The mahout's weapon descends with a terrific crash on his skull, and for a second he is restrained! The tiger springs up in sudden suspicion, and, in that half second, there's a flash, and a hoarse bark from Diggs' .375 high velocity!

The great striped creature collapses without a sound or a stir; and then, amid the trumpeting of the two charging elephants, and the excited snorting of the monkeys, we are on the top of that tiger! Completely out of control of the plucky mahouts, the two elephants are now trampling the huge dead body. Now they leave it, and stampede round the place and then come charging back to the attack, with redoubled fury. The pommelling given the dead tiger each time is awful! Diggs' mahout, a big strong driver, by dint of terrific struggling with the tusker, prevents him from goring the body with his tusks, and spoiling the magnificent skin.

An hour had passed since the exciting episode, and the two elephants had at last calmed down. We had been shaken up terribly, and were glad to alight and rest on the ground. Diggs blew his powerful whistle, which the chauffeur and the factotum seemed to understand, for they left the car on the road, and came up to us on foot. We needed them to help pad the tiger. There was just sufficient light left—a flicker of twlight—to examine the tiger and pad him.

"What happened," asked Colonel J. K.; "how is it that you didn't fire, Colonel Mac?"

"My rifle was empty," groaned Colonel Mac. "When

Diggs made the elephants parade and they began their antics, I thought they were going to run away; and, thinking the empty rifle would be safer to carry, I unloaded—worse luck! In the excitement that followed, I forgot to re-load, a clear case of *lapsus calami*. I shall never get over the terrible disappointment!"

"I thought," said Diggs, "that you had missed the spot, and had not seen the tiger, lolling like a dog! I was manœuvring the elephant to give you a shot, when you whispered what the trouble was; though this beauty was nearly lost, we had a wonderful experience! Another second and he would have gone," said Diggs; "he has paid dearly for his curiosity!"

"Would that I had bagged him, with such a beautiful shot through the head," said Colonel Mac, as he unrolled a small fifty foot tape, and we commenced to measure the tiger.

It was nine feet, eight and half inches, a splendid animal! Every bone in his body was a pulp, but luckily, his skull and skin were intact. Diggs and I recognised him as the big tiger we had been tracking for days, and the one that saved us from the wild tusker and which we lost over the kill the day previously. The beautiful mane was conspicuous—and, here it was!

Tired out, we sat down to dinner at 10 o'clock that night at Buxar Camp, after the great experiences of the day.

"Extraordinary," said Diggs, with his eyes half closed, "that all our deliberate attempts to bag this tiger for days past, should fail, and that we should get him in the end by a mere chance! It is another instance of preconceived intention meeting with failure. I never dreamt I should have had to fire this evening, and had no intention. The whole occurrence was sudden, and I only made up my mind on the spur of the moment; so that, all through the skirmish, the tiger's suspicion was disarmed!"

And then he added to Colonel Mac:

"Had the elephants not been excited—a state I was obliged to get them into in order to draw the tiger out—I should have exchanged my loaded rifle for yours, and you would have had the shot."

"My bad luck!" murmured the Colonel.

# CHAPTER XXII

## A WHISTLE AVERTS A TRAGEDY

THE next morning we remained in camp and decided to visit some pools later on, high up in the Ramganga River, abounding with the "mahseer" and the trout. We could do the greater part of the distance in a car—some six miles, and sent two of our baggage elephants—our trained hunters having been ordered a rest—on ahead, to take us, from the spot where our car would pull up, another two miles to the fishing ground.

We started off in high spirits, using the Standard car, with our fishing gear and rifles. It was an exciting six-mile run—now along the perilous banks of the river, now through dense forest, and now suddenly round a precipitous mountain ridge where one might easily come into collision with wild elephants. We disturbed a black bear by the side of the road, that shuffled down the valley grunting angrily. This valley seemed to be well stocked with the beautiful sambhur and spotted deer. We heard many alarm cries and a panther roaring in the distance. Carnivora were apparently on the move, making a selection for their next meal. But we were bent on fishing, and spurted on wherever we could run safely on top gear.

It was about 3 o'clock in the afternoon and we were on the banks of a picturesque river with a cascade of water below us. Diggs had just climbed up to us, after looking at some tracks in the river bed. He packed up all the beautiful imitation flies which he had spread out for our inspection. The jungles are full of surprises, and one has often to change one's plans to meet an opportunity. We agreed to await the chance of a shot at a tiger, and postpone our original intention of fishing, though some "mahseer" were jumping in the pool, and enjoying their shower bath under the spray most temptingly. We sent our baggage elephants some three hundred yards into the forest to our left to graze quietly and wait until our whistle was sounded. Taking careful cover we loaded our rifles and waited, listening meanwhile to a lecture from Diggs on flies and fly-fishing. The sound of the waterfall drowned his subdued voice, which was not likely to be heard by an approaching animal, however good its hearing.

"Fly-fishing is a great science," said Diggs, "and one that requires more than a lifetime to master. There is no fisherman alive who could tell you all about the numerous varieties of flies; or even something more than a mere smattering about the twenty to thirty principal ones. Each fly has its particular season; and not only must you use the right fly in season, but the right one at the particular time of day, or you would arouse the suspicion of our friends in the water, and seldom or never get a bite. So often have fishermen complained to me that a certain fly was worse than useless, and that he could not understand why it was ever made, unless purely as a money-making scheme.

"But big fly-manufacturing firms, like Hardy Brothers, Alnwick, put new flies into the market from real observation. As a matter of fact, so little is known about the habits of these flies, and when they are supposed to come into season, that fly-fishing is yet purely guess work, and almost entirely in its infancy. Almost invariably the wrong fly is used during the particular month, and time of day, with, of course, unfruitful results.

"And then," continued Diggs, "there are minute details, such as weather conditions, sunny and cloudy days, light and shade on the surface of water—and even ripples—all of which play a very important part in the movements and habits of these flies—governed greatly by their coloration—and a corresponding part in the habits of the different varieties of fish that rise to them. To possess a knowledge of those deep secrets would be invaluable.

"It may not be generally known," went on Diggs, "as it is a matter of my own private information, which I have gained from very studious observation, that some fish that rise to bait like the 'mahseer' and trout, have two wonderful gifts of vision. One is a double refraction of light in their eyes, when an object on the surface of the water is duplicated, as in certain crystals, when two distinct images are seen. The object of this is to induce fish into deceptive tactics in pursuit of their food, or they would run a risk of starving. A fly, for instance, on the surface of the water, would see a fish rising straight up at it, every time, and would very rarely be caught. What happens is this:

"When a fly alights, a fish, say, at a depth of two to three feet, actually sees two flies on the surface of the water; and he rises every time to the refracted shadow or the unreal one, for some inexplicable reason—probably because the image looks brighter. This disarms the suspicion of the fly. The fish now scarcely touches the surface of the water, when he suddenly darts across to the real fly, which he seldom misses. Their tactics pass unnoticed by most fishermen, as they are very deceptive and quick. I have lain quietly overhanging a pool in these hill streams for hours at a time in the quest of this study, and it is a conclusion which I have carefully arrived at. The brain of the fish is not very great, and he could not deliberately pursue such tactics, without being helped by nature, in some special development of the wonderful eye lens.

"The other extraordinary gift in the power of the fish's eye, is an adaptable penetration which enables the fish to actually separate the elementary colours, from a homogeneous compound colour. With the only exception of green, and perhaps a few varieties of entirely black and white flies, neither a 'mahseer' nor a trout will rise to a fly of a purely elementary colour unless compounded with distinct shades of the same colour. On the other hand, if you make an imitation paper fly, and paint it with an even shade of, say, purple—which is a compound—and flick it on the surface of a pool on a bright sunny day, there will be a rise and a rush across every time; but, of course, the imitation would not be good enough for a bite.

"In connexion with this, it is a remarkable fact that the more gorgeous flies, decked in a variety of bright colours, will only drop down on the pools on dull cloudy days, or where there are shades and shadows, or patchy light on the surface of the water. This is another provision of nature to help the fish; for, when the light in the water is so bad that the fish are unable to distinguish the colours in a homogeneous compound, the gorgeous colours, in external decoration of the fly, are openly exposed for them. With 'mahseer' and trout—and I take it with most fish that live a good deal on flies—the rule is that only the gorgeous flies are fed upon—those that are openly decked out in many colours; or such flies the colours of which are hidden in the scheme of a homogeneous compound, the case in which the wonderful eyes of the fish come into play, and recognise the gorgeous element. The compound coloured flies only alight on bright sunny days, when the hidden coloration can be distinguished in some marvellous way. That these fishes do not feed on flies with elementary coloration is another curious and wonderful thing. It may be that such flies are not good for them.

"Thomas' *Rod in India*, a standard work," said Diggs, "gives the 'mahseer' up to 150 lb. Good records of 104 and 103 lb. were caught in 1917 by a Mr. Murray Ainsley in Coorg, in the Kali Nadi Hills of the Western Ghats. In this part of India, 'mahseer' attain their maximum size, where they have been known to grow up to 200 lb. Mr. Murray Ainsley's records were caught with Luscombe's spoon and his steel-centred rod. A record for the Himalayas is 101 lb. caught up the Kauriala River in Nepal, in the 'Nineties, by Mr. Hercules Ross, Commissioner of Kamaon."

Diggs stopped; something seemed to arrest our attention, and we looked round. The sun is dipping in the west behind the high canopy of trees, splashing the lofty mountains in front with a golden glow, that tints the red crowded slopes of hanging rhododendrons, and, seeking the secluded haunts of many a waterfall and streamlet, sends a firework of lightning streaks darting up, to glitter on the bare rocks of the topmost heights like circlets of great jewels suspended from neck to neck.

Suddenly, from the deep shades across the river bed, come the thrilling alarm cries of a herd of cheetal, the sharp high notes of the hinds mingling with the deeper bellowing of the stags; that now and again drown the hoarse call of the ever-dashing cascade, and carry far down the densely wooded valley.

We are looking straight down in the front of us, scanning the edge of the forest beyond the river, but there is nothing visible yet—no sign of stripes or spots! Just bare stretches of sand, about fifty or sixty yards wide, on the opposite side of the cascade of water, meet the eye to the right and left; and nothing more but the dark forest in front—that makes the sandbed stand out whiter than ever—and the gorgeous sun-set on the mountains; still sparkling from summit to summit, leaving some bare heads decked with golden caps, that appear to be getting smaller and to be fading!

Nothing more to be seen or heard, but the invisible spotted deer that are calling loud and frantically; and through it all, like a tremendous background, the absorbing sound of the cascade that almost deadens the senses! Hot alarm, certainly, but jungle alarms we have often heard before, from the smallest bird to the biggest deer—and cheetal will persist in calling, even when out of danger; for a tiger or a panther usually gives up the chase when spotted, and adopts other tactics—yet what is it?

In the whole surroundings, there is something uncanny that seems to agitate us—something inexplicable. A glance at each other tells us that each is feeling the peculiar sensation, and for some unknown reason our breasts heave, and we sit pale and tight, looking anxiously about, though there is nothing apparently to threaten us in our safe position.

We can hear our two elephants in the jungle behind us. They are attempting to trumpet. Diggs just glances at us, as if to express a moment's surprise at the absence of the familiar hollow sound on their heads, of the flat part of the mahout's iron weapon. Then he turns his head slowly to the front again; in which direction we are all keeping a careful look out: But for the occasional tremulous call from a nervous hind, the alarm cries of the spotted deer seem to have stopped, and nothing but the monotonous sound of the falling cascade is heard now.

"Ugh!" that uncanny feeling again! But we are

suddenly fascinated with the view in front. The whole herd of spotted deer has emerged from out of the dark forest, and the animals are spreading out over the sands, coming nearer and nearer the water. The hinds, as is usual, are leading the way, and the stags—some with beautiful antlers—are straggling behind, and following lazily with the sluggish gait of the buffalo.

All of a sudden Diggs draws our attention to the right. There is just a streak of something long and grey passing rapidly over the sand; then it gets hidden among the rocks at the edge of the water, about a hundred yards down the river.

"A panther," whispers Diggs. "He'll be stalking up in front of us presently, under cover of the rocks, to seize a cheetal!"

Scarcely has this been said, when a sudden terrorised "ugh!" escapes Colonel J. K. who is sitting a little behind us. I glance at him, and see that he is in a shrinking attitude, staring up at something close beside him. At that very instant Diggs and Colonel Mac move slightly, glance up behind, and, with ashen faces, suddenly seem glued to the rocks against which they are reclining. The crash of the falling water makes it impossible to hear any kind of sound at the back of us.

Slowly, I turn my head too, and look behind. Two great slaty-coloured trunks of trees, emerging above the grass, seem to have suddenly got planted, three or four paces behind our backs. From the level of the grass, my eyes follow the huge upright logs, up, up, up! Good Heavens!

The shock was so terrific, that I, too felt stunned—frozen to death! A huge wild elephant stood over us! The big ears were pressed back against his great head, and the endless trunk, as it seemed in the terror of the moment, hung straight down. He seemed to be taking in the situation preparatory to trampling us down, and tearing us to pieces. He was a tuskless elephant, too, a "Makhna"—that are more dangerous than any others—and his eyes were swollen and half closed, and were pouring with matter, which ran down the length of his trunk. He was as round as a balloon, with an exuberance of flabby flesh on him, which made him look most unhealthy and aggressive—a dreadful nightmare!

It is impossible to say how long we lay there in a benumbed state gazing up at him in horror, and entirely at his mercy; but it seemed an awful eternity. The sudden shock putting us out of action, probably saved our lives; for the slightest movement, or a shot fired at such close quarters, would have irritated or challenged the brute, with disastrous results. I was dimly conscious of the spotted deer calling frantically again, and thought of the panther being there waiting to be shot, when, suddenly, a loud whistle rang out, and split the very air. There came a tremendous grunt, as the huge brute backed several paces. Then Diggs blew his whistle violently again. "Now fire, one of you," he exclaimed, and two rifle shots immediately rang out. The horrible brute turned, emitted a terrific roar, and crashed back into the forest from where he came, trumpeting far into the depths of the jungle. The whistle had saved us.

We now understood what had happened. The mahouts had got scent of the wild elephant, and had taken their elephants out of the way. The attempt at trumpeting which we had previously heard, came from the wild one. The brute had stalked up slowly behind us, under cover of the sound of the falling cascade, which drowned all other sounds, and we never heard him coming up! Colonel J. K. said that he felt his arm being suddenly tugged, and he turned round, only to shrink back quickly from the protruding trunk, that had actually grabbed him!

There was no sign of either the cheetal or the panther, they had all been frightened away. Carrying our fishing tackle and rifles, we stalked back quietly to camp on foot. The mahouts said that their elephants had bolted back, and that the wild elephant had chased them a little distance. Diggs said that, as soon as he recovered from the sudden shock, he thought of the whistle, and got it quietly out of his pocket, knowing how much elephants objected to such unusual sounds. "Even that was a risk," he said, "at such close quarters, but it was the only thing to be done."

## CHAPTER XXIII

### ON THE TRACKS OF A MAN-EATING TIGER

I WAS stopping a few days with my friend Denis, who was a great motorist and incidentally a great shikarri too. He lived in a small sub-Himalayan station, and was not far from the Terai forests where big game abounds. He kept only two cars ; a Ford and a Dodge, both four-seaters. He believed in no others. We had received news of a man-eating tiger which was in the habit of carrying off local traders and poor villagers, who frequented a certain fair in a jungle village about twenty miles distant. The tiger himself would visit the fair and had taken up his quarters in some scrub jungle close by.

Denis set his old car going—and a wonderful car it was—and we started, taking in the back seat an old grey-haired patriarch of the jungle village in question, who was my friend's favourite shikarri, and, as I discovered, a very intelligent man too.

The " Hatia," or village fair, was to be held that day, within two miles of which the tiger lived. We bumped along the usual rough, unmetalled, district road, and were passing through the scrub jungle, the tiger's abode, when, of course, the old car broke down. We were on the horns of a dilemma, as the tiger was sure to pay us a visit. The old shikarri and I were told off to keep guard with our rifles loaded, while my friend and his chauffeur tried to put new life into the worn-out hurdy-gurdy. Our idea was to get all the men we could from the "Hatia" and organise a beat. The shikarri and I kept watch in the back seat; he keeping his eye on the jungle on one side and I on the other. But the old fellow began to get talkative.

"Let us discuss Hanumanza, one of Hanuman's greatest Generals," he said suddenly.

"Why," I said, becoming interested in the whole attitude of the old man, "I have never heard of Hanumanza."

"Haven't you?" said he. "No tiger will dare come near us if we keep him in mind."

"Go on," said I, and he told us the following amusing legend (believed in by all the village folk) in beautiful Hindustani.

"Well," he said, "Hanumanza was also a great monkey-god who helped Hanuman in his wars against the King of Ceylon. Here is the story of how he instituted the first village fair." And he waxed eloquently witty while we were waiting, *nolens volens* for the man-eater.

"Hanumanza arrived one morning at the very spot where our fair is now held. It was dense jungle. He came with instructions from Hanuman, from whom he had received the Feudatory Proprietorship of the whole of this sub-Himalayan country, to encourage trade among the people.

"Hanumanza reclined on a mango tree and turned his head at the tinkling sound of bells from the distant village, as the cattle moved out; he heard the crackling of the dry leaves close by, and, to his surprise and delight, beheld five fair maidens from the village, coming down to the rivulet for water with 'chatties' on their heads. It was the delightful mango season, and the path led under his tree. Now Hanumanza, thrilled with the joy of all nature around him, found a sense of humour arising, which tickled him into a playful mood. He let his gigantic tail fall to the ground, and, turning the end up in imitation of a cobra's hood, he made it sway angrily from side to side in the middle of the pathway, to arrest the merry maidens on their quest. Then came the young damsels in the highest spirits, making as much noise as the chattering seven sisters in an adjoining bamboo clump.

" Chuckling with delight, Hanumanza hid himself with great care in the thick foliage of the tree, as the foremost girl shrieked and, in terror, dropped her chatty on the snake's head. This hurt Hanumanza, but he merely winced. The maids behind, however, with more presence of mind, armed themselves quickly with thorny sticks. Now Hanuman, who was a thousand miles away and could see the whole occurrence with his telescopic eye, was also touched with a sense of joviality, and chuckled too, as, at that very moment, he deprived Hanumanza of the power to withdraw his tail, while leaving him still the sense of feeling. Four of the maidens then set about belabouring Hanumanza's tail. In vain did he implore them to desist; but each time he spoke, Hanuman turned his words into hisses, so that the maidens redoubled the violence of their blows.

" Now it so happened, that one maiden who was the most beautiful of the five, and who had not joined the others in the attack, rebuked them for not respecting the cobra, who was an offspring of the god Siva, the destroyer. This damsel's name was Kasunda, and on hearing her words of advice Hanumanza gazed at her, and was enraptured with her beauty as well as her good sense. When, taking Kasunda's advice, the other maidens desisted from further beating his tail and he regained his muscular activity, he drew up his sore appendage, much puzzled as to what had happened. The maidens watched the supposed snake going up the tree, and started in a fright when they beheld the terrible appearance of its owner. But Hanumanza addressed them courteously, disclosing his real identity, and delivered a homily on maidenly behaviour and the respect that was due to all living creatures. While he showered praises upon Kasunda, he censured the others for their gross action, finally accusing them of attempting to steal, by brutal onslaught, the tip of his tail for a keepsake.

" The four maidens avowed their innocence and implored his forgiveness, but he said there was an enchantress among them, and that he could not forgive them until the real culprit was discovered, who might be the one who saved his tail in order to possess it herself later. And, saying this, he eyed Kasunda, who blushed deeply, and hotly denied the existence of grounds for any such suspicion against herself. But Hanumanza put her at her ease, and made her blush deeper still by answering that an enchantress was fit to be the wife of a god, and that there was no shame attached to being born such a high personage. Now Kasunda turned her back upon him and was greatly perturbed in turn. She had no doubt he was a god after the patient endurance of pain he had exhibited and, though she felt reluctantly drawn towards him, she was determined to assert the truth and uphold her maidenly modesty. And so she shook her head, and her raven tresses shone in the sun.

" After Hanumanza had thus appealed to her vanity and her understanding and had failed, he resorted to various kinds of stratagem, to discover through the medium of the senses whether the girl had a sneaking regard for him, as she had now left him more disturbed and perplexed than ever. He worked through the four senses, making each play a part but without success, until he came to the fifth sense, that of feeling or touch. He then amiably agreed to postpone the discussion, as to whether she had enchanted his tail so that he could not pull it up, and ordered the maidens to bring him a chatty full of fresh cow's milk, as he said he needed that which was both food and drink. But as Hanumanza ordered that only one should fetch the milk, the girls hesitated; each was too afraid to return through the forest alone! Feeling aggrieved at the little faith they put in his protection, Hanumanza became obstinate, and finally threatened them all, if one did not go. Kasunda being the bravest of the lot, moved off to obey, flashing back over her shoulder that she would bring back poison instead of milk, if she returned alive. On hearing this, Hanumanza was again troubled; and when Kasunda returned with the milk, she found him greatly incensed, with the girls trembling by. When he came down from the tree, the wide-necked chatty was placed before him, but he refused to drink.

"Thereupon Kasunda twitted him with the fact that she had gone through the jungles alone trusting in him, and that it was his turn to trust her. Feeling ashamed of himself, Hanumanza accepted her challenge, but on the condition that she should stroke his tail; as he was anxious to test the degree of affection (if any) in her touch!

"Now it so happened that while he was absorbed in his enjoyment of the milk, the end of his tail slipped into an ant's hole, and those little 'tradespeople' soon nipped off six inches of the end. Kasunda was unaware of this while conscientiously stroking his tail, and was surprised and indignant when Hanumanza leapt up, holding his bleeding appendage and accusing her of the brutality. By this time all the people of the village had collected and there was a great stir.

"Now, she thought it was another miracle of his, made with the deliberate object of sporting with her, so she determined to fling back his base joke. She suddenly opened the girdle round her waist and, to everybody's surprise, produced an old piece of spare cord, which she carried for her chatty, and flung it to the village folk saying that she was the guilty one; and that that was the tail which they should enshrine in memory of the noble creature who had threatened the innocent lives of five helpless maidens.

"Hanumanza knew the length of his tail and quickly picked up the cord. Comparing it with the stump behind him, he found that it tallied exactly in length with the severed tail end. He then ordered a search to be made for the missing appendage, and none being able to find it, he declared Kasunda to be an enchantress who had made the wonderful miracle of transforming his tail end into a cord, in order to preserve it, and he took her words of scorn as a truthful confession and offered Kasunda marriage.

"Kasunda blushed deeply, and though she tried to explain the whole occurrence none would believe that she was innocent of the miracle. Then all the people declaring that a god and a goddess should be united, performed the marriage ceremony under a peepul tree.

"And there is a peepul tree in the fair on ahead," said the old shikarri, pointing to the place, "from which a cord still hangs, under which a prosperous bazaar is held once a week."

The story had hardly concluded when, suddenly, alarm cries from a herd of cheetal inside the forest close to our right front, made us come quickly to attention, and a moment later, several beautiful spotted deer dashed across the road in front of the car. Some carters, who were coming up behind, suddenly stopped their carts in a line and called out for help.

The old shikarri had Denis' rifle, a .500 double barrel express, in his hands. It was by the grand old maker, Alexander Henry, whose rifles are now almost extinct. With the death of the renowned Alexander Henry, there passed out of existence a make which was the pride of every sportsman of reputation, and the envy of all those who were unable to equip themselves with this superb weapon.

I was handling a .375 high velocity magazine—a comparatively small bore, but one of the more modern rifles which for accuracy was most effective. Provided accuracy can be depended upon; there is great advantage in a light weapon. A shot with a small bore rifle can be placed in a vital spot with a greater degree of confidence than with a heavy bore, which has, on the other hand, the advantage of stopping power. In the earlier days of shikar, when the more general method adopted of shooting on foot, was in vogue, a big bore heavy rifle was looked upon as something essential. But in those days the sporting instinct (in the matter of shikar) was not so acutely developed as in the present times. But to the story. It was a second-hand car that had broken down, and the very first time that my friend had experienced any trouble with it.

"This is no time to rack your brains over the idiosyncrasies of the engine," I said quietly to Denis. "If the car won't go, she won't. We had better all crowd into the two seats without delay, as I don't like the signs in the jungle. The tiger must be somewhere close by. And, for goodness' sake," I added, "take your rifle from the old man here, who really appears to be quite dotty."

It was ten o'clock in the morning, and as bitterly cold as it can sometimes be in the month of December at the foot of the Himalayas. A cold damp mist—as if the cloak of night, determined to prove its impenetrable density, had refused to fold and lift—still lay across the high canopy of the Terai forest, defying the struggling rays of the welcome sun. Great vertical and horizontal beams fell deflected over our heads, until they crossed and recrossed each other in a network of resplendency encompassing the entire heavens with great broad crimson girdles.

"How gorgeous that is," said Denis, as he entered the car quickly, and took his seat at the back, alongside of me, hugging his beautiful .500 express. He instantly took the warning from me and instructed the chauffeur and his old shikarri to take their seats in front; and we awaited further developments after the scared cheetal had bounded across the road.

The last call of the cheetal rang through the silent trees of the forest to our left, as we heard one scampering through the undergrowth, and then, suddenly, the forest on either side of us lay still, and became as quiet as a graveyard. A chilly breeze, that had kept up a flutter among the tree tops, seemed to die away entirely. Our nerves were now strained to the utmost, as we glanced anxiously around. We had the hood of the car up owing to the cold mist; and while Denis and I took it in turn to peep through the oval window at the back, the two Indians in front were bobbing their heads in and out of the car, looking about them desperately. Now and again would come the soft wail of the shikarri's tragic voice, breathing out the name of Hanumanza, half doubtfully, as if he knew he was appealing in vain, and yet persisted in the forlorn hope of being heard by his deity.

"He is a lame tiger—this one," said Denis in subdued tones, "and a cold-blooded brute too," he added. "The Thanadar of the police station tells me that he never missed his depredations on this road, twice a week —on 'Hatia' or Bazaar days, and that the monster usually roars to paralyse with fear the poor people who pass along this beaten track on their way to the fair."

It must be remarked here that a man-eating tiger can become very bold, and sometimes breaks through all the well-established habits of his species in the matter of hiding his identity, of stalking with the greatest care, and killing by surprise.

"I hear," continued Denis in an awe-stricken whisper, "that only three days ago, during the last fair, the brute walked casually up to a crowd of men and women, who were trembling in horror on this very road—after they had been treated to his terrible roars for a space of half an hour—and seized a shrieking young woman most deliberately, shouldering her and carrying her off into the jungle for his midday meal."

I inquired whether Denis had his rifle loaded; and we were both on the point of looking at our rifles to make certain, when we were startled at the most uncanny, terrorising sound. There was deadly silence as we stopped whispering. The two poor Indians in front turned round to look at us, and their eyes seemed to be bulging out in fear; the blood froze in our veins, but we shuffled round to face the direction.

"Keep your head and be steady, for God's sake," whispered Denis.

"Yes," I said; and my voice sounded far away; the next instant it was drowned!

Through the misty gloom—as if dusk was approaching—and the solemn stillness of the forest, came the roar of the wandering man-eater, like the distant boom of a big gun rolling up its last pent-up volume in a climax of deep sound, that seemed to shake the very ground, and, in scattered diffusion, die away far into the jungles beyond us. Again—as remarked in an earlier chapter—how the poor sambhur and the spotted deer in the forest must quake in fear at those dreaded sounds, those awful guttural depths that begin in the high staccato of the tabby cat's "mee-ow," and gather in terrific volume, till they roll by all stricken creatures in a clap of thunder. Very soon roar seemed to follow roar; and after each thunderous peal an ominous silence prevailed.

"What is that!" exclaimed Denis suddenly, in a husky voice, as the dreadful suspension of a prolonged silence seemed to make our nerves shake violently. The two Indians had got beyond the stage of speech, and were trembling pitifully. I looked up at Denis almost at the same time; for both of us distinctly heard the far-off hooter of a car. It must have been a mile away, coming down the same road—there was no other.

We had but scarcely turned our heads a moment to listen, when suddenly a deafening shriek from the chauffeur at the wheel, in front of Denis, made us turn sharply round again.

We could scarcely believe our eyes. Denis' rifle was instantly at the shoulder with the muzzle up against a monstrous grinning head that had in its jaws—between its yellow fangs—the loose khaki sleeve of the driver's right arm. An enormous striped shoulder was lurched over, resting on the side of the car, with a great forearm and paw pressed round the driver's waist, as if the intention was to lift the poor man out bodily. Standing on his hind legs, the mighty brute's head and neck were on a level with the steering wheel. The dreaded monster had slunk out of the forest suddenly, like a cat, and moving with the rapidity and silence of a streak of lightning, before the accompaniment of thunder, was on the top of us before we were aware of it.

Click—click! There was no report from Denis' rifle, and my heart sank.

I could see down the brute's huge throat, as he turned

with the spluttering of a steam engine to threaten us behind. A terrible grin and growl warned us again, as my rifle came up instantly, pointing straight at his face.

I pulled my trigger—but there only came the sickening sound of a click! A roar followed; and the brute almost lifted the driver, who lay limp and unconscious with pain and fear.

I jerked the bolt back of my rifle, and saw a misfire, and then the cartridge jammed. At the clashing sound of the metal, as I pulled and tugged in vain, the ghastly brute redoubled his grip, and roared fiercely. His hot breath blew in at us, as if from the flue of a furnace.

Ho—o—t—hoot, hoot!—quite close, came the low hoarse sound of what seemed heavenly music to our ears; and then came the whirlwind rush of a revolving engine—declutched.

The monster tiger let go his grip, and limped back to the edge of the forest, about fifteen paces away, where he stood, puzzled for a moment at the sound of the newly arrived car. "Sahib! your cartridges," said Denis' brave cook, as he came round from behind and handed them in. "You left them in the bungalow!"

My rifle, too, was now in order. The tiger stood before us, and with the hair standing on his neck and with arched back, he put his head down and emitted a terrible roar. The next instant a volley rang out, and we heard the echo from a distant ridge. A dull thud on the ground followed.

We had at last rid the neighbourhood of the famous man-eater. He was a huge beast, measuring 10 ft. 3 in. My friend's Dodge, in which his cook, who could drive a car, had so timely arrived, was throbbing behind our disabled Ford, as we revived the driver, with our brandy flask and did all we could for his horribly mauled arm. It was broken in three places. Denis drove him home at once in company with the old shikarri, and the cook and I followed shortly afterwards in the Dodge, with the dead tiger.

The cook said that he knew we had gone out after the dreaded man-eater, and, after we had left, he looked round the bungalow ; and found to his surprise that Denis had left his cartridge bag behind. He followed us up in Denis' Dodge car, in the nick of time, to save us all from a tragedy. It was lucky for us that my friend had such a plucky and enterprising cook. The whole incident was an example of what can happen sometimes, even amongst the most experienced shikarries.

BAD LUCK OF LOT DRAWING
(the guarding of the cars)

BRITISH ENTERPRISE
THE GREAT " SARDAR CANAL " HEAD-WORKS
NEAR NEPAL

# CHAPTER XXIV

## THE LAME GHOST BULL

ARMED with a pickaxe, a shovel, a Gurkha knife and a good hatchet, it is wonderful what rough roads and jungle-grown cart tracks a car can be helped through. In the extreme north of the Bahraich district, some seventy or eighty miles from the first low range of the Himalayas, there lies an immense tract of Government reserve forest, known in the Forest Department as the "Charda Range." Bahraich is one of the most northern jungle districts of the old province of Oudh which had Lucknow as its capital. My brother, Colonel J. K., and an Opium Officer (well-known shikarries), and I joined a Christmas party arranged by the Deputy Commissioner of Bahraich.

The Charda Camp for which we were bound lay two miles south of the Nepal frontier, and our party consisted of five guns. We had brought out two cars, delighted and surprised at their success over the rough unmetalled road, through typical gigantic sal forests—intersected by rivers from the Himalayas, which brought us on our second day's march to a picturesque camping ground, called "Salbani." We had four trained elephants with us, for "howdah" work in inaccessible places. They would usually be sent on in advance to await us at likely spots for big game shooting, and assistance in case of "breakdowns," and in crossing dry river beds. Bullock carts were used for our tents and heavy baggage.

We had another twenty-five miles to accomplish before

reaching Charda, and retired early full of expectations the next day, as our forest guards, and thoroughly reliable shikarries of the jungle villages, had regaled us with thrilling news. A number of tigers had recently strayed down from Nepal, owing to shooting across the border, and swamp deer (the Gond) were on the increase in certain large swamps conveniently situated. There were also buffalo and wild cattle in the neighbourhood. It is the latter, however, to which the following extraordinary experience relates.

A cold misty morning in the middle of December saw us trying to start our two cars; one a veteran Standard and the other a recently purchased "Ford-Royce"—excellent for its high clearance. We were soon leaving "Salbani" behind. The forest line lay a beautiful vista before us, piercing the depths of primeval forests for many miles, and emerging at right angles to a boundary line, a hundred foot wide, running due east and west, and dividing the two territories, Nepal on the north side and British India on the south. By mutual agreement, both Governments help to maintain this boundary which is a costly upkeep, owing to the vast clearing of grass and undergrowth that has to be done annually to keep it well-defined. The Nepal Foresters who guard their frontier, live, two or three together in grass-thatched huts, built in the centre of small jungle clearings which are three to four miles apart, and extend in this order, down the entire length of the Nepal boundary. These short sturdy watchers are armed with rifles and the short Nepalese sabre, the Kukri, in the use of which they are expert. Fiercely and jealously they guard their frontier, and no one dare cross over who does not hold a thoroughly authentic passport into their country. The intrusion of foreigners is strictly prohibited, and a trans-border pass is most difficult to obtain. For State emergency only, a few high officials on either side hold passports.

Mr. B., the Deputy Commissioner—this official designation approximates to the rank of Governor on a small scale over the limits of a district under its jurisdiction—was anxious to make inquiries into the whereabouts of a jungle tribe, known as "Tharoos," who were inhabitants of a forest village situated within a few miles of Charda. Owing to an extraordinary superstition, these poor people had fled from the village and nobody knew where they had gone. It was a complete mystery, and we were determined to visit the deserted village and investigate the matter.

Along the forest line, the dusky chill of early morning began to glow faintly. A cold damp mist rose over the canopy of the forest, shot with rays of shimmering crimson that delicately veiled the interlaced branches of gigantic trees towering on either side of us. Dew began to sparkle everywhere, falling on the dense undergrowth and dry leaves below like noisy rain, as we moved along, carefully, down the dripping vista.

In front of our cars, spotted deer and sambhur dashed across the road at intervals, but our fingers were too benumbed with the cold to use our rifles and we awaited the warmth of the sun. To shoot birds on the wing out of a moving car is thrilling sport. As the sun began to rise over the tree tops and disperse the night mists, we pulled up to put the hoods of the cars down, and had an hour of grand flash-shooting at jungle fowl, our cars moving at about fifteen miles an hour, at a distance of about half a mile apart. The sporting jungle cock in his gorgeous winter plumage of red and gold, and the beautiful black partridge, seemed to be on the move, and were constantly crossing over our heads from one side of the road to the other. By the time that we pulled up at a steep hill stream, half way to Charda, we had added a goodly bag to our camp larder, including three hares, and that rare bird, a Florican. Here we found three of our shikarries (wood-craftsmen) and two of our elephants awaiting us; and glad we were of the assistance afforded by these great beasts of burden to haul our cars over the heavy sand and up the opposite steep bank.

We were soon in the throes of a momentous discussion with an experienced forest guard and our chief shikarri, Goman Sing, as to the best motorable road to the deserted village. We learnt of a short cut that took a zigzag course through almost impervious timber and undergrowth, crossing many deep nullahs and small streams, and decided to risk it, to the great consternation of the shikarries; who had all joined and were examining the cars with that philosophic calmness which the Oriental shows on his face, when obliged to look upon some unusual performance on the part of the white man. To bring a "Shaitan Howah-Garry" (devilish conveyance) into a country where only the sublime creak of the bullock cart, the roar of the tiger and the trumpet of the tusker should be heard, seemed to surpass their understanding.

Goman Sing shook his head and addressed the Deputy Commissioner: "These things cannot proceed further," he said. "Your honour had better return them to Salbani, and look with some favour upon our ancient means of jungle transport; the humble but invincible bullock cart, and Ganesh, our God the Elephant of slow but certain movement." The others of the advisory committee grinned in acquiescence. They pressed us very earnestly to avoid the short cut, and looked frightened when we refused.

"Whatever means of transport you select, it will be

very inadvisable, your honour," said Goman Sing, " to take the short cut, when the long way round is open to you."

The Deputy Commissioner, Mr. B., turned to the Opium Officer, with the remark that further discussion would be futile, as the superstition about the deserted village being haunted, extended to a dread of this particular cart track.

" I have always found," said the Opium Officer, " that these jungle superstitions, if followed up carefully, lead to the discovery of some remarkable habits of wild animals unknown before. They are always worth investigation." We questioned Goman Sing further.

"It is an unearthly lame bull," Goman Sing said in a shaking voice; " the ghost leader of the herd of wild cattle that live all 'round the deserted village; and the short cut is this terrible monster's main line of patrol, where certain death meets the intruder—even 'Ganesh,' the Elephant, cannot protect us."

This explained the desertion of the village, and we encouraged the old hardy Gurkha woodsman to enlighten us, as to the cause of their belief, before starting on the perilous track.

With his scared companions standing close behind him —even the Mahomedan mahouts shivering on the necks of their elephants that had been brought up, and were now standing like statues—Goman Sing gave the following brief history of the case. His low, tremulous voice was the only sound that broke the impressive stillness of the jungles, that seemed to hang like something tangibly heavy. The gorgeous vista of the straight forest line seemed to penetrate it, and the rays of the sun struck obliquely through the thinning mist, throwing faint shadows of the trees across the road.

" Twenty years ago," began Goman Sing, " in the city

of Lucknow, there was a high caste Brahmin who desired to possess the power of raising the dead. He studied the necessary magic and invocation under a very holy Ascetic, and was, in due course, ordered to go out and practise among the out-castes or untouchables. The lowest and most shunned of these poor beings is the 'Chandala'; the offspring of the forbidden union of a Brahmin woman with a low caste man. He is the scum of the earth.

"A Chandala died, and was thrown away to be devoured by jackals. The Brahmin came to where the body was lying and commenced his incantations. He succeeded in resuscitating one half of the body, or the entire length down one side, when, in sudden terror, he forgot the rest of the 'holy formulas.' Panic-stricken, the Brahmin bolted, but was followed by the shuffling body of the half alive 'Chandala,' calling out after him, 'half-done, underdone, undone!' The miserable Brahmin fled from city to city, but could not get away from the awful shuffling sound and terrible cry of the wretched apparition—that even penetrated stone walls—howling to be made whole.

"The Ascetic, under whom the Brahmin had studied, had expired; and there was no other holy man possessing such powers, to whom the Brahmin could go for help. He fled to the jungle, and found his way to this village last year. The poor village people heard his prayers to the great God, Vishnu the Protector, who granted him death and transmigration; his soul passing into one of the living bulls of the wild herd, for protection from the 'Chandala.'

"Soon after this, the apparition arrived at the village by the short-cut, crying out 'half-done, underdone, undone!' Then the village people heard his prayers, too, for redress, to the great God 'Siva' the Destroyer, who changed the Chandala into the dreaded lame Ghost Bull—twice as large as the biggest bull of the wild herd, and many times as fierce."

Looking around him as if afraid to speak again, Goman Sing raised his arms tragically and continued in a low hoarse whisper:

"This mighty limping Ghost Bull, the raging spirit of the Chandala, shuffles up and down this cart track, emitting deafening bellows in challenge to the wild herd. By the mandate of 'Siva,' the herd has to respond and send forth a bull to dispute the leadership. Nearly every second day, a bull of the herd is slain in broad daylight! By calling out all the bulls in turn, the Ghost will eventually meet his enemy—the bull sanctified with the Brahmin's soul—and the fight will be momentous. It will be a struggle for mastery between the great Gods Vishnu and Siva, and the heavens will quake! It means instant death, your honour," repeated Goman Sing, "to anybody who dares to tread the patrol of the dreaded God Siva."

"When did the village people decamp?" inquired the Deputy Commissioner.

"In the beginning of the monsoons," replied the old veteran. "Day after day the Ghost bellowed in their midst until a wild bull would appear, when the startled people would suddenly see a huge, limping spectre—like a shadow, that would instantly kill the living bull and melt away. One day," concluded Goman Sing, "a Sadhu priest came into the village, by a circuitous route, and took all the people away. They have not been heard of since!"

We were now a solemn-looking party. Respect for the agitated feelings of our men, and the weird deathly stillness of the forest, broken at intervals by the frightened alarm cries of various deer, all contributed to impress us deeply. After directing us on to the haunted cart track, Goman Sing begged permission to accompany us and to share our fate, but we insisted upon his going direct to the Charda Camp with the others, and we made no attempt to start until we had seen all the shikarries safely off, on the backs of the two elephants, including our two Indian chauffeurs. We merely instructed Goman Sing, if we were not in camp by five o'clock in the afternoon, to come and await us on the forest line, on the north side of the village, about the distance of a mile, bringing the elephants with him.

"Coming events throw their shadows before!" There is no maxim more applicable to the jungles; but one has to be in the "know" to recognise the shadows, or the various causes in the shape of signs and sounds which may lead to the bag of a tiger or a panther. We were determined to find a way through and explore the place. As our cars throbbed slowly down the winding cart track—breaking into the stillness uncannily—the very atmosphere seemed to be spirited with a strange mysticism of ill-omen, which seemed to hang over the forest trees like a heavy cloud.

We lead in the same order as before; the Opium Officer, the Deputy Commissioner and his guest in the Standard, while the Colonel and I bring up the Ford, keeping about fifty yards behind the front car. But for the sharp curves, and the jungle that has to be constantly cut away in the middle of the track, we find the passage tolerably motorable. There are long delays in crossing steep banked nullahs, and in felling the overhanging boughs of trees that sweep the track.

After two hours hard work—having accomplished a distance of about five miles, we suddenly come winding out into a large open space covered with grass about two or three feet high, and interspersed with the prickly shrub of the wild plum. It looks like a continuous glen stretching far to our left front. On the right side of the cart track, the high tree forest stands up like a mighty wall. The track seems to be turning into the open glen, and we stop our cars to look for signs of the deserted village. It is early in the afternoon, but the sun seems still obliterated with the morning mist intervening, leaving a dull gloomy effect like a cloudy day. Far down the glen, we can catch a glimpse of a few broken down mud walls in between huge cotton trees with their straight symmetrical branches pointing, like warning arms, over the canopy of the forest.

The doors of the two cars are ajar, and we are standing on the ground with our lunch baskets open. Nothing untoward having occurred so far to disturb our mental tranquillity—the felling operations have brought us back to realities—we are now in the best of spirit, munching sandwiches and pouring out frothing beer. "Extraordinary superstitions one meets with out in this country of wonders and disappointments," whispers Mr. B, the Deputy Commissioner, "the poorer people bury facts in life and live in imagination and,"—but his concluding remarks were quickly cut short!

A thunderous bellow, coming from somewhere close to our left front, makes us all jump up to our feet. Our rifles are seized and we get into the cars, standing up and looking over the open grass. No animal of any kind is visible, and we naturally think we are mistaken in the direction of the sound. But, presently, we see the grass shaking not more than fifty to sixty yards from our position, and, the next moment, another deafening bellow —the challenge of an angry bull to a fight—rolls through the silent jungle. We actually see some dust rising from the grass, as if hoofed up in rage, and yet there seems nothing. A horned animal, as large as a bull, would be clearly seen in the comparatively short grass where the dust hangs.

It is incomprehensible, and we turn to look at each other with bloodless faces during the stillness that follows. Mysterious manifestations are beyond our mentality of fact and common sense; but this occurrence before our very eyes, conforming to the exact details appertaining to the ghost, is staggering beyond words. We step cautiously out of the cars for a whispered confabulation.

"We must wait for the next bellow and walk over that bit of ground on foot," said the Opium Officer, "and then search round the whole glen. Never mind about stalking, we must race round quickly, leaving our cars here. Ghost or no ghost, I have certain very strong suspicions."

Scarcely have the last words been whispered, when loud snorting and another bellow seems to shake the ground, so close does it seem, but nothing—nothing is visible! The Opium Officer is just on the point of moving forward, and we about to follow him, when he suddenly halts dead and gives a suggestion to the right front. From this opposite direction another bellow resounds, and to our astonishment we see a monster bull coming up rapidly, making the dry grass rustle and breaking fallen twigs under his heavy hoofs with reckless disregard of the laws of the jungle. On comes the brute shaking his enormous curved horns, and stopping every ten paces to lower his great head and bellow! At each such demonstration, a cloud of dust rises up to screen him for a few seconds. We bend low under the cover of some bushes and curving grass in the front of the cars, utterly bewildered, and watch the huge bull walk right up to the spot from which the original challenge first came thundering out. But there is no fierce opponent to meet him! A dead silence prevails, and the huge bull stands with head erect and nostrils expanded, apparently as much surprised and puzzled as we are, in our cramped position. Fortunately we are on the leeward side of him, with ourselves and the two cars well hidden, and he has not the slightest suspicion of our close presence.

The picture is a grand one—but remains only for a second or two more. The Opium Officer nudges the Deputy Commissioner and whispers something in his ear. His head then turns slowly round towards us with a broad smile upon his face—which, if not explanatory, was at least comforting. He spells one word in the dumb alphabet which makes our hearts beat doubly quickly. "Be ready," the spelling concludes. A slight rustle in front—what is it? An enormous elongated form has suddenly emerged from the low grass, and there are two mighty paws hugging the "thick-set" neck of the monster bull, whose great horned head is suddenly thrown up, and he falls forward with a deep groan. The next instant, a great striped animal with a gigantic cat's head gives a clear view of formidable bulging shoulders, and a volley flashes out immediately! There follows a rush, and a roar, a distant echo—as if from hills far to the north—of the rifle shots, and breathless silence! Nothing is visible—just the grass and open view as before, as if nothing had occurred. At a signal from the Opium Officer we remain sitting—crouched. Not a word for half an hour till he breaks the stillness.

"A huge tiger, by jove!" exclaimed the Opium Officer, "and we've bagged him!"

We merely gaze at the speaker, thrilled and amazed.

"It is the ghost," continued the Opium Officer. "I have known a tiger before to imitate perfectly the bell of a sambhur, and even a cheetal in order to get his mutton easily and lazily; but here, enacted in front of us, is a case of a tiger actually calling out a wild bull, resorting to every trick—even to the raising of dust—to perfect his camouflage! I should never have believed it, had I not been an eye-witness to such a feat this afternoon."

We found a splendid specimen of a tiger, 9 ft. 10½ in. in size, lying stretched out, some eighty yards away from the vanquished bull, whose neck had been broken by the tiger's sudden and mighty wrench. We were a second too late to save the bull. There was a single hit only on the tiger—the vital shoulder shot, and we decided to draw lots for him in camp, after dinner. The excitement had been too great for accurate shooting. Coveting up the two animals with broken branches, we started up our cars and moved off towards our camp at Charda, in wonder and delight. We found the faithful Goman Sing awaiting us, at the place arranged, with the two elephants, and we sent a party back with two buffalo carts, which we commandeered on the way, to load up and bring home the lucky bag.

The shikarries expressed little surprise at the turn of events; all Goman Sing said was, that the tiger had come to witness the bull fight and had killed the bull, as the ghost had decamped owing to our presence. That the tiger was the creation of "Siva," the Destroyer, and was in duty bound to support the ghost. Some weeks later, the Deputy Commissioner heard of the deserted village people. They had crossed over into Lakhimpur, an adjoining district, further to the west, and had settled down in the estate of a big Zamindar (landowner).